The Onset of Literacy

Peg Sahg

COGNITION Special Issues

The titles in this series are paperback, readily accessible editions of the Special Issues of *COGNITION: An International Journal of Cognitive Science,* edited by Jacques Mehler and produced by special agreement with Elsevier Science Publishers B.V.

VISUAL COGNITION, Steven Pinker, guest editor

THE ONSET OF LITERACY: Cognitive Processes in Reading Acquisition, Paul Bertelson, guest editor

The Onset of Literacy
Cognitive Processes in
Reading Acquisition

edited by
Paul Bertelson

A Bradford Book
The MIT Press
Cambridge, Massachusetts
London, England

First MIT Press edition, 1987

Reprinted from *Cognition: International Journal of Cognitive Science*, Volume 24 (1986). The MIT Press has exclusive license to sell this English-language book edition throughout the world.

Printed and bound in the United States of America.

Library of Congress Cataloging-in-Publication Data

The Onset of literacy.

"A Bradford book."
Bibliography: p.
Includes index.
1. Reading. 2. Literacy. 3. Word recognition. 4. Language awareness in children. I. Bertelson, Paul
LB1050.42.057 1987 428.4 86-27367
ISBN 0-262-52125-3 (pbk.)

Contents

The onset of literacy: Liminal remarks*

PAUL BERTELSON

Université libre de Bruxelles

Abstract

As an introduction to the Special Issue, a tutorial examination of recent developments important to understand current research on reading acquisition is offered. The accent is put on the interrelations between studies of skilled adult performance, of effects of neurological damage and of early reading. The central puzzle of reading research is to identify the causes of the specific difficulties which acquiring literacy appears to entail. The problem has generally been attacked through correlational methods, based on the comparison of better and poorer achievers. The merits and shortcomings of that approach are examined and the need for linking differential studies to a general theoretical conception of the reading process and of its development is emphasized. The line of studies stemming from the hypothesis that a major difficulty in acquiring alphabetic literacy is to manipulate language at the level of phonemic segments is examined, and also the way the results of these studies can be related to current theories of lexical access. The limitations of the approach consisting of deriving hypotheses about development from theories of the adult stage are discussed and illustrated by data from studies of the reading performance of both children with normal reading achievement and developmental dyslexics. Finally, the possibility that sources of acquisition difficulties might be found at levels beyond that of word recognition is discussed.

*The author's work on reading is being supported by the Belgian Ministère de la Politique scientifique (Action de Recherche concertée "Processus cognitifs dans la lecture") and by the Fonds de la Recherche fondamentale collective (Convention 2.4505.80). This paper owes much to the discussions that took place at the symposium on "Information Processing in early Reading" which the author organized within the 1984 International Congress of Psychology in Acapulco and at which several of the articles in the Special Issue were originally presented. Thanks are due to Ruth Campbell, Bob Crowder, Emilia Ferreiro, Uta Frith, Isabel Liberman, Jacques Mehler, Karalyn Patterson and Tim Shallice for stimulating discussions of several of the present topics, and to Jesus Alegria, Alain Content, Béatrice De Gelder, Daniel Holender and José Morais for critical comments on former versions of the paper. Requests for reprints should be addressed to Paul Bertelson, Laboratoire de Psychologie expérimentale, Université libre de Bruxelles, 117 Av. Adolphe Buyl, 1050 Bruxelles, Belgium.

Traditions of research on reading

Psychological research on reading has in the last 15 years or so gone through a remarkable process of acceleration. As a result, reading is today one of the most actively investigated topics in cognitive psychology.

As is usually the case when sudden progress occurs in a field of inquiry, the present development has resulted from the converging effects of extrinsic and intrinsic factors. The main extrinsic factors are the practical problems arising from the difficulties encountered by many children in acquiring literacy. Intrinsic factors are conceptual and methodological developments in cognitive psychology, psycholinguistics and neuropsychology that have made it possible to deal with complex issues which in earlier times appeared to defy rational analysis.

Three main research traditions have been involved in those developments: the experimental analysis of skilled adult readers' performance, the neuropsychology of acquired reading disorders and the study of reading development. Communication has however not been equally distributed between these three fields of inquiry.

During the 1970s, a close interaction has developed between the people working with normal adults and with neurological patients. The critical event here has probably been the adoption by specialists of the two fields of the same conceptual framework, that of the information processing approach, that is, the view of the cognitive apparatus as a network of partially autonomous functional units, sometimes called "modules", which can be analyzed both through experimental manipulations and through observation of the effects of brain damage. As a result, the most influential contemporary ideas regarding the architecture of the apparatus involved in basic processes such as word recognition and sentence understanding (see the book by Ellis, 1984, for an excellent simple presentation) are based on evidence from these two fields. For instance, the classical dual-route model of lexical access finds its origin in efforts by experimental psychologists to analyze the role of phonological conversion in written word recognition. It received a decisive impetus when Marshall and Newcombe (1973) showed that the complementary symptoms of the patients they called "deep" and "surface dyslexics" could be interpreted as providing a double dissociation between two procedures for identifying written words. The dual-route model has more recently come under attacks based on arguments from both experiments with normal readers and studies of dyslexic patients (Henderson, 1982; Humphreys & Evett, 1985).

There are certainly differences in emphasis on different aspects between the experimental and the neuropsychological traditions. Neuropsychologists, for instance, have generally been mainly interested in the general architecture of the processing system, and have not been very specific about details of procedures, while experimental psychologists have concentrated more on the latter aspects. It is nevertheless clear that a close and fruitful dialogue has been established between the two traditions.

Until recent years, the study of acquisition and of development has to some extent stayed away from that dialogue and has followed a path of its own.

There are historical reasons for that situation. In the early pre-1914 psychological research on reading, as reviewed by Huey (1908) in his classic book, studies of development and of the adult state were well integrated. That line of research virtually disappeared during the behavioristic era—with the notable and significant exception of studies of the directly observable phenomenon of eye movement. Practitioners—clinicians, educators, physicians—developed their own conceptions of the nature of reading. Whatever research there was concentrated on problems of diagnosing and predicting acquisition failures, and there was by and large little concern for the analysis of the reading process itself. It is during that period that some views of the etiology of reading retardation, which have exerted a strong influence on remediation and teaching practices up to now, were formulated. Most conspicuous among them are Orton's notion that dyslexic children, because of delayed lateralization of brain function, have difficulties with spatial orientation, which in reading manifest themselves in inversions of letter sequences and mirror-image confusions, and also various proposals that linked reading difficulties to some lag in the maturation of holistic perception capacities (e.g., Bender, 1957).

Research relevant to understanding reading performance resumed within experimental psychology in the 1950s, with New Look work on word recognition. Within cognitive psychology, identification of tachistoscopically presented words soon became one of the most intensively studied experimental tasks. This focusing originally was not only due to the role of word recognition in reading, but also to questions of technical expediency: written words are a category of perceptible objects regarding which our knowledge can be more rigorously described and measured than, say, things in the everyday environment, and on the other hand, written words can be presented under controlled conditions more easily than spoken ones. Nevertheless, this research was the basis for the elaboration of models of the mental lexicon which then played a central role in analyzing the reading process (Forster, 1976; Morton, 1979).

In that line of inquiry, developmental aspects have rarely received serious consideration. When new directions of research on reading acquisition developed in the late 1960s, the main influences came from linguistics, psycholinguistics and phonetics, with cognitive psychology only in the background, as examination of the very influential collection of papers published by Kavanagh and Mattingly (1972) shows.

There are many signs however that the gap between developmental and other studies of reading might be filling fast. Several contributions to the present issue are representative both of a movement toward integration and of the difficulties that lie in its path.

Reading is difficult

The notion that some particular difficulty is attached to the process of reading acquisition has consistently provided reading research with both its principal practical incentive and its main theoretical challenge.

Learning to read is difficult in at least two senses.

First, it is difficult to the extent that it requires instructional support of the kind generally provided by schools. That feature puts reading and writing in a different category of skills from speaking and understanding speech, which develop in practically all hearing children independently of any deliberate effort on the part of the adults. Exactly how much instruction is necessary to get the child started on the path to literacy, we do not know. Cases of children who supposedly learned to read "by themselves" have been reported (Torrey, 1979) but the reports generally do not contain the critical information about the amount of support provided by the environment. On the other hand, the spontaneously acquired script-related skills of some pre-school children may have little relation to actual autonomous reading. The point is well documented for the capacity to recognize familiar graphic patterns such as brand names in the work of Masonheimer that **Barron**[1] describes in this issue. The performance of pre-readers with such material is apparently closely tied to the habitual graphic appearance, and plunges to near zero when the same names are presented in ordinary print.

The second form of difficulty is the one encountered by that substantial minority of school-attenders who progress slowly in reading and writing, and sometimes leave school without having attained the minimum level of mastery necessary for practical reading. These children are often found to have normal intelligence and to be adequately motivated, hence the notion of some specific disability responsible for their particular problems with the written medium.

---

[1]References to the papers appearing in the present issue are printed in boldface type.

The opinion has often been held that research concerned with the sources of developmental reading disorders should concentrate on the second form of difficulty and considerable efforts have been made selecting the subjects supposed to be affected by the hypothetical specific reading disability. It can be doubted however that these efforts were justified. Both Carr (1981) and Stanovich (1982a) note that there is little evidence that the pattern of deficiency depends very much on how the sample of deficient readers is selected.

The question of the right research population has generally been associated with the notion of a so-called biological determination of reading disorders: the most extreme deficient readers would be those with a problem of biological origin. The assumption is not unreasonable, but it does not rest on any strong base of data, so that for the time being it is better to consider the two issues as orthogonal. The problem of possible biological roots of reading disorders is one that none of the contributors to the present issue addresses. The reason, I shall propose, is not that the possibility is being denied. Many demonstrated facts, such as the strong association of reading disorders with gender, support it. The question is rather one of research strategy. We need a good description of reading performance at its own behavioral level before the relation of that description to aspects belonging to other levels of description can be fruitfully examined.

The locus of the difficulty:
Differential psychology of good and poor readers

The major part of research on acquisition has been aimed at localizing the sources of learning difficulties. It has generally used the correlational approach, in one of its main variants: either groups of poor and proficient readers have been tested for capacities that might be involved in reading acquisition, or correlations have been measured between reading skill and other capacities within one sample.

The classical evaluation of earlier work is to be found in the book by Vellutino (1979) and reviews of more recent contributions have been provided by Carr (1981) and by Stanovich (1982a, 1982b). For a more selective but highly readable presentation, see the recent little book by Bryant and Bradley (1985).

The main casualties of Vellutino's critical scrutiny have been the various theories that located the origin of reading difficulties in visual perception, whether of the Orton or of the Lauretta Bender variety. Correlations that had been presented as supporting the role of visual perception repeatedly disappeared once the tasks were redesigned in order to isolate the visual component from more general cognitive or linguistic processes. Several studies by Vellutino and his collaborators have shown that retarded readers are inferior to non-retarded ones in *naming* written words but not in *copying* them, and that they commit left–right confusions in naming but not in copying. Regarding orientation mistakes, Stanovich (1982a) notes that a number of studies have now shown that although they are observed often in the reading of poor readers, they do not occur *proportionately* more often than in better readers, and are thus not characteristic of retarded reading. Carr (1981, p. 75) concluded his own review of that research by the remark that "visual discrimination theories thus appear to be unique in that the factor supposed by many of them to underlie the entirety of dyslexia may not account for any of it". Theories that saw the origin of dyslexia in a general capacity for cross-modal integration of all sorts of materials or in serial order recall appear to fare equally poorly. Vellutino argued convincingly that many results which have been quoted in favor of the preceding views are flawed by lack of control for possible common factors such as intelligence, motivation and verbal coding capacities.

On the positive side, Vellutino's major conclusion was that the main difficulties encountered by poor readers reside in the linguistic domain, in operations concerned with the phonological aspects and possibly the syntactic ones, but not with semantics. These were important conclusions which, as **Shankweiler and Crain** claim in this issue, cleared the way for more detailed exploration.

While there can be little doubt as to the importance of Vellutino's monumental effort, one point which its outcome makes clear is that the correlational approach is more efficient at eliminating groups of factors as possible sources of important difficulties than at identifying the particular operations which poor readers cannot perform.

This state of affairs is linked to some extent to the well-known limits of the differential method. Correlations do not allow causal inferences. If poor readers are also poor in skill X, it does not follow automatically (a) that deficiency in X is the origin of poor reading. Another possibility is (b) that literacy, or some of the activities necessary to attain it, promote X. And it can also be the case (c) that literacy and X are both influenced by some common factor, such as intelligence, socio-economic status or motivation for school achievement. And of course, these three types of relations are not mutually exclusive, and we should expect most observed correlations to reflect various combinations of the three. These problems of course arise only when a significant correlation has been obtained. The interpretation of non-correlation is much simpler: if poor readers perform on X as well as better ones, then X is unlikely to be one cause of reading retardation. This asymmetry in the interpretability of positive versus negative results would explain why the differential approach is so much better at eliminating groups of possibilities than at finer grain analysis.

Several ways of dealing with the problems of interpreting correlations have been developed within the differential tradition. The influence of intelligence or of social class has often been controlled for by use of groups matched on those variables or of partial correlation techniques. To partial out the backward effect of reading experience on correlated capacities, one can use the reading-age match advocated by Bryant and Bradley (1985), which consists of comparing retarded readers with non-retarded ones matched on reading ability: any difference between such groups can obviously not have been caused by differences in reading experience. The method has however not been used very often. Other approaches which have been applied with some success to disentangle factors of reading acquisition are partial correlations between measures taken at different points during acquisition (Perfetti, Beck, & Hughes, 1981) and path analysis (Torneus, 1984).

The most tricky question for the interpretation of correlations is certainly the possible influence of unknown third factors: how do we know that there is not some common cause we have not thought of? Probably the best answer is the solution, advocated persuasively by Bryant and Bradley (1985), of using a correlational and an experimental approach in parallel. If children trained on X progress in reading faster than control subjects, a causal link from X to reading performance is demonstrated. Of course, it does not follow automatically that causality does not operate in the reverse direction also. Semi-naturalistic experiments, where one tries to influence overall reading proficiency (Bradley & Bryant, 1983), are costly in terms of time and effort, and can only be attempted to check on well explored hypotheses. For faster analyses, one may prefer to simulate aspects of reading acquisition in the laboratory and there are some interesting examples of the application of that strategy (Ehri, 1984; Treiman & Baron, 1983; Reitsma, 1983).

The solution advocated by Bryant and Bradley is thus a convergent appeal to the differential and the experimental approaches. As they note, the weaknesses and strengths of the two methods combine very well. The experimental approach provides more efficient control on effects and the differential approach provides the necessary check that the variables one is manipulating in the laboratory are relevant to actual reading.

The preceding discussion has been focused on the choice of methods for testing predictions, and thus misses what is probably the main limitation of the differential approach: the fact that it has too often consisted of testing a series of disconnected local predictions. What is needed is a more integrated strategy, where the question of the origin of reading difficulties is related to a general theory of reading performance and of its development.

Phonological awareness and explicit analysis of speech

Of all plausible loci for reading acquisition difficulties, one has in recent years drawn more attention than any other: the ability to analyze speech into phoneme-level units. The main cause of that concentration is no doubt that, unlike for other possible origins, the present notion was backed by an articulate set of theoretical proposals. These proposals, which took form in the early 1970s (see Liberman, 1973 and the book edited by Kavanagh & Mattingly, 1972, for early formulations, and the twin papers by Gleitman & Rozin, 1977, and Rozin & Gleitman, 1977, for a more extensive presentation; also the collection of papers edited by Sinclair, Jarvella, & Levelt, 1978) resulted from the convergence of lines of thought from developmental psycholinguistics, generative linguistics, the biology of language, experimental phonetics and the history of writing systems.

The basic idea was that of a fundamental difference between the skills involved in dealing with print and with speech. Speaking and listening are *primary linguistic activities* (Mattingly, 1972) which emerge through maturation of some universal pre-wired machinery, hence the fact that all children allowed some minimal linguistic input become expert with great facility. These activities, however, are largely automatic and only their end product reaches consciousness. In the absence of specific tuition, the speaker-hearer will become aware mainly of the meaning of utterances and be much less prepared to take account of more superficial aspects such as syntax and phonology. Reading, on the other hand, like versification, is a *secondary linguistic activity* and involves *meta-linguistic* knowledge. Reading a particular orthography would involve explicit, conscious manipulation of the linguistic units which the written symbols stand for: mapping speech segments onto the characters makes it possible to decipher text into some phonetic rendering which can then be dealt with by the existing speech interpretation mechanisms (Liberman et al., 1977). That means that the student must be able to represent speech as a succession of units at the corresponding levels, and attaining such *linguistic awareness* ("phonological awareness" is the familiar expression, but it can normally be used only in relation with submorphemic units) would be the main difficulty some children encounter in learning to read.

Linguistic awareness was conceived as possessing several levels, words and possibly morphemes being accessed more easily than syllables and syllables more easily than phonemes. Learning to read in different writing systems would as a consequence be more or less difficult according to the accessibility of the linguistic units being mapped onto the characters. Logographic systems, which represent words or morphemes, would be easiest and alphabetic ones, which represent phonemic segments, would be the most difficult, with

syllabaries somewhere in between. One early study that was seen as supporting the conception was one by Rozin et al. (1971) showing that children who
had failed learning to read simple words written alphabetically could rather
easily learn to read the same words represented by Chinese logographs. Gleitman and Rozin (1977) linked the problem of levels of linguistic awareness to
Gelb's (1963) conception of the history of writing systems. They suggested
that the order in which the logographic, syllabic and alphabetic principles
were introduced reflects the difficulty of access to the corresponding levels
of description of language.

The phonological awareness hypothesis has stimulated an extremely active
line of developmental investigations of the ability to manipulate language at
the level of submorphemic units, a group of capacities that will be designated
here by the term "speech analysis". On the other hand, the more theoretical
aspects of the hypothesis, which have been elaborated by Rozin (1978) in an
important paper, have not received much further attention. There has been
very little discussion, for instance, of the status of the attribute of "consciousness" or of the nature of those aspects of primary linguistic activity that are
supposed to be accessed. A general discussion of the methodological issues
is presented by De Gelder (1986).

The empirical work has demonstrated a robust correlation between speech
analysis and reading performance. Better readers have been shown to perform better on a wide range of speech analysis tasks, even when differences
in general intelligence and socio-economic status have been controlled for.

A good deal of work has been devoted to analysing the source of the
correlation. Three papers in the present issue (**Read et al., Morais et al.** and
Mann) deal with that problem, so that the basic data need not be examined
in detail here.

There is evidence both for effects of speech analysis capacity on progress
in reading and for effects of reading acquisition on speech analysis.

Evidence for the influence of speech analysis ability on progress in reading
has come from two types of studies. First there are longitudinal studies showing that performance on speech analysis at one stage predicts later progress
in reading performance. To interpret these data, it is of course necessary to
make sure that at the time it was measured, speech analysis ability had not
yet been influenced by reading experience. The danger exists not only when
the initial test of analysis ability is carried out after the start of reading
instruction, but also when it takes place shortly before, at a time when some
children can receive various types of reading tuition at home. There are a
few studies in which the contamination can probably be ruled out. The best
known is the monumental study by Bradley and Bryant (1983) where correlations, which survived controls for general intelligence and memory span,

were obtained between a test of the ability to categorize words on the basis of sound similarity, carried out at 4 or 5 years of age, and performance on standard reading and writing tests 3 or 4 years later. Using sophisticated partial correlation techniques, Perfetti et al. (1981) have provided what looks like convincing evidence for causal influences of phone deletion and addition capacities on subsequent progress in word decoding and spelling.

The other form of evidence comes from experiments where training on some speech analysis ability has been shown to improve reading capacity. Here also, the best known contribution is the training experiment carried out by Bradley and Bryant with a sub-sample of the population of their longitudinal study. Giving children who had scored poorly on sound classification extensive tuition on that kind of activity enabled them to score better on the final reading tests than equally poor performers trained on semantic manipulations. The superiority, however, was significant only for children trained on both sound classification and letter–sound correspondences. Results going in the same direction have been provided by Lundberg and his collaborators at Umeå (Oloffson & Lundberg, 1983) and by several other groups.

The main demonstration that, on the other hand, reading acquisition can influence speech analysis comes from the sudden improvement in segmentation ability that generally follows the beginning of reading instruction. Several studies have suggested that the improvement is time-locked to reading instruction and not to chronological age: it can be shifted on the age axis when instruction begins one year later, as for example in Denmark (Skjelfjord, 1976), or for the children who are older at the beginning of the school year (Alegria & Morais, 1979) and it does not occur in illiterates who at adult age perform at the same low level as pre-school children (Morais et al., 1979). On the other hand, the improvement depends on the content of instruction: it is delayed when a whole-word method rather than a phonic method is being used (Bruce, 1964; Perfetti, Beck, & Hughes, 1981; Alegria et al., 1982).

Another line of evidence comes from demonstrations that orthographic knowledge is being used in speech analysis tasks. Ehri and Wilce (1979) have shown that in the phoneme counting situation, children are influenced by the number of letters in the corresponding orthographic representation: they count for instance one more unit in PITCH than in RICH. **Mann** describes similar tendencies in the phone counting performance of her Japanese subjects. Findings of that sort could be taken as simply revealing weaknesses in the tests designed for measuring phonological awareness. They might also be seen as demonstrations of changes of forms of speech processing brought about by the acquisition of literacy. They would add to a corpus of data showing for example that pronunciation is influenced by spelling (Kerek, 1976), that apparent location of extraneous noises in spoken sentences can be influenced by direction of writing (Bertelson, 1972) and that rhyming decisions concerning pairs of spoken words are influenced by their spelling (Seidenberg & Tanenhaus, 1982). The result of Brady, Shankweiler and Mann (1983) that good readers are better at recognizing noise-masked speech could also imply some use of orthographic knowledge in listening to speech.

There has been a tendency to ask regarding the relation between speech analysis and reading some version of the familiar "chicken and egg" question: is segmentation ability a prerequisite of reading acquisition, or one of its consequences? This is not a very fruitful way of looking at the problem. The reason is that entities such as reading acquisition and the emergence of speech analysis capacities are both too global to expect to observe a unidirectional causal relation between them. Only by analyzing both processes into simpler episodes can one hope to reach a level of description at which unidirectional influences would be found. Frith's (1985) insightful analysis of the interaction between reading and writing during development might here show the way.

The question asked by Morais et al. (1979) in the illiterates study was simply whether speech analysis can develop spontaneously, through maturation of the linguistic machinery and/or practice of speech communication, or whether it requires more specific experience. The inability of the illiterates seemed to imply the necessity of some specific kind of experience. It was not claimed, however, that only reading instruction can provide that experience, simply that possibly effective alternatives were not available to the population in question. On the other hand, the result was not inconsistent with the notion of an important role of speech analysis in reading acquisition: one plausible reason why the ex-illiterate subjects performed better in the tests could be simply that the curriculum of the literacy classes included some form of tuition in manipulation of language segments.

The first three papers in this volume each throws some new light on the issue.

(1) **Read et al.** show that literate Chinese who only learned the logographic characters perform in phonetic segmentation at the same low level as preschool children and adult illiterates, whereas those who also received instruction in the alphabetic "pinyin" system are comparable to second-grade European children and to alumni of Portuguese adult literacy classes. Mann shows that Japanese first-graders who have learned both syllabic "kanas" and logographic "kanji" cannot perform phonetic segmentation as well as American first-graders. These results are consistent with the notion that the form of phonological awareness promoted by learning to read a particular writing system depends on the level of the linguistic units which that system maps onto the characters.

(2) The fact that logographic literate Chinese are at the same low level as

Portuguese illiterates has important implications for the interpretation of the latter subjects' performance. In the Portuguese situation, the subjects who took the opportunity of literacy classes may have been the more enterprising and intelligent ones, and their superior performance in speech analysis could be due to some unknown extent to these pre-existing superiorities. The non-alphabetic Chinese had presumably had no opportunity to learn the alphabetic characters at the time they had gone to school, so that the argument of selection does not apply to the Chinese study. Was the factor an important one, one would have obtained a smaller inter-groups difference in the latter study.

(3) **Morais et al.** address the question of the degree of specificity of the difference in speech manipulation capacity between illiterates and ex-illiterates. Two aspects of specificity are considered. The first concerns the type of phonological unit that must be manipulated. Illiterates perform as poorly as in the previous study with consonants, in both a deletion and a detection task. But they perform at a non-negligible level in tasks involving syllabic segments and also in rhyme detection. These results are consistent with those obtained with pre-readers, who also are much better at judging rhyme and manipulating syllables than at manipulating phonetic segments, and who progress much more in the phonetic skills than in the other ones when they learn to read. The findings would suggest that some forms of speech manipulation are acquired up to some point spontaneously, although they can still be improved by specific training, but that manipulation of particular phonetic units, consonants, requires training.

(4) The second aspect of the specificity question concerns the possibility that part of the superiority of literate subjects would be due to general cognitive abilities rather than to specific linguistic or metalinguistic ones. This is of course a question that currently commands much attention in psycholinguistics. **Shankweiler and Crain** in this issue argue strongly against the notion that difficulties of reading acquisition might originate in general non-linguistic cognitive capacities. Authors working in different traditions have been attracted by such a notion. Lundberg (1978) for instance has proposed that the condition for attaining phonological awareness may lie in the Piagetian process of decentration. Treiman and Baron (1981) on the other hand have given serious consideration to the notion that the onset of speech segmentation abilities might be a reflection of a general progress in the capacity to deal in analytic fashion with parts and local features of all sorts of patterns, linguistic or not. **Morais et al.** address the question by giving their subjects a musical segmentation task, and find no difference between illiterates and ex-illiterates. The finding goes against an interpretation in terms of a general analytic capacity, but of course the fact that both groups perform nearly at floor level

invites caution in the interpretation. Other relevant aspects of the results are that the level of difficulty of the tasks depends essentially on the type of unit that must be manipulated, and little on the type of instruction.

(5) **Mann**'s main finding is that Japanese children appear eventually to acquire the ability both to count phonemes and to delete them without being taught the alphabet. That finding no doubt creates problems for the notion of the non-spontaneity of phonetic segmentation. Mann considers the possibility that exposure to a *phonological orthography* promotes the development of speech analysis up to phonetic segments, but rejects it on the basis of **Read et al.**'s data on non-alphabetic Chinese readers. Chinese orthography, she reasons, has phonetic radicals, hence is a phonological orthography. One important consideration might be that those phonetic radicals stand for whole morphemes, so that, although they require attention to the sound aspect of language, they do not engage the reader in submorphemic segmentation proper. One possibility which **Mann** does not consider might thus be that the critical experience for reaching segmentation into phonemic units would be exposure to a *submorphemic orthography*. Another factor which might have its importance is the fact, mentioned by the author, that a few kana characters actually stand for sub-syllabic segments. Kanas are thus not pure syllabaries. One should consider the possibility that manipulating some particular letter-phoneme correspondences might be sufficient to get children started on phonemic segmentation. The finding that pre-readers given experimental tuition on particular phones readily transfer the effect of the training to other phones (Content et al., 1982) is favorable to that sort of conception. Also relevant is Treiman and Baron's (1983) result showing that among pre-readers trained to segment syllables, the most successful subjects gave evidence of spontaneously segmenting syllables they had not been trained on.

(6) **Read et al.** observe that some of their alphabetic subjects could no longer read pinyin well, yet could perform the segmentation task. They conclude that "the segmental conception acquired with alphabetic literacy may persist even when the literacy itself is dormant". In a similar vein, **Morais et al.** note that differences in segmentation ability between their better and poorer readers are small compared to those between poorer readers and illiterates. These findings are relevant to the distinction between two ways in which reading instruction can promote speech analysis. On one hand, we have the possibility that reading instruction involves direct teaching of segmentation or the imposition of exercises designed to promote it. That is the possibility considered by Bertelson et al. (1985) when they suggested that the relation between speech analysis and reading instruction is a part–whole one. On the other hand, literacy, especially the availability of stored alphabetic representations of words or other units, provides, as we have mentioned al-

ready, new ways of dealing with speech. The two results mentioned above go definitely in the direction of a direct influence of school activities on speech analysis, rather than of an indirect influence mediated by literacy.

Theories of lexical access

The theoretical question that has attracted the greater amount of attention during the period we are considering concerns the organization of the part of long-term memory—the *mental lexicon*—which contains information about words (or morphemes: the question whether whole words, morphemes or both are represented in the lexicon will not be considered here) and the procedures through which that information is retrieved in reading—*lexical access*. The most influential notion, generally called the *dual-route concept-ion*, has been that there are two access procedures: an *indirect* or *phonological* procedure, in which a phonological representation of the word is assembled by application of letter–sound correspondence rules, and is used to find the address of the word in the input register normally used for speech perception; and a *direct* or *orthographic* procedure which involves no phonological recoding and uses an orthographic input register specially developed for the sake of reading.

The two-step procedure of indirect access is only possible in so-called "phonographic" writing systems (Gelb, 1963), syllabic and alphabetic ones, that represent submorphemic segments of language and it would, as a matter of fact, provide their main advantage over logographic systems. The assembly can be accomplished without understanding, for instance by a foreigner ignorant of the language, by using the rules linking characters to language segments. Explicit indirect reading can be observed in some beginning readers who are heard "sounding out" phonetic approximations and replacing them afterwards by correct pronunciations, presumably after lexical access has taken place. It is a reasonable extrapolation from these observations to expect indirect reading to occur covertly during silent reading, through some internal representation of the speech sounds.

One great attraction of the notion is that it describes a parsimonious solution to the problem of making sense of print, one that takes advantage, in parasitic fashion, of existing speech interpretation facilities. It has been especially attractive to students of reading acquisition, because it offers a method through which the beginning reader can deal with words that have not been taught at school, and so become autonomous. There is little doubt that confidence in the phonological awareness hypothesis has been reinforced by the notion that segmentation is necessary to allow indirect reading. Liberman et al. (1977) have formulated the notion very explicitly. The main problem with the direct strategy, they write, is "that it is self-limiting. It does not permit the child to read words not previously encountered in print ... . Only if the child is able to use the more analytic strategy" (deciphering by rules), "can he realize the important advantage of an alphabetically written language. Given a word that is already in his lexicon, the child can read it without specific instruction although he has never before seen it in print; or given a new word which he has never before heard or seen, the child can closely approximate its spoken form and hold that until its meaning can be inferred from the context or discovered later by his asking someone about it."

The role of indirect access was much emphasized in the early 1970s. One argument for its existence was derived from the everyday observation that we can read words we have never seen before, like foreign words, neologisms and the pseudo-words that flash in psycholinguistic laboratories. At the experimental level, the two main classes of arguments were the effects of homophony in the lexical decision task (it takes longer to decide that the pseudo-word we see is not a word if it sounds like a real word) and the effects of orthographic regularity on word naming latency (words with regular spellings are pronounced faster than those with irregular spellings). Some authors tried to argue for an exclusive use of the indirect procedure (e.g. Rubenstein, Lewis, & Rubenstein, 1971). That position however could not cope with a series of arguments based on experimental analysis of adult readers' word recognition performance (e.g., homophony with real words does *not always* increase the time necessary to categorize pseudo-words in the lexical decision task), on clinical data (e.g., deep dyslexics who cannot read non-words can still read some words) and also on everyday observation (e.g., we understand and pronounce correctly words with wild spellings, we discriminate between homophones and detect misspellings). One had as a consequence to accept the existence of an access procedure involving no phonological recoding. The details of such a procedure have not been much specified in the literature on lexical access but on the other hand a great deal of the work concerned with building models of visual word recognition (see Henderson, 1982, Chapters 9 and 10) is actually focused on that question.

Towards the middle of the decade, there was a quasi-general consensus on some form of dual-route position. Coltheart (1978) provided the most explicit formulation, which has also been the most influential. One feature of his formulation which has had important consequences is his insistence that phonological assembly must be based on rules operating at the level of graphemes and phonemes, and not of units of varying sizes, as the more liberal conception defended in several papers by Shallice (e.g., Shallice & McCarthy, 1985) allows. The model provided two routes, the indirect and the direct one, into the lexicon, and also a non-lexical route from grapheme-to-phoneme conversion to pronunciation. So, in a sense, it was a three-route model. As used by psychologists, who are mainly interested in describing how normal readers comprehend text, the "dual-route" label generally refers to the two procedures available to access the lexicon. However, with the increasing application of the model to the word naming performance of dyslexic patients, there has been a growing tendency to use the same expression in reference to the distinction between lexical and non-lexical obtention of phonology. The resulting confusion has often gone unnoticed. Going back to Coltheart's formulation, another important step was taken when he proposed on the basis of the then available evidence that in a language with a deep orthography, like English, words are in actual reading recognized by the direct route most of the time, and the indirect route plays only a back-up role to allow reading of unknown words.

The dual-route conception has come under rather serious criticisms in recent years. One argument is based on experimental data showing that, as common sense would have predicted, people sometimes use orthographic similarity with already known words to derive the pronunciation of a new one (Glushko, 1979; Marcel, 1980). This suggests a form of indirect reading in which phonological assembly makes use of lexical information, a possibility for which there is no provision in the standard model. The other argument, which has been most persuasively developed by Henderson (1982), is that the model lacks a plausible mechanism for combining the outputs of the lexical and of the extra-lexical routes. If, following the principle of a "horse-race" model, the routes remain independent up to pronunciation, one is led to the absurd prediction that readers will on a number of occasions produce regularized pronunciations of irregular words: that happens a lot in surface dyslexics, but very seldom in normal readers. The silly prediction can only be avoided by assuming that the lexical route is always faster than the non-lexical one, but then there is no explanation for the effect of orthographic regularity on pronunciation latencies.

These problems have led authors to propose either purely lexical models (Henderson, 1982) or some modified dual-route one allowing interactions between the two processes (Patterson & Morton, 1985). Those models have in turn been criticized for lack either of parsimony or of predictive power. The procedure for assembling phonology on the basis of analogies has in particular been sometimes insufficiently specified and at other times very costly in terms of computational space.

There is a recurrent tendency to describe debates like the present one in revolutionary terms. One may prefer the less martial view that application of the dual-route conception has revealed weaknesses which will impose adaptation, making provisions for instance for several phonological assembly procedures or for integration of assembled and addressed phonology. Of course, the problem is that once a conception with wide implications has to be reorganized, all the consequences of each modification do not become apparent immediately. For the time being, the situation is certainly fluid, as examination of the recent treatment by Humphreys and Evett (1985) and of its commentaries will show.

Early word recognition

As we have noted already, the notion of an important function of indirect lexical access in early reading has figured prominently among conceptions of reading acquisition and has been seen as explaining the observed link between phonological awareness and reading performance. Here, one must note an important distinction made by Jorm and Share (1983) between two different roles of indirect access and early reading. Indirect access would serve on one hand as a back-up procedure for reading words for which no orthographic address is yet available, and on the other hand as a self-teaching device for developing the orthographic lexicon. The idea here is that each successful application of indirect access would function as a trial in a conditioning experiment, creating an association between the orthography of the printed word and the phonological representation which has been accessed. The authors suggest in addition that very few encounters with a new word would be enough to establish an orthographic address, so that from very early on, one should expect children to use in parallel indirect access with some words and direct access with other ones. That young children can assimilate specific orthographic representations very fast has since been shown convincingly by Reitsma (1983).

One can ask how this view of reading acquisition developed within the dual-route conception would be affected by the current controversy around that conception. In particular, would the notion that phonology could be assembled through an analogy procedure, and not only through application of conversion rules, make it difficult to understand the role of segmentation abilities? As a matter of fact, it is probable that most conceivable analogy-based procedures involve segmentation of language up to phonetic segments. The choice between conversion rules and analogies as basis for assembling phonology would then have no important implication regarding the function of segmentation capacity. The main advantage of indirect reading, giving the child autonomy for developing his vocabulary of visually recognizable words, by taking advantage of spoken words knowledge, is obtained whether phonology is assembled by rules or by analogy. Inversely, the fact that segmentation capacity is important would provide no argument for either side in the controversy.

On the other hand, one should not automatically assume that the use of conversion rules and of analogies for assembling phonology would be operations which appear at the same time during development. Marsh, Friedman, Welch, & Desberg (1981) in their model of the development of reading skill propose that the use of analogies is one of the latest acquisitions, occurring well after children have mastered letter–sound correspondences. The recent findings of Goswami, described in this issue by **Barron**, might indicate caution in adopting that particular conclusion. But these are the sort of considerations we shall turn to later on.

Several authors have derived from dual-route theory the prediction that beginners would use indirect access more often than more skilled readers, and have tried to put it to the test of experiments. **Barron** reviews that work thoroughly. It is clear that no coherent picture emerges.

Some of these studies can be criticized at the level of validity, since they are based on tasks with remote relations to actual reading. It might be worth noting that those studies that are based on actual reading performance, those by Doctor and Coltheart and by Seidenberg and his group, yield results more favorable to the hypothesis than the other ones. One particular aspect of the validity problem has been noted by Jorm and Share (1983). It follows from their view that from early on children will use the direct procedure to read those words they have already read a few times, so that the chance of observing indirect access in a particular study will depend on which words the investigators have chosen to present. The authors note that experimenters who study word processing in young children will generally use high frequency concrete words which are familiar even to their younger subjects, and which are likely to be identified by the direct procedure. Special precautions would be necessary to observe their specific behavior in the presence of genuinely unknown words.

Barron takes a radical position regarding the application of dual-route theory to reading development. His central thesis is that the two procedures offered by dual-route theory cannot account for the characteristics of early word recognition as revealed by recent investigations of children's actual reading performance. The essential message of his paper, as I read it, would be that although deriving hypotheses about development from knowledge of the adult stage might have been acceptable as a starting strategy, the time has now come to turn to actual developmental data. That is a position that goes much beyond the more familiar criticism of dual-route theory as a model of adult performance.

Much work, going back to observations by Biemiller (1970), has shown that many children pass through an early stage where their knowledge concerning text consists of paired associations between particular features of the written representation and whole-word pronunciations, for a limited vocabulary of words, generally those that have been taught at school. Frith (1985) calls that stage the *logographic stage*. It has often been assumed, especially by advocates of look-say methods, that possession of a vocabulary of sight words would allow the child to infer pronunciation rules and discover orthographic analogies, and thus become an autonomous reader. This optimistic expectation has not been supported by research. It would appear that the principle of logographic reading is non-productive. In Seymour and Elder's (1986) study of a group of first-graders taught reading by a look-say method, the children appeared unable to read words they had not learned at school, and their errors consisted mainly of substitutions of other learned words. On the other hand, responses were generally chosen on the basis of part only of the available visual evidence, as is typical of performance in paired-associates learning (Gough & Hillinger, 1980): word length and community of salient letters, mostly in initial or terminal position, appeared to be important sources of confusions.

From the present point of view, the important implication of these results is that there is no continuity between early logographic reading and the direct orthographic reading of the skilled adult, where typically all the available orthographic evidence is taken account of (see Ehrlich & Rayner's, 1981 finding that a small change in a single interior letter of a word highly predictable from the context still disrupts reading performance).

The critical event that would allow the child to escape the limitations of logographic reading would be the acquisition of letter–sound correspondences. These correspondences would be applied first to some critically located letters—essentially the first and last ones—and only later in a systematic left-to-right fashion. Following Ehri and Wilce (1979), the initial usage of letter–sound correspondences would be as mnemonic devices for memorizing word pronunciations. The child would thus pass through a stage where he would use both the feature-whole-word associations typical of the logographic stage and particular letter–sound correspondences to get at the pronunciation of written words. Such a mixed strategy is different both from the exhaustive phonological assembly assumed to take place in indirect reading and from the complete orthographic identification typical of direct access.

In Frith's (1985) conception of reading development, after passing through the early *logographic stage* and an intermediate *alphabetic stage*, the child would reach an *orthographic stage* characterized by the context-dependent use of pronunciation rules, the use of analogies and the recourse to morphemic decomposition. The view developed by Marsh in several papers (e.g., Marsh et al., 1981) is very similar. Frith makes the interesting suggestion that one reason why the studies purporting to establish the developmental sequence of direct and indirect reading have produced ambiguous results might be that response patterns characteristic of both logographic and orthographic reading have indistinctly been taken as reflecting direct access.

One final remark invited by views of reading acquisition which involve some relatively invariant succession of stages, is that much too little is known about the influence of the curriculum on such succession. The majority of specialists agree that this factor must be very influential, but have done little to document that belief.

Developmental and acquired reading disorders

Although the majority of students of reading difficulties have proceeded as if there was only one pattern of reading retardation which research had to define, there have been recurrent attempts at defining sub-types of developmental dyslexia. Boder (1973) for example has proposed that one can distinguish *dysphonetic* dyslexics, whose deficiencies lie essentially in deciphering skills, *dyseidetic* ones who are mainly deficient in visual recognition and mixed cases combining the two deficiencies. One reason why the possibility of sub-types has generally been disregarded is that the traditional approach based on group means is not well adapted to their detection. If, as Boder's data suggested, there is a majority of dysphonetic types among dyslexics, mean performances on batteries of tests will presumably reveal the pattern typical of dysphonetic dyslexia. On the other hand, the definition of sub-types poses problems to which there is no ready-made solution. Yet, the notion that, in the acquisition of a complex activity such as reading, there would be one single weak step, is one many people felt uncomfortable with. With the adoption of the information processing framework and its insistence on analysis into modular sub-systems, the problem became acute.

In recent years, several investigators have started performing in-depth studies of the pattern of reading performance of individual retarded readers. The method is one that has been used extensively with dyslexic patients and the results have been likened to those obtained with the patients. One case resembling phonological dyslexia has been described by Temple and Marshall (1983) and two other ones by Seymour and McGregor (1984) and by Campbell and Butterworth (1985). Cases resembling surface dyslexia have been described by Coltheart et al. (1983) and by Seymour and McGregor. These results would seem to support the position of Boder, to the extent that her dysphonetic type resembles phonological dyslexia and her dyseidetic one sur-face dyslexia.

The extension of single-case methodology to the study of developmental dyslexia is no doubt due to an important extent to the success of its application to work with patients. One should not forget however that there might be important differences between acquired and developmental disorders. The paper by **Bryant and Impey** draws our attention to these differences, and we shall briefly consider the general problem before commenting on the authors' more specific contribution.

A simple-minded view of the relation of acquired to developmental reading disorders would be to expect a one-to-one mapping between acquired and developmental *syndromes*. That view is difficult to defend. As Ellis (1985) notes, acquired dyslexic syndromes are not well defined. As a matter of fact, one might argue that the syndrome concept is one that has been used in cognitive neuropsychology for historical reasons but which is fundamentally alien to its theoretical options. A growing number of cognitive neuropsychologists are now distancing themselves from the syndrome concept, and adopt the position that the classification issue is not critical to the task of relating patients' performance to a model of cognitive operation, and in fact creates unnecessary complications (Caramazza, 1986). The same considerations would apply equally to the study of developmental disorders. The definition of syndromes or sub-types entails problems of frontiers between categories of dyslexic subjects and also between dyslexic and non-dyslexic subjects, which should better be avoided (Ellis, 1985) and single-case methodology offers just that possibility.

A more sophisticated view is that acquired and developmental symptoms can be understood with reference to a same model of normal reading. The same components of the model could be affected through brain damage or through failure to develop normally. That is the view expressed for example by Temple and Marshall (1983).

That conception is still unsatisfactory for the reason, mentioned by **Bryant and Impey**, that data on developmental disorders should be related not to a model of the adult stage, but to a model of the development process. The point is one that should sound familiar to readers of the **Barron** paper. If we take seriously the notion that different components of the adult system appear during different stages, which succeed each other following a more or less obligatory sequence, it becomes implausible that any pattern of symptoms that damage to the adult system can produce can also result from some developmental accident. The argument has been persuasively developed by Frith (1985), taking her own interactive model of the development of reading and spelling as a framework. Brain damage can presumably affect selectively a relatively early developing component—say grapheme-phoneme conversion—and leave a later component—say morphological parsing—intact, while there is no way in which developmental arrest could produce that sort of situation.

Bryant and Impey show that patterns of reading performance resembling those observed in single-case studies of developmental dyslexics are found also in younger non-retarded subjects scoring at the same level on standard measures of reading proficiency. That is an important finding, which, as they note, earlier work of Jonathan Baron and Rebecca Treiman already predicted to some extent. These findings raise a very general question for any theory of development, and not only for theories of developmental dyslexia. The problem is that the same pattern of behaviour can be a normal state of affairs, which will smoothly make place for a different one, at a certain age, and signal developmental arrest at another age. Being much better at reading words than nonsense is a normal transitory pattern at 10 years but becomes a dyslexic symptom at 16. One could certainly find a number of similar examples in other domains. But how does one account for them? Given that the authors have chosen to give the question a rather polemical form, there is a hope that some readers will be provoked into offering an answer.

Beyond words

If Woody Allen ever made a picture on reading research, there might be a scene in which the main character, a distinguished expert on lexical access, is confronted by an intelligent layperson with the remark that "There is more to reading than just recognizing words". "Yes, yes of course!" would be the hero's immediate response, followed after a while by the somewhat reluctant query: "But what sort of things, for instance?".

It is true that contemporary reading research is to a great extent focused on the processes of word identification. This state of affairs is however not simply due, as some would have it, to academic psychologists' incapacity to deal with broad complex issues. There exists, as a matter of fact, a strong current of sophisticated research on the comprehension of phrases, sentences and larger units of text (see Mitchell, 1982, for an excellent review). On the other hand, there are serious reasons, based in part on the results of that research, to assume that in reading, just as in speech comprehension, "words are where the action is" (Cole & Jakimik, 1978).

The question we have to consider concerns the respective weights of processes specific to word recognition and of processes specific to comprehension of higher-order units in the determination of overall reading skill. It is not whether comprehension is important: nobody has to my knowledge denied that the function of reading is to understand the message intended by the writer. The problem is to locate the weak components in the chain of operations leading to comprehension. We are thus back to the problem of the locus of acquisition difficulties. Three answers have been proposed: (1) the main difficulties rest with comprehension, and poor readers are those who fail to use higher order knowledge to guide lower-level processing; (2) the main difficulties rest at the word-processing level, and poor comprehension results from deficient word recognition; (3) there are independent sources of difficulty at the two levels.

The notion of a critical role of higher-order comprehension processes was one that fitted well with the dominant beliefs of the cognitive psychology of the 1960s, which had inherited from New Look psychology a strong bias in favour of top-down types of influences. Neisser (1967) called reading "visually guided thinking". The crucial capacity leading to efficient reading was supposed to be the use of context to help the recognition of individual words (Smith, 1971). Hochberg (1970), who produced probably the most elegant presentation of the whole position, assumed also that the choice of fixation points was controlled continuously by expectations derived from already interpreted text. The position led to the practical conclusion that teachers should stress comprehension rather than word recognition, and has served as theoretical basis for advocating global approaches to reading instruction.

The results of research have not supported the notion that better readers are characterized by higher reliance on context. First, studies of eye movements have revealed that fluent readers fixate about every word in a text, and show no tendency to skip highly predictable ones (McConkie & Zola, 1981). On the other hand, better readers appear not to use context more than poorer ones, when reading text. Perfetti, Goldman and Hoagaboam (1979) found that the word naming times of superior 5th grade readers were *less* affected by prior presentation of a congruent sentence context than those of poorer readers, and a number of other studies reviewed by Stanovich (1982b) have found either equal or greater reliance on context in poorer readers. Stanovich (1980) has suggested an "interactive-compensatory" hypothesis, according to which readers compensate for deficiency in one source of information about words by relying more on information from other sources. Poor readers would rely more on context because they process words less efficiently. Better readers would depend on contextual facilitation much less because they access lexical information faster. The notion is strongly supported by the results of Perfetti and Roth (1981) who found that skilled readers increase their reliance on context when they read degraded print, a situation in which word recognition is presumably slower.

That context-free word recognition capacity is an important determinant of overall reading skill would thus seem to be well established. The remaining question is whether comprehension processes have a contribution of their own. This is a complex question regarding which no clear-cut conclusion can probably be reached at the present time.

One problem is to isolate a contribution which is specific to reading. We can of course expect comprehension processes to be to a large extent common to reading and speech understanding. So, we should not be surprised by data showing that good readers, that is, children who are competent at making sense of written sentences, are also good at understanding spoken sentences, and that they are for example more successful than poorer readers in the task of guessing missing words in sentences (Stanovich, 1982b). One could well hold that such performances do not belong properly to the study of reading, and sympathize with Crowder's (1982) suggestion that "the proper subject of reading leaves off more or less where comprehension begins". Crowder takes the examples of an hypothetical study of metaphor understanding by braille readers, which, he claims, should normally not be considered as belonging to the field of braille reading.

The problem however is too complicated to be reducible to a matter of definition. It might be the case that some comprehension operations do not proceed likewise in reading and in listening, because of the particular ways in which the data are being obtained in the two situations. One obvious difference lies in the various possibilities for retracing, checking or simply slowing down which are available to the reader and not to the listener (**Shankweiler and Crain** in this issue note however that they may be less available to the unskilled reader).

Another reason why comprehension might proceed differently in reading and in listening lies in the hierarchical relation between comprehension and word recognition: inaccuracy or slowness at the lower level might create difficulties at the higher level. This "transmitted difficulty" notion, which has been introduced some years ago by Perfetti and Lesgold (1977), is one component of the general conception presented here by **Shankweiler and Crain**.

In their ambitious paper, these authors develop a particular view of the causes of the difficulties in dealing with complex syntactic constructions which have been observed in poor readers. This view is then integrated into proposals for a general conception of the origins of reading acquisition difficulties. We shall consider these two aspects in turn.

Regarding syntactic difficulties, the authors argue that they do not reflect a lag in the development of syntactic structures but rather a limitation at the level of processing, namely at that of working memory. They refer to earlier work by Crain with pre-school children where it was shown that similar types of difficulties in dealing with spoken sentences could be eliminated by lessening the burden on working memory. On the other hand, they discuss results by Shankweiler and by other Haskins investigators, which make difficulties for a structural lag interpretation. Fowler's recent finding that poor readers who are inferior in the task of correcting syntactic errors are not on the task of judging grammaticality, is here particularly suggestive. Finally, the authors question arguments raised against a working memory interpretation by Byrne and by Crowder.

One critical aspect of the authors' conception is that working memory is viewed, following Baddeley, as composed of buffer stores (only one of which, the "articulatory loop", is relevant here) and a control processor (Baddeley's "central executive"). Within that conception, poor readers' syntactic deficiencies are linked to working memory in two ways. The first link is direct: poor readers are people with less powerful working memory, which makes it more difficult for them to perform parsings involving storage of long strings of words, in both listening and reading. The other link is indirect and follows the familiar transmitted difficulty pattern. The mechanism which is supposed to affect the transmission involves however the central processor, and this assumption puts Shankweiler and Crain's proposal apart from other ones. Earlier conceptions (e.g., Daneman & Carpenter, 1980) involved the buffer component of working memory: the slower word recognition of poor readers imposes storage of identified words for longer periods of time before parsing. Shankweiler and Crain consider another possibility which is that the central executive is involved in word recognition, so that less efficient word recognition will deplete the resources available for syntactic processing.

What they suggest is thus that a single factor, deficient working memory, explains the whole pattern of symptoms of the poor reader. It would affect reading efficiency directly at both the levels of lexical access and of syntactic processing, and exert in addition an indirect multiplicative effect on syntactic processing by a process of transmitted difficulty.

A general phonological deficit?

Although speech analysis difficulties are, among the symptoms of the poor reader, those that have received the greater amount of attention, others have also been considered with varying frequencies. As listed by **Shankweiler and Crain**, they comprise, beside difficulties with complex syntactic constructions, which have been discussed in the preceding section, *object naming difficulties, anomalies of speech perception* (which presumably comprise the delays in acquisition mentioned by many authors) and *deficient working memory*.

Several authors have tried to find some underlying structure to that pattern of symptoms, and it has for instance been suggested that a general deficiency in "phonological processing" might be involved (Jorm & Share, 1983; Stanovich, 1982b). The trouble with that sort of proposal is that, in the absence of a more detailed description of a process linking the different symptoms, we are left mostly with a form of explanation by naming.

Shankweiler and Crain suggest that the sort of working memory deficit they envisage might be at the root of the whole set of difficulties. It will not escape the reader that this suggestion is a departure from the previous adherence of Haskins investigators to some form of phonological awareness conception. On the other hand, the notion would certainly need much further elaboration before it becomes a testable hypothesis. Since the authors do not develop their proposal in much detail in the present paper, this is not the place for a thorough discussion, and only some preliminary remarks will be made.

The fundamental problem is again to describe the process by which the proposed basic deficiency produces the different symptoms. Baddeley (1979) has provided a rather explicit proposal about the way working memory may be involved both in performing grapheme-phoneme translations and in holding the obtained segments until lexical access has been achieved, but no similar description is available for difficulties in speech perception or in object naming. Another problem is that working memory plays an ubiquitous role in all sorts of skills and one would need an explanation of how limitations at its level would affect reading performance specifically. There is a large literature on that topic, in which the Haskins work figures prominently, but there is neither space nor time to discuss it in adequate detail here.

Finally, some of the data reported in the present issue might create difficulties for the hypothesis. For instance, it is not clear how it would explain the differences in speech analysis capacity between illiterates and ex-illiterates or between alphabetic and non-alphabetic Chinese readers.

References

Alegria, J., & Morais, J. (1979). Le développement de l'habileté d'analyse consciente de la parole et l'apprentissage de la lecture. *Archives de Psychologie, 1983*, 251–270.

Alegria, J., Pignot, E., & Morais, J. (1982). Phonetic analysis of speech and memory codes in beginning readers. *Memory and Cognition, 10*, 451–456.

Baddeley, A.D. (1979). Working memory and reading. In P.A. Kolers, M.E. Wrolstadt, and H. Bouma (Eds.), *Processing of visible language, vol. 1*. New York: Plenum.

Barron, R.W.G. (1986). Word recognition in early reading: a review of the direct and indirect access hypotheses. *Cognition, 24*, 93–119, this issue.

Bender, L. (1957). Specific reading disability as a maturational lag. *Bulletin of The Orton Society, 7*, 9–18.

Bertelson, P. (1972). Listening from left to right vs. right to left. *Perception, 1*, 161–165.

Bertelson, P., Morais, J., Alegria, J., & Content. A. (1985). Phonetic analysis capacity and learning to read. *Nature, 313*, 73–74.

Biemiller, A.J. (1970). The development of the use of graphic and contextual information as children learn to read. *Reading Research Quarterly, 6*, 75–96.

Boder, E. (1973). Developmental dyslexia: prevailing diagnostic concepts and a new diagnostic approach. In H.R. Myklebust (Ed.), *Progress in learning disabilities, vol. 2*. New York: Grune & Stratton.

Bradley, L., & Bryant, P.E. (1978). Difficulties in auditory organization as a possible cause of reading backwardness. *Nature, 271*, 746–747.

Bradley, L., & Bryant, P.E. (1983). Categorizing sounds and learning to read: a causal connection. *Nature, 301*, 419–421.

Brady, S., Shankweiler, D., & Mann. V. (1983). Speech perception and memory coding in relation to reading ability. *Journal of Experimental Child Psychology, 35*, 345–367.

Bruce, D.J. (1964). The analysis of word sounds by young children. *British Journal of Educational Psychology, 34*, 158–170.

Bryant, P.E., & Bradley L. (1985). *Children's reading difficulties*. Oxford: Blackwell.

Bryant, P.E., & Impey, L. (1986). The similarities between normal readers and developmental and acquired dyslexics. *Cognition, 24*, 121–137, this issue.

Campbell, R., & Butterworth, B. (1985). Phonological dyslexia and dysgraphia in a highly literate subject: a developmental case with associated deficits of phonemic processing and awareness. *The Quarterly Journal of Experimental Psychology, 37A*, 435–476.

Caramazza, A. (1986). On drawing inferences about the structure of normal cognitive systems from the analysis of patterns of impaired performance: the case for single-patient studies. *Brain and Cognition, 5*, 41–66.

Carr, T.H. (1981). Building theories of reading ability: on the relation between individual differences in cognitive skills and reading comprehension. *Cognition, 9*, 73–113.

Cole, R.A., & Jakimik, J. (1978). Understanding speech: how words are heard. In G. Underwood (Ed.), *Strategies of information processing*. London: Academic Press.

Coltheart, M. (1978). Lexical access in simple reading tasks. In G. Underwood, (Ed.), *Strategies of information processing*. London: Academic Press.

Coltheart, M., Masterton, J., Byng, S., Prior, M., & Riddoch, J. (1983). Surface dyslexia. *The Quarterly Journal of Experimental Psychology, 35A*, 469–495.

Content, A., Morais, J., Alegria, J., & Bertelson, P. (1982). Accelerating the development of phonetic segmentation skills in kindergartners. *Cahiers de Psychologie cognitive, 2*, 259–269.

Crowder, R. (1982). *The psychology of reading: an introduction*. New York: Oxford University Press.

Daneman, M., & Carpenter, P.A. (1980). Individual differences in working memory and reading. *Journal of Verbal Learning and Verbal Behavior, 19*, 450–466.

De Gelder, B. (1986). Phonological awareness reconsidered. (Unpublished manuscript) Tilburg University.

Ehri, L.C., & Wilce L.S. (1979). The mnemonic value of orthography among beginning readers. *Journal of Educational Psychology, 71*, 26–40.

Ehri, L.C. (1984). How orthography alters spoken language competencies in children learning to read and spell. In J. Downing and R. Valtin (Eds.), *Language awareness and learning to read*. New York: Springer.

Ehrlich, S.F., & Rayner, K. (1981). Contextual effects on word perception and eye movements during reading. *Journal of Verbal Learning and Verbal Behavior, 20*, 641–655.

Ellis, A.W. (1984). *Reading, writing and dyslexia: a cognitive analysis*. Hillsdale: Lawrence Erlbaum.

Ellis, A.W. (1985). The cognitive neuropsychology of developmental (and acquired) dyslexia: a critical survey. *Cognitive Neuropsychology, 2*, 169–205.

Forster, K.I. (1976). Accessing the mental lexicon. In R.J. Wales and E. Walker (Eds.), *New approaches to language mechanism*. Amsterdam: North-Holland.

Frith, U. (1985). Beneath the surface of developmental dyslexia. In K.E. Patterson, J.C. Marshall & M. Coltheart (Eds.), *Surface dyslexia: neuropsychological and cognitive studies of phonological reading*. London: Lawrence Erlbaum.

Gelb, I.J. (1963). *A study of writing*. 2nd edn.. Chicago: University of Chicago Press.

Gleitman, L.R. & Rozin, P. (1977). The structure and acquisition of reading I: Relations between orthographies and the structure of language. In A.S. Reber & D.L. Scarborough (Eds.), *Toward a psychology of reading*. Hillsdale: Lawrence Erlbaum.

Glushko, R.J. (1979). The organization and activation of orthographic knowledge in reading aloud. *Journal of Experimental Psychology: Human Perception and Performance, 5*, 674–691.

Gough, P.B., & Hillinger, M.L. (1980). Learning to read: an unnatural act. *Bulletin of the Orton Society, 30*, 179–195.

Henderson, L. (1982). *Orthography and word recognition in reading*. London: Academic Press.

Hochberg, J. (1970). Components of literacy: speculations and exploratory research. In H. Levin & J.P. Williams (Eds.), *Basic studies on reading*. New York: Basic Books.

Huey, E.B. (1908). *The psychology and pedagogy of reading*. Reprint. Cambridge, MA: MIT Press.

Humphreys, G.W., & Evett, L.J. (1985). Are there independent lexical and non-lexical routes in word processing? An evaluation of the dual-route theory of reading. *The Behavioral and Brain Sciences, 8*, 689–740.

Jorm, A.F., & Share, D.L. (1983). Phonological recoding and reading acquisition. *Applied Psycholinguistics, 4*, 103–147.

Kavanagh, J.F., & Mattingly, I.G. (1972). *Language by ear and by eye*. Cambridge, MA: MIT Press.

Kerek, A. (1976). The phonological relevance of spelling pronunciation. *Visible Language, 10*, 323–338.

Liberman, I.Y. (1973). Segmentation of the spoken word and reading acquisition. *Bulletin of The Orton Society, 23*, 65–77.

Liberman, I.Y., Shankweiler, D., Liberman, A.M., Fowler, C., & Fisher, W.F. (1977). In A.S. Reber & D.L. Scarborough (Eds.), *Toward a psychology of reading*. Hillsdale: Lawrence Erlbaum.

Lundberg, I. (1978). Aspects of linguistic awareness related to reading. In A. Sinclair, R.J. Jarvella & W.J.M. Levelt (Eds.), *The child's conception of language*. Berlin: Springer.

Mann, V.A. (1986). Phonological awareness: the role of reading experience. *Cognition, 24*, 65–92, this issue.

Marcel, A.J. (1980). Surface dyslexia and beginning reading: a revised hypothesis of the pronunciation of print and its impairment. In M. Coltheart, K.E. Patterson & J.C. Marshall (Eds.), *Deep dyslexia*. London: Routledge & Kegan Paul.

Marsh, G., Friedman, M.P., Welch, V., & Desberg, P. (1981). A cognitive-developmental approach to reading acquisition. In T.G. Waller & G.E. McKinnon (Eds.), *Reading research: advances in theory and practice, vol. 3*. New York: Academic Press.

Marshall, J.C., & Newcombe, F. (1973). Patterns of paralexia: a psycholinguistic approach. *Journal of Psycholinguistic Research, 2*, 175–199.

Mattingly, I.G. (1972). Reading, the linguistic process and linguistic awareness. In J.F. Kavanagh & I.G. Mattingly (Eds.), *Language by ear and by eye*. Cambridge, MA: MIT Press.

McConkie, G.W., & Zola, D. (1981). Language constraints and the functional stimulus in reading. In A.M. Lesgold & C.A. Perfetti (Eds.), *Interactive processes in reading*. Hillsdale: Lawrence Erlbaum.

Mitchell, D.C. (1982). *The processes of reading*. Chichester: Wiley.

Morais, J., Bertelson, P., Cary, L., & Alegria, J. (1986). Literacy training and speech segmentation. *Cognition, 24*, 45–64, this issue.

Morais, J., Cary, L., Alegria, J., & Bertelson, P. (1979). Does awareness of speech as a sequence of phones arise spontaneously? *Cognition, 7*, 323–331.

Morton, J. (1979). Word recognition. In J. Morton, & J.C. Marshall (Eds.), *Psycholinguistic series, vol. 2.* Cambridge, MA: MIT Press.

Neisser, U. (1967). *Cognitive psychology.* New York: Prentice.

Oloffson, A., & Lundberg, I. (1983). Can phonemic awareness be trained in kindergarten? *Scandinavian Journal of Psychology, 24,* 35–44.

Patterson, K.E., & Morton, J. (1985). From orthography to phonology: an attempt at an old interpretation. In K.E. Patterson, J.C. Marshall & M. Coltheart (Eds.), *Surface dyslexia: neuropsychological and cognitive studies of phonological reading.* London: Lawrence Erlbaum.

Perfetti, C.A., Beck, I., & Hughes, C. (1981). Phonemic knowledge and learning to read. Paper presented at meeting of American Society for Research in Child Development, Boston.

Perfetti, C.A., Goldman, S.R., & Hoagaboam, T.W. (1979). Reading skill and the identification of words in discourse context. *Memory and Cognition, 7,* 273–282.

Perfetti, C.A., & Lesgold, A.M. (1977). Discourse comprehension and sources of individual differences. In P.A. Carpenter & M. Just (Eds.), *Cognitive processes in comprehension.* Hillsdale: Lawrence Erlbaum.

Perfetti, C.A., & Roth, S.F. (1981). Some of the interactive processes in reading and their role in reading skill. In A.M. Lesgold & C.A. Perfetti (Eds.), *Interactive processes in reading.* Hillsdale: Lawrence Erlbaum.

Read, C.A., Zhang, Y., Nie, H., & Ding, B. (1986). The ability to manipulate speech sounds depends on knowing alphabetic reading. *Cognition, 24,* 31–44, this issue.

Reitsma, P. (1983). Printed word learning in beginning readers. *Journal of Experimental Child Psychology, 36,* 321–339.

Rozin, P. (1978). The acquisition of basic alphabetic principles; a structural approach. In C.A. Catania & T.A. Brigham (Eds.), *Handbook of applied behavior analysis.* New York: Irvington.

Rozin, P., & Gleitman, L.R. (1977). The structure and acquisition of reading II: The reading process and the acquisition of the alphabetic principle. In A.S. Reber & D.L. Scarborough (Eds.), *Toward a psychology of reading.* Hillsdale: Lawrence Erlbaum.

Rozin, P., Poritzky, S., & Sotzky, R. (1971). American children with reading problems can easily learn English represented by Chinese characters. *Science, 171,* 1264–1267.

Rubenstein, H., Lewis, S.S., & Rubenstein, M.A. (1971). Evidence for phonemic recoding in visual word recognition. *Journal of Verbal Learning and Verbal Behavior, 10,* 645–657.

Seidenberg, M.S., & Tanenhaus, M.K. (1982). Orthographic effects on rhyme monitoring. *Journal of Experimental Psychology: Human Learning and Memory, 5,* 546–554.

Seymour, P.H.K., & Elder, L. (1986). Beginning reading without phonology. *Cognitive Neuropsychology, 3,* 1–36.

Seymour, P.H.K., & McGregor, C.J. (1984). Developmental dyslexia: a cognitive experimental analysis of phonological, morphemic and visual impairment. *Cognitive Neuropsychology, 1,* 43–82.

Shallice, T., & McCarthy, R. (1985). Phonological reading: from patterns of impairment to possible procedures. In K.E. Patterson, J.C. Marshall & M. Coltheart (Eds.), *Surface dyslexia: neuropsychological and cognitive studies of phonological reading.* London: Lawrence Erlbaum.

Shankweiler, D., & Crain, S. (1986). Language mechanism and reading disorder: a modular approach. *Cognition, 24,* 139–168, this issue.

Shankweiler, D., & Liberman, I.Y. (1972). Misreading: a search for causes. In J.F. Kavanagh & I.G. Mattingly (Eds.), *Language by ear and by eye,* pp. 293–318. Cambridge, MA: MIT Press.

Sinclair, A., Jarvella, R.J., & Levelt, W.J.M. (Eds.) (1978). *The child's conception of language.* Berlin: Springer.

Skjelfjord, V.J. (1976). Teaching children to segment spoken words as an aid in learning to read. *Journal of Learning Disabilities, 9,* 297–306.

Smith, F. (1971). *Understanding reading.* New York: Holt, Rinehart & Winston.

Stanovich, K.E. (1980). Toward an interactive-compensatory model of individual differences in the development of reading fluency. *Reading Research Quarterly, 16*, 32–71.

Stanovich, K.E. (1982a). Individual differences in the cognitive processes of reading: I. Word decoding. *Journal of Learning Disabilities, 15*, 485–493.

Stanovich, K.E. (1982b). Individual differences in the cognitive processes of reading: II. Text-level processes. *Journal of Learning Disabilities, 15*, 549–554.

Temple, C.M., & Marshall, J.C. (1983). A case study of phonological developmental dyslexia. *British Journal of Psychology, 74*, 517–533.

Torneus, M. (1984). Phonological awareness and reading: a chicken and egg problem? *Journal of Educational Psychology, 76*, 1346–1358.

Torrey, J.W. (1979). Reading that comes naturally: the early reader. In T.G. Waller & G.E. MacKinnon (Eds.), *Reading research: advances in theory and practice, vol. 1*. New York: Academic Press.

Treiman, R., & Baron, J. (1981). Segmental analysis ability: development and relation to reading ability. In T.G. Waller and G.E. MacKinnon (Eds.), *Reading research: advances in theory and practice, vol. 2*. New York: Academic Press.

Treiman, R., & Baron, J. (1983). Phonemic analysis training helps children benefit from spelling-sound rules. *Memory and Cognition, 11*, 382–389.

Vellutino, F.R. (1979). *Dyslexia: theory and practice*. Cambridge MA: MIT Press.

Résumé

Cette introduction passe en revue des développements récents dont la connaissance est indispensable pour comprendre la recherche actuelle sur l'acquisition de la lecture. L'accent est mis sur les rapports entre l'étude de la performance adulte, celle des effets des lésions neurologiques et celle du développement de la lecture. Le problème central de ces recherches est d'identifier les causes des difficultés spécifiques auxquelles semble se heurter l'acquisition de la lecture. En général, ce problème a été abordé par des méthodes correlationnelles, fondées sur la comparaison des performances des bons et des mauvais lecteurs. Les mérites et les défauts de cette approche sont discutés, et on insiste sur le besoin de rattacher les études différentielles à une conception théorique générale du processus de lecture et de son développement. On examine le courant d'études issu de l'hypothèse selon laquelle une des difficultés majeures de l'acquisition de la lecture alphabétique réside dans la manipulation du language au niveau des segments phonémiques, et on discute la manière dont les résultats de ces études peuvent être reliés aux théories actuelles de l'accès lexical. Les limites de l'approche qui consiste à tirer des hypothèses sur le développement à partir de théories relatives au stade adulte sont décrites et illustrées par des données sur la performance d'enfants normaux et dyslexiques. Enfin, on discute la possibilité que les difficultés d'acquisition de la lecture trouvent leur source à des niveaux supérieurs à celui de la reconnaissance des mots.

The ability to manipulate speech sounds depends on knowing alphabetic writing*

CHARLES READ

University of Wisconsin, Madison

ZHANG YUN-FEI

Beijing Normal University

NIE HONG-YIN

China Central Institute for Nationalities

DING BAO-QING,

Beijing Normal University

Abstract

Chinese adults literate only in Chinese characters could not add or delete individual consonants in spoken Chinese words. A comparable group of adults, literate in alphabetic spelling as well as characters, could perform the same tasks readily and accurately. The two groups were similar in education and experience but differed in age and consequently in whether they had learned an alphabetic writing system in school. Even adults who had once learned alphabetic writing but were no longer able to use it were able to manipulate speech sounds in this way. This "segmentation" skill, which has been shown to contribute to skilled reading and writing, does not develop with cognitive maturation, non-alphabetic literacy, or exposure to a language rich in rhymes

*The research reported in this paper was funded by the Wisconsin Center for Education Research, which is supported in part by a grant from the National Institute of Education (Grant No. NIE-G-81-0009). The opinions expressed in this paper do not necessarily reflect the position, policy, or endorsement of the National Institute of Education. Charles Read is Professor of English and Linguistics at the University of Wisconsin-Madison. Zhang Yunfei is Professor of the English Language at Beijing Normal University. Nie Hongyin is Lecturer on Ancient Chinese and Chinese Phonology in the Central Institute for Nationalities, Beijing. Ding Baoqing is Teacher of the English Language at Beijing Normal University. We wish to thank Jonathan Baron, Paul Bertelson, Lynette Bradley, Peter Bryant, Lila Gleitman, Isabelle Liberman, Jose Morais, and Rebecca Treiman for helpful comments on an earlier draft. They are not responsible for remaining errors and infelicities. Reprint requests should be addressed to Charles Read, Department of English and Linguistics, University of Wisconsin, Madison, WI 53706, U.S.A.

and other segmental contrasts. It does develop in the process of learning to read and write alphabetically.

For more than a decade, evidence has been accumulating that learning to read and spell in an alphabetic writing system depends upon the skills known as *phonemic segmentation*: the ability to conceive of spoken words as sequences of phonemic segments and to identify and locate those segments within words and syllables. Liberman (1971) was among the first to identify this relationship. Gleitman and Rozin (1977) and Rozin and Gleitman (1977) argued persuasively that segmentation skill is crucial to alphabetic reading. Considering the unique invention of alphabetic writing and their experience in teaching a syllabic writing system for English to children who had had difficulty with the alphabetic one, they claimed (p. 133) that:

> the basic barrier to initial progress [in reading] is in the realization of the segmentation of speech.

Several studies have found segmentation skill to be a significant predictor of success in early reading, even when the effects of educationally potent variables such as IQ and family status have been taken into account (Blachman, 1983; Bradley & Bryant, 1983; Lundberg, Olofsson, & Wall, 1980; Mann & Liberman, 1984; Zifcak, 1978). Liberman, Liberman, Mattingly, and Shankweiler (1980) reviewed studies of the development of segmentation skill and the use of phonological analysis in reading. They pointed out that segmentation is inherently difficult because speech is more like a stream than like a row of buckets: what we think of as discrete phones actually overlap and influence each other. Learning segmentation constitutes a major obstacle for some beginning readers, they concluded.

Liberman (1982) presents a view of reading and reading disability based on the premise that segmentation is crucial to reading alphabetic writing.

> In contrast [to the hearer or speaker], the reader and writer must be something of a linguist—able, at the very least, quite deliberately to divide utterances into the constituent segments that are represented by the characters of the orthography.

Liberman cites several studies which show that poor reading can be predicted from poor segmentation skills (p. 34) and that the skilled reader uses the phonological structure of words, and therefore must be able to segment (p. 38).

Making the relationship more specific, Treiman and Baron (1981) showed that "segmental analysis correlates most highly with one aspect of reading ability—use of spelling-sound rules" (p. 194). Treiman and Baron (1983) reinforced that conclusion by showing that specific training in phonemic analysis helps preschool and kindergarten children learn to use such rules in learning to read.

In short, it appears that a crucial step in learning to read and write alphabetically is learning to conceive of speech as a sequence of discrete segments. It is a difficult step for some learners, perhaps because this conception is only indirectly related to both sound and meaning, the aspects of language that we are normally aware of. Segmentation facilitates learning to read primarily by making it possible for the reader to use spelling-sound rules, an ability which is part of skilled reading.

Another question about the relation between segmentation and literacy is that of cause or effect: is segmentation a prerequisite to literacy, a consequence of literacy, or both? Bradley and Bryant (1978) addressed this question by comparing older poor readers with younger good readers. Because of the substantial difference in age (3½ years, on the average), the two groups were the same in reading and spelling achievement, but nevertheless they differed greatly in segmentation skill, measured by judgments of rhyme and alliteration. This result suggests that the difference in segmentation ability between good and poor readers cannot be solely an *effect* of differences in reading achievement or experience; it may therefore be a partial *cause* of those differences.

Next Bradley and Bryant (1983) combined a longitudinal study with a training study. The former showed substantial correlations (about .50) between prereaders' ability to recognize sameness of sounds and their success in reading and spelling 3 years later. Segmentation accounted for significant variance in reading, even beyond the strong effects of IQ and memory. The training study showed significant effects (on reading and spelling performance) of training prereaders to recognize sameness of sounds. Separately, neither of these two kinds of evidence would permit us to infer causation, but together they indicate that sound recognition skills do contribute to reading success. They do not show that the causation is in one direction only: that learning to read does not also enhance segmental analysis. The effects of sound categorization skill and training were large enough to be important in planning pedagogy. For example, the training accounted for 4 months of additional development within a period of 2 years.

How does segmentation skill develop?

Given this persuasive evidence that segmentation skill is strongly and causatively related to reading and writing performance, we have investigated part of the question, under what conditions does this skill develop? In particular, does segmentation ability develop without reading instruction, on the basis of cognitive maturation and experience with spoken and even written language?

Significance

The answer to this question bears on a theoretical issue: is alphabetic literacy the only linguistic performance that relies on a segmental conception of language? Are there other activities that might foster this conception, such as rhyming and alliteration in verse, committing and correcting speech or comprehension errors that interchange segments ("Spoonerisms"), or distinguishing pairs of words that differ in just one segment ("minimal pairs"), like *pin* and *tin*?

On the practical side, the answer may affect our view of children who have difficulty in learning to read and write. Do they simply lag behind their peers in developing a conception of spoken language that comes about normally with maturation and linguistic experience? If so, they might be better served by beginning reading instruction later, and adults of low literacy might be able to develop the skills that eluded them as children. Or do people rarely develop a segmental conception of language without learning to read and write alphabetically? In that case, we can not expect other linguistic experiences to help those who find literacy difficult, and second-language learners whose native language is written nonalphabetically, such as Japanese or Chinese, may lack a conception which underlies the writing system of the language they are trying to learn.

The Morais experiment

Morais, Cary, Alegria, and Bertelson (1979) investigated whether segmentation ability can develop over time *without* literacy, that is whether it can be an effect of cognitive development and experience with spoken language alone. They compared literate and illiterate adults in rural Portugal, finding that the former, but not the latter, could add and delete consonants at the beginning of words. They conclude,

> Awareness of speech as a sequence of phones is thus not attained spontaneously in the course of general cognitive growth, but demands some specific training, which for most persons, is probably provided by learning to read in the alphabetic system.

Comparing alphabetic and nonalphabetic *literates*, rather than literates and illiterates, would be a somewhat more direct test of the Morais et al. hypothesis, and it might avoid possible differences between literates and illiterates in intelligence and experience with language. Following Shankweiler and Liberman (1976), Morais et al. suggest a study of the development of segmentation skills in children learning nonalphabetic writing, as in Chinese. (Chinese characters represent one-syllable morphemes, not phonemes). But they cite Liberman, Shankweiler, Liberman, Fowler, and Fischer (1977):

> Unfortunately, a pure test will be hard to make. Children in the People's Republic of China are now being taught to read alphabetically before beginning their study of logographic characters (Liberman et al., 1977, p. 213 fn.)

This last statement is essentially correct, but a comparison of alphabetic and nonalphabetic literates is still possible in China. Most adults who completed primary school before 1958, who are now more than 35 years old, have not learned alphabetic writing, while most younger people *have* done so. We conducted a study like that of Morais et al. with workers in Beijing who fit these two patterns.

Since 1958, an official alphabetic writing system known as *Hanyu pinyin* has been taught in primary schools, particularly in a period of about 4 weeks in first grade, just before the children begin to learn to read Chinese characters. For the Beijing dialect, *pinyin* is essentially a phonemic representation, in Roman letters. It is used mainly in primary schools and in some contexts for foreigners; it is not used in ordinary communication, as in newspapers and books. As a result of the long-standing interest in Romanization, *pinyin* appears below the Chinese characters on the signs of some hotels and stores. These signs aid foreign visitors who can recognize some words that they have heard spoken, but to most Chinese adults, they are mere decoration.

Method

Our method was like that of Morais et al. except for changes which followed from differences between the two languages or the subjects.

Subjects

Our two groups of subjects were adults literate only in Chinese characters (the nonalphabetic group) and adults who had also learned *Hanyu pinyin* (the alphabetic group). Subjects were assigned to these two groups on the basis of whether they reported having learned any alphabetic writing system in school. We checked this self-report with the dates of their schooling. Before the segmentation task, we tested each subject in the alphabetic group, asking him or her to read aloud 10 simple words printed in *pinyin* on cards.

The two groups were similar in occupation and environment; all were workers at Beijing Normal University and lived on the campus. The subjects in both groups were gardeners, waitresses, cooks, tailors, and nursery teachers. All but one subject in each group was female. As Table 1 shows, the groups differed primarily in age and to a lesser extent in years of schooling.

Comparing literates with illiterates who had had opportunities to learn to read, as in Morais et al. (1979), one might fear that the two groups differed in relevant skills, that is, that the illiterates had failed to learn to read, or chosen not to try, because they lacked skills like segmentation. In our sample, neither group had much opportunity or motivation to learn to read alphabetically as adults, because *pinyin* is not used among native-speaking adults. For that reason, we believe that the major difference was that of alphabetic instruction in primary school, which reflects age, not self-selection.

Tasks

As in Morais et al., each subject's task was to add or delete a single consonant at the beginning of a spoken syllable. Chinese syllables lend themselves to this procedure: they consist of a syllabic nucleus, such as /a/, with or without a single initial consonant, such as /d/, and a single final nasal (or retroflex) consonant, such as /n/; thus /a/, /da/, /an/, and /dan/ are possible syllables; there are no consonant clusters, initially or finally. Because of this syllable structure, Chinese provides a strong test of whether adults without training in alphabetic spelling can learn to add or delete initial consonants. It should be relatively easy to learn to do so in Chinese, where every syllable has either one initial consonant or none and there are many pairs of words that differ in just this respect. In both poetry and prose, there are also many rhyming

Table 1. *Subjects' mean ages and mean years of schooling*

Group	N	Mean age	Mean years of schooling
Alphabetic	12	33	10
Nonalphabetic	18	49	7

words, which might stimulate the tacit development of a segmental conception of language.

In this experiment, the phoneme to be added or deleted was /d/, /s/, or /n/; thus there were six conditions in all (add /d/, delete /d/, etc.). Subjects were assigned to conditions randomly in equal numbers.

The arrangement of tasks within each condition also followed that in Morais et al.; there were three sections, as outlined in Table 2. In the first (training) section, the experimenter explained the task and presented five examples followed by ten training trials. As an example of adding an initial consonant, for instance, he pronounced the consonant, the rime, and the result, e.g., /s /, /an/, /san/. In the training trials, he encouraged the subject and corrected the response, giving repeated examples if necessary. In the two experimental sections, the experimenter read each stimulus syllable and waited for the subject's response; he did not indicate whether the response was correct.

In the nonalphabetic group, three subjects were assigned to each condition; thus three subjects were to add /d/, three were to delete /d/, and so on. In the alphabetic group, there were two subjects in each condition. All stimuli and targets were possible syllables in Chinese; thus, for example, the non-words included /dɔ́ŋ/ but not /djɔ́ŋ/, which is not a possible syllable in the phonological structure of Chinese.

Scoring

Each subject was interviewed individually in a quiet room. Three judges were present at each interview. Two of these, trained in phonetic transcription, transcribed each response; the third judge simply wrote down whether the response was correct. One transcriber and the third judge were native speakers of Chinese; the former was a native of Beijing, and the latter had lived there for many years. When the two transcribers agreed on whether the response was correct, that judgment was accepted. When they disagreed, the

Table 2. *Arrangement of tasks in all conditions*

Section	No. of items	Stimulus	Target	Examples: Add/delete	Feedback, correction
Training	10	Nonword	Word	ōng ⟨--⟩ dōng	yes
Exptl.	10	Word	Word	ai ⟨--⟩ dai	no
Exptl.	10	Nonword	Nonword	ou ⟨--⟩ dou	no

opinion of the third judge was accepted. A correct response was one which added or deleted the single initial consonant in one integrated production, without changing the syllable nucleus. The two transcribers agreed more than 80% of the time; most disagreements were about whether the subject had produced a single integrated syllable, rather than about what phones he or she had produced.

Results

There were no significant differences by phoneme (/d, s, n/) or by task (add vs. delete), so we have ignored these variables in subsequent analysis. Only the trials with nonword targets provide unambiguous evidence of segmentation skill; on the other trials, a subject might produce some correct responses merely by seeking a real word that "sounds like" the stimulus. Even that strategy requires a degree of phonetic awareness, however, so we have not ignored the trials with real-word targets.

The basic result was a large difference in the proportion of correct trials between the alphabetic and non-alphabetic groups, for both word and nonword targets, as shown in Table 3.

These results are strikingly similar to those of Morais et al., shown in Table 4.

There was very little overlap between individuals in the two groups, as shown in Figure 1 for nonword trials and in Figure 2 for all trials.

A two-way analysis of variance shows that mean score differs significantly by alphabetic literacy ($p < .0001$) and by word vs. nonword target ($p < .01$), and there is no significant interaction (see Table 5).

Table 3. *Main results by group*

Group	N	Percent correct	Mean	S.D.
		Nonword targets		
Alpha	12	83	8.3	1.4
Nonalpha	18	21	2.1	2.4
		Word targets		
Alpha	12	93	9.3	0.9
Nonalpha	18	37	3.7	3.5

Table 4.   *Main results of Morais et al. (1979)*

Group	N	Percent correct: nonwords	Percent correct: words
Literate	30	72	~89
Illiterate	30	19	~36

Figure 1.   *Number correct in non-word trials analyzed by group (Each * represents one subject)*

Number correct	Alpha group	Nonalpha group
10	**	
9	*****	*
8	**	
7	*	
6	**	*
5		*
4		
3		**
2		***
1		*****
0		*****

Thirteen of the 18 nonalphabetic subjects attempted the task a second time immediately after the first try, with a different phoneme target but the same operation (adding or deleting). For these subjects, the median change in score was zero, on both word and nonword targets. However, one subject did improve greatly on nonword targets, from one item correct on the first try to all ten correct on the second. Evidently, given enough instruction and practice, some individuals can learn to do this task without alphabetic literacy.

Figure 2.   *Number   correct.   All
trials by group (Each *
represents one subject)*

Number correct	Alpha group	Nonalpha group
20	*	
19	****	
18	**	
17	**	*
16	*	*
15	*	
14	*	
13		
12		
11		**
10		
9		*
8		*
7		*
6		
5		*
4		**
3		***
2		
1		***
0		**

Table 5.   *Analysis of variance
2 × 2 repeated measures*

Factor	F	df	$p <$
Alpha literacy	55.75	1/28	.0001
Word vs. nonword	7.64	1/28	.01
Interaction	<1		NS

Errors

Like those in Morais et al., our subjects tended to give a real-word response
on trials with a nonword target. In Chinese, it is possible to give a response
that is identical to the target in its sequence of phonemes, differing only in
tone. Such responses are of particular interest: a predominance of them might

indicate that the subject can perform the phoneme manipulation but does not understand that the target is not a real word. For both groups, just 10% of incorrect responses (on nonword trials) were of this type. Other typical errors were simply to repeat the stimulus, to repeat the stimulus with a different tone, or to add the wrong consonant. Most of these latter two errors yielded real words. A few subjects who were to add a consonant consistently produced it in isolation (with a vowel if necessary), followed by the stimulus syllable.

Discussion

Clearly, these results confirm those of Morais et al., as shown in Tables 3 and 4. Our alphabetic group performed very much like Morais et al.'s literates, and our nonalphabetic group performed very much like their illiterates. This result allows us to make Morais et al.'s conclusion more specific: it is not literacy in general which leads to segmentation skill, but alphabetic literacy in particular.

The main exception, namely the nonalphabetic subject who was correct on 9 of the 10 nonword targets (and 8 of 10 word targets), seems to have known some *pinyin*. She was a 30-year-old tailor, the youngest of the nonalphabetic subjects, who admitted to having learned 'a little' about *pinyin* from her son. (We could not give her the test of reading *pinyin* that was given to the alphabetic subjects, however, because she had already denied that she could do so.)

In fact, some of our alphabetic subjects were no longer able to read alphabetic writing well. A 36-year-old cook with a primary school education, for example, said that she had learned *pinyin* from her children. She was able to read only 5 of 10 words correctly on our pretest, but she correctly deleted the initial segment on 14 of 20 experimental trials. At least two other subjects in our alphabetic group were no longer fluent in *pinyin*; on the pretest, they read words slowly and with difficulty, sounding out each letter. Yet both of them were correct on 17 of 20 experimental trials. From these cases we infer that the segmental conception acquired with alphabetic literacy may persist even when the literacy itself is dormant.

The task which we (and Morais et al.) used, adding or deleting a consonant at the beginning of a syllable, though well-suited to Chinese syllable structure, is among the more difficult manipulations of individual speech sounds (Bruce, 1964). Tasks which require less conscious and deliberate manipulation of segments (such as judgments of rhyming and alliteration, akin to the tasks in Bradley & Bryant, 1983) might not yield so sharp a distinction between alphabetic and nonalphabetic literates.

One might wonder whether this sharp distinction came about in part because our alphabetic subjects were familiar with the task; was a similar task used in teaching them to read *pinyin*? In fact, an exercise like our addition task is used in teaching, but any direct effect on this experiment must surely be weak: our alphabetic subjects had learned *pinyin* 27 years earlier, on average. Moreover, there is not a classroom exercise like our deletion task, but we found no difference between addition and deletion scores for either group.

Even alphabetic writing is taught in terms of syllables and morphemes in China. Letters are presented as spellings of syllables, indeed words, not phonemes; each letter has a particular syllabic value. For instance *g* is said to spell *gē* (older brother); the word *guān* (to close) is presented as the liaison of *gē* and *wān* (to bend). Similarly, Chinese dictionaries typically include a table of syllables, written in both *pinyin* and characters. In this table, there are about 21 syllables (words) representing possible initials (syllable onsets) and 35 representing finals (rimes). All other Chinese words are conceived of as combinations of those syllabic units. Thus the concept of individual phonemes remains implicit in both the school lessons and the dictionaries.

One might also wonder whether all of our subjects had not been exposed to segmentation in the "phonetic radicals" that are a part of many Chinese characters, indicating the pronunciation of the word represented. For example, the character for "eight," pronounced *bā*, occurs in the character for "to cling," which is also pronounced *bā*. But one crucial difference between these radicals and alphabetic writing is that the radicals always represent a whole syllable. When that syllable is not pronounced *exactly* like the one that it cues, the difference is almost always in the initial consonant and/or the tone, not the rime. For example, the character for "to exude an aroma," as for flowers or wine, pronounced *gìn*, contains the radical for "heart, mind," pronounced *xīn*. Thus these so-called phonetic radicals suggest phonemic segmentation only in a constrained and implicit way, as do rhyming words, speech errors, and minimal pairs. Exposure to such examples is evidently not sufficient for most people to develop a segmental conception of language that makes possible more explicit manipulations.

Conclusion

Learning to read and write alphabetically requires conceiving of speech as a sequence of phonemes and skill in locating and identifying phonemes within syllables. Morais et al. (1979) showed that that skill does not develop spontaneously. We can now add that it does not develop even with 7 years of schooling and 40 years of reading and writing nonalphabetically in a language rich in implicit examples like rhymes, minimal pairs, and phonetic radicals, not to mention Spoonerisms. Once a segmental conception has developed, however, it may outlast the fluency in reading. This is not to say that no educational or linguistic experience other than reading instruction could produce segmentation skill; in fact, one nonalphabetic subject learned to perform our task well, given a second set of trials. However, in both Morais et al. and in the present study, we see very large differences in segmentation skill according to alphabetic literacy, with almost no overlap between groups, despite substantial differences in language, culture and education between the two populations.

From these strong connections between alphabetic literacy and phonemic segmentation, we can gain a greater understanding of children and adults who have difficulty in learning to read, and of second-language learners confronting alphabetic writing for the first time. To read and write alphabetically, they must not only acquire specific reading skills, but more basically, they must learn to segment spoken syllables into phonemic units. That skill, and the conception of language that underlies it, does not ordinarily develop by itself, even with nonalphabetic literacy and many examples of words that differ in just one segment. For most people, it evidently requires explicit instruction.

References

Blachman, B.A. (1983). Are we assessing the linguistic factors critical in early reading? *Annals of Dyslexia, 33,* 91–109.

Bradley, L., & Bryant, P.E. (1978). Difficulties in auditory organization as a possible cause of reading backwardness. *Nature, 271,* 746–747.

Bradley, L., & Bryant, P.E. (1983). Categorizing sounds and learning to read—a causal connection. *Nature, 301,* 419–421.

Bruce, D.J. (1964). The analysis of word sounds by young children. *British Journal of Educational Psychology, 34,* 158–170.

Gleitman, L.R., & Rozin, P. (1977). The structure and acquisition of reading I: Relations between orthographies and the structure of language. In A.S. Reber & D.L. Scarborough (Eds.), *Toward a psychology of reading: the proceedings of the CUNY conference.* Hillsdale, NJ: Erlbaum.

Liberman, I.Y. (1971). Basic research in speech and lateralization of language: some implications for reading disability. *Bulletin of the Orton Society, 21,* 71–87.

Liberman, I.Y. (1982). A language-oriented view of reading and its disabilities. In H. Myklebust (Ed.), *Progress in learning disabilities,* Vol. 5. New York: Grune & Stratton.

Liberman, I.Y., Liberman, A.M., Mattingly, I., & Shankweiler, D. (1980). Orthography and the beginning reader. In J.F. Kavanagh & R.L. Venezky (Eds.), *Orthography, reading, and dyslexia.* Baltimore: University Park Press.

Liberman, I.Y., Shankweiler, D., Liberman, A.M., Fowler, C., & Fischer, F.W. (1977). Phonetic segmentation and recoding in the beginning reader. In A.S. Reber & D. Scarborough (Eds.), *Toward a psychology of reading: the proceedings of the CUNY conference.* Hillsdale, NJ: Erlbaum.

Lundberg, I., Olofsson, A., & Wall, S. (1980). Reading and spelling skills in the first school years predicted from phonemic awareness skills in kindergarten. *Scandinavian Journal of Psychology, 21*, 159–173.

Mann, V.A., & Liberman, I.Y. (1984). Phonological awareness and verbal short-term memory: can they presage early reading problems? *Journal of Learning Disabilities, 17*, 592–599.

Morais, J., Cary, L., Alegria, J., & Bertelson, P. (1979). Does awareness of speech as a sequence of phones arise spontaneously? *Cognition, 7*, 323–331.

Rozin, P., & Gleitman, L.R. (1977). The structure and acquisition of reading II: The reading process and the acquisition of the alphabetic principle. In A.S. Reber & D.L. Scarborough (Eds.), *Toward a psychology of reading: the proceedings of the CUNY conference.* Hillsdale, NJ: Erlbaum.

Shankweiler, D., & Liberman, I.Y. (1976). Exploring the relations between reading and speech. In R. Knights and D.J. Bakker (Eds.), *The neuropsychology of learning disorders: Theoretical approaches.* Baltimore: University Park Press.

Treiman, R., & Baron, J. (1981). Segmental analysis ability: Development and relation to reading ability. In G.E. MacKinnon & T.G. Waller (Eds.), *Reading research: Advances in theory and practice*, Vol. 3. New York: Academic Press.

Treiman, R., & Baron, J. (1983). Phonemic analysis training helps children benefit from spelling-sound rules. *Memory and Cognition, 11*, 382–389.

Zifcak, M. (1978). Phonological awareness and reading acquisition in first grade children. (Doctoral dissertation, University of Connecticut, 1977.) *Dissertation Abstracts International*, 1978, *38*, 6655A-6656A. (University Microfilms No. 78-6156).

Résumé

Des chinois adultes ne connaissant que l'écriture logographique se sont avérés incapables d'ajouter ou d'effacer des consonnes individuelles dans des mots chinois parlés. Un groupe comparable d'adultes, connaissant à la fois l'écriture logographique et l'écriture alphabétique, pouvaient effectuer les mêmes tâches sans difficulté. Les deux groupes avaient une éducation et une expérience comparable, mais des âges différents, et avaient donc eu des expériences différents en ce qui concerne l'apprentissage de l'écriture alphabétique à l'école. Même des adultes qui avaient appris l'écriture alphabétique mais n'étaient plus capables de s'en servir étaient capables de manipuler de la sorte les sons linguistiques. Cette capacité de "segmentation", dont on a pu montrer qu'elle contribue à la lecture et à l'écriture, ne se développe pas avec la maturation cognitive, l'acquisition d'un système d'écriture non-alphabétique, ou l'exposition à une langue riche en rimes et autres contrastes. Par contre, elle se développe au cours de l'apprentissage de la lecture et de l'écriture alphabétique.

Literacy training and speech segmentation

JOSÉ MORAIS*
PAUL BERTELSON
LUZ CARY
JESUS ALEGRIA
*Université libre de Bruxelles and
Universidade de Lisboa*

Abstract

New groups of illiterate and ex-illiterate adults, comparable to those of Morais et al. (1979), were given a battery of tasks designed to assess the specificity of the effect of literacy training on speech segmentation. As in the previous study, a strong difference was observed between the two groups on the task of deleting the initial consonant of an utterance. The illiterates displayed the same incapacity to deal with phonetic segments in a detection task and in a progressive free segmentation task. Their performance was better, although still inferior to that of ex-illiterates, on both deletion and detection when the critical unit was a syllable rather than a consonant, as well as in a task of rhyme detection. No significant difference was observed in a task of melody segmentation, on which both groups performed poorly. The high specificity of the differences in performance level implies that they cannot result to an important extent from differences in general ability or motivation between the two groups of subjects. They rather mean that while sensitivity to rhyme and analysis into syllables can develop up to some point in the absence of the experience normally provided by reading instruction, analysis into phonetic segments requires that experience. Finally, in a picture memory task, the illiterates showed a phonological similarity effect, which is consistent with other results suggesting that the use of phonological codes for short-term retention does not require explicit phonetic analysis.

*We thank Alain Content, Béatrice De Gelder, Régine Kolinsky, Leonor Scliar-Cabral, and three anonymous referees for helpful comments on a previous version. This work has been partially subsidized by the Belgian Ministère de la Politique et de la Programmation scientifiques (Action de Recherche concertée "Processus cognitifs dans la lecture"). Reprint requests should be addressed to José Morais, Laboratoire de Psychologie expérimentale, 117 Av. Adolphe Buyl, B-1050 Bruxelles, Belgium.

Introduction

There is a well documented correlation between the acquisition of alphabetic reading and the ability to deal with speech at the level of sub-morphemic units (see Content, 1984, for a review). Pre-school children generally perform poorly on speech analysis tasks and the majority make important progress once engaged in reading instruction (Alegria & Morais, 1979; Calfee, Linda-mood, & Lindamood, 1973; Liberman, Shankweiler, Fischer, & Carter, 1974; Rosner & Simon, 1971). On the other hand, poor or retarded readers exhibit lower performance on such tasks than more proficient ones (Bradley & Bryant, 1978; Calfee et al., 1973; Helfgott, 1976; Liberman, 1973; Morais, Cluytens, & Alegria, 1984; Treiman & Baron, 1981).

The reason behind the correlation lies presumably in the fact that, since alphabetic writing represents language mainly in terms of phonemic units, the ability to analyze utterances into such segments would be necessary to acquire text-to-speech and speech-to-text conversion procedures. The role of these procedures in ongoing fluent reading is still a matter of debate but one very likely function, especially in the early stages of acquisition, would be to allow the student to derive pronunciations for words he has not yet encountered in the written form, and thus to increase in autonomous fashion his vocabulary of visually recognizable words (Jorm & Share, 1983).

The correlation would thus reflect the fact that speech analysis is a crucial sub-component of developing reading skill (Bertelson, Morais, Alegria, & Content, 1985). One central question then concerns the conditions of emergence of that ability. Specifically, one is led to ask to what extent the underlying competence develops spontaneously, as an aspect of general cognitive and linguistic growth, and to what extent it requires specific instruction.

There is evidence of a very strong effect of reading instruction on speech analysis. In a study carried out in an agricultural area of southern Portugal, the present authors compared phonetic segmentation ability in illiterate adults and subjects of comparable age and socio-economic background who had attended literacy classes as adults (Morais, Cary, Alegria, & Bertelson, 1979). The task was either to add a particular consonant at the beginning of a spoken utterance or to delete the initial consonant. The illiterates performed at the same low level (less than 20% correct responses) as first-grade Belgian children at the beginning of reading instruction whereas ex-illiterates reached a level comparable to that of second graders (more than 70% correct).

Those results would thus suggest that phonetic segmentation is not attained in the absence of some specific training. For most people, that training is provided within school reading instruction, but it is possible to provide it independently and prior to reading instruction. Work from our laboratory (Content, Kolinsky, Morais, & Bertelson, 1986; Content, Morais, Alegria, & Bertelson, 1982) and from other ones (Fox & Routh, 1984; Olofsson & Lundberg, 1983) has now established that pre-school children can be taught speech analysis independently of reading proper.

On the other hand, several studies have revealed non-negligible performance on some forms of phonological manipulation in pre-school children (Bradley & Bryant, 1983; Fox & Routh, 1975) and the level attained on those tasks predicts later reading achievement to some extent. Such findings have been proposed as demonstrations of an autonomous development of speech analysis skills which would thus function as prerequisites to reading acquisition (Bryant & Bradley, 1985).

There is no necessary contradiction between these findings and the notion that acquiring phonetic segmentation requires specific instruction. First, the speech analysis capacities displayed by some pre-readers are not necessarily the effects of spontaneous growth. They may be the product of more or less informal instruction at home, which in educated families can range from exposure to phonologically oriented games to straightforward teaching of letter-sound correspondences. The range of such opportunities which are available to illiterates is presumably more limited. On the other hand, specific instruction may be necessary to acquire some speech analysis capacities while others may develop more spontaneously. The cases of analysis into phones and into syllables are apparently different. Analysis into phonetic segments is presumably required by the consonant addition and deletion tasks which neither pre-school children nor adult illiterates can perform well at all. Analysis into syllables is performed to a non-negligible level by pre-school children (Liberman et al., 1974). Another capacity which seems to be present in pre-readers is sensitivity to rhyme and other sound aspects of utterances (Knafle, 1973, 1974; Lenel & Cantor, 1981). The "sound classification" task which the children tested by Bradley and Bryant (1983) could perform reasonably well at 4 or 5 years and which was predictive of their later success in reading involves either sensitivity to rhyme (SIT different form PIN and WIN; HAT different from POT and COT) or to identity of initial CV-segment (HILL different form PIG and PIN). These tasks can be performed by recording identity or non-identity at each phone position (e.g., SIT, PIN, WIN: 1st position, all different; 2nd position, all identical; 3rd position, SIT different from PIN and WIN). Such a procedure clearly involves sub-syllabic analysis. But one cannot at this stage eliminate the possibility or recourse to less analytic procedures, based on overall similarity. Treiman and Baron (1981) have shown that in a CV classification task, pre-readers tend to put together utterances that are globally similar rather than those that share one particular phone. Thus, it is possible that pre-readers' success in tasks involving rhymes and other sound relations does not reveal any particular segmentation capacity, but a different ability which might be called *sensitivity to sound similarity*.

The results of the comparison between illiterates and ex-illiterates are not sufficient, however, to establish the existence of a specific effect of literacy training on level of speech analysis. They might also reflect more general differences between the two groups of subjects, due to general experience gained during the literacy class, to the opportunities consequent upon literacy, or because of pre-existing intellectual or motivational level. For instance, the illiterates might have difficulties with analytical tasks in general rather than specifically with analysis of speech. Or they might find it especially difficult to infer a rule from examples.

There are some arguments which point toward a specific effect of reading instruction. Alegria, Pignot and Morais (1982) have found that first-grade pupils taught by a whole-word method performed more poorly (15% correct responses) on the task of inverting initial and final consonants of a CVC syllable than children of the same age taught by a phonic method, involving specific tuition on letter–sound correspondences (58% correct). Interestingly, the two groups did not differ significantly when the task required to invert *syllables*. Read, Zhang, Nie and Ding's (1984) result showing that it is only the learning of alphabetic writing that promotes phonetic segmentation goes also clearly in the direction of a specific effect of the content of instruction.

To examine the question of specificity further, it was necessary to analyze the differences between illiterates and ex-illiterates in more detail. To that purpose, new groups of subjects drawn from populations comparable to those of the original study, were submitted to a battery of tasks exploring a wider range of capacities.

(a) Several *speech segmentation tasks* were used. The task of deleting the initial phone of a spoken utterance was applied with two different targets: a stop consonant in a consonant-vowel (CV-)context (the deletion task of Morais et al., 1979) and a vowel in a VCV-context where it constituted a syllable by itself. As in the previous studies, the rules were demonstrated through examples. During the test phase, on some trials the target was presented in the same context as in the examples. On those trials, extrapolation from the examples unambiguously dictated deletion of the initial phone. On other trials, the context was such that the initial phone could form a cohesive cluster with the following element: for the vowel, a VCCV-context where it formed a syllable with the following consonant, for the stop consonant a CCV-context where it made part of a consonantic cluster. These trials provided transfer tests: according to his interpretation of the rule, the subject could here delete either the initial phone alone or the whole cluster.

(b) One reason for working with targets of different degrees of accessibility is to separate difficulty in accessing the particular type of linguistic unit from difficulty in inferring the deletion rule from the examples: if the difficulty lies in understanding the task, changing the target should make no difference. Another approach to the same problem consists in giving more explicit instructions. Speech analysis capacity was also evaluated in a *progressive free segmentation task* (Fox & Routh, 1975), where the subject is asked explicitly to produce smaller and smaller parts of an utterance.

(c) Progressive segmentation shares with initial segment deletion the feature that the subject must produce the remaining part of the presented utterance, and any difficulty may rest in this production as well as in isolating the target segment. The subjects were also submitted to a *detection* task involving only attention to particular units: they had to localize phonetic or syllabic targets in spoken sentences.

(d) The task of deleting the initial note from a short *musical sequence* was included. It makes it possible to examine the extent to which the difference between illiterates and ex-illiterates is located specifically in the analysis of speech and not in a more general capacity to analyze all sorts of materials into constituent elements.

(e) As proposed above, *detection of rhyme* is a task that requires attention to some sound aspect of speech but not necessarily to its phonological structure. Illiterates appear to be sensitive to rhyme in poetry. The authors are acquainted with illiterate adults who enjoy rhyme and engage in rhyming games during popular festivities. If, as we expected, our illiterate subjects showed reasonably good performance on rhyme detection, that would indicate that their inability in phonetic segmentation does not reflect a more general inability to focus on the sound properties of speech.

(f) A final task involved *remembering series of pictured objects with rhyming vs. non-rhyming names*. Inferior performance on rhyming series would reflect the use of speech-related codes in short-term memory. Conrad (1971) first used the present type of task with children of different ages and found no effect of rhyming before 6 years. Alegria and Pignot (1979), on the other hand, observed an effect in preliterate 4-year-olds, but smaller than in older children. The use of phonological representations in short-term memory might thus be correlated with reading acquisition in the same way as speech analysis capacities, and the illiterates–ex-illiterates comparison may shed light on the origin of that correlation also.

Method

Subjects

The experiment was run in an agricultural area of south Portugal and in a Lisbon shanty-town. Subjects, 21 illiterate people (I subjects) and 20 ex-illiterates (Ex-I subjects) were all of peasant origin. The Ex-I subjects had began learning to read at ages ranging from 18 to 40 years by attending classes of elementary instruction for adult illiterates.

I subjects, 3 males and 18 females, were aged 25 to 60. Ten of them, 2 males and 8 females, tested in the agricultural district, were all employed in agricultural cooperatives, and of the remaining 11, tested in Lisbon, 8 were servants, 2 fruit sellers and 1 a mason. None had received any reading instruction at any time.

Ex-I subjects, 5 male and 15 female, were aged 17 to 60. Eight, 2 male and 6 female, were tested in the agricultural area. They included 3 agricultural workers, 3 servants and 2 industrial workers. Of the remaining 12, tested in Lisbon, 10 were servants and 2 industrial workers.

The Ex-I subjects were administered a reading test at the end of the experiment. It consisted of reading as fast and as accurately as possible 111 current words, most of them (86) nouns, the majority disyllabic (40) and trisyllabic (41), typed in lower case. The results showed a clearly discontinuous distribution, suggesting the presence of two types of subjects who will be called *better* and *poorer* readers. Better readers read at more than 60 words/min and did not make errors. Poorer readers read at a rate considerably inferior to 60 words/min, with long pauses, and occasionally made errors. Nine of the better readers had received some kind of certificate after completing the literacy course. Among the poorer ones, three had obtained a certificate and the remaining five were still attending class. There was no systematic difference regarding age, sex or occupation between the two subgroups.

Tasks and procedure

   1. Segmentation of speech (SS)

The subject had to delete the initial segment of a pseudo-word provided orally by the experimenter. There were 40 experimental trials. In half of them, the initial segment was the consonant [p] followed either by a vowel or by one of the consonants [l] or [r] (e.g.: [púb(ə)], [plúku], [prál(ə)]). In the other half, it was the vowel [ʌ] followed either by a CV syllable—in which case it was a syllable by itself—or by [ʃ] or [r] forming a syllable with the initial vowel (e.g.: [ʌbɔ́pu], [ʌʃpél(ə)], [ʌrdím(ə)]). Half the subjects first worked with [ʌ] and then with [p], and the other half had the reverse order. For each target ([p] and [ʌ]) the rule was illustrated by 15 introductory trials, where a correction procedure was used: when the subject failed to produce the correct response, the experimenter provided it. On those trials, [p] was always followed by a vowel and [ʌ] always constituted a syllable. The subject was told that his task was to delete the beginning "sound" of each utterance. On the experimental trials, no correction was provided and the subject was told that he was going to work with "meaningless words".

2. Segmentation of melodies (MS)

The subject had to reproduce the last three notes of a four-note melody played by the experimenter on a toy xylophone. To avoid making the task excessively difficult, only the two extreme plates of the scale, those producing the low-pitched C and the high-pitched C were used, and the remaining plates were hidden under a screen. The subject was first familiarized with the situation by having him play the two notes himself on the xylophone. The test consisted of five introductory trials, to illustrate the rule, followed by nine experimental trials. In the introductory trials, a correction procedure was used. The subject was told that the task was to delete the beginning "sound" in the sequence of four provided by the experimenter and to repeat the remaining three exactly in the same order. Half the subjects saw the experimenter play the sequences, the other half did not.

3. Progressive segmentation of speech (PS)

The experimenter uttered a sentence orally and the subject was asked to say only part of it, then only part of the part, and so on until he could go no further. This procedure was applied to each of five sentences, four to seven words long.

4. Detection of target sounds in auditorily presented speech (AD)

The subject listened to recorded sentences and had to localize a target previously enunciated by the experimenter. The stressed syllable [tá], the phone [ī], the unstressed syllable [tʌ] and the phone [k] were successively used as targets. Each target appeared once at the beginning of a word in each of five sentences. There were no introductory trials. The subject was instructed to listen to the sentence and to indicate the word which contained the target.

5. Rhyme detection (RD)

Five pictures of common objects were displayed on the table, and the experimenter pronounced their names. The first picture, the target, and one of the other ones represented objects with rhyming names, and the task of the subject was to point to the latter. Twenty-five series were used. The instruction was to indicate the picture which had the same sound at the end or produced a rhyme with the target.

6. Recall of pictures with rhyming and non-rhyming names (R)

Three series of 10 black-and-white pictures of common objects were used. In one of the series (R), the depicted objects had rhyming names: JANELA (window), CAPELA (chapel), VITELA (veal), etc. In the other two series, NR1 and NR2, no pictures had rhyming names. The testing started with 6 to 10 training trials where the cards of series NR1 were used throughout. On the early trials, the experimenter first showed 5 cards in succession, each time naming the depicted object. Each card was exposed for about 2 s, then placed face down on the table. As soon as the 5 cards had been shown, the experimenter exposed a strip of cardboard supporting the whole series of 10 cards, and the subject was asked to place each of the previously presented cards, without turning it up, on the corresponding one on the strip. This required that the subject recall both which cards had been shown and the order in which they had been presented by the experimenter on that particular trial. The cards were then turned up to show any mistake. During successive training trials, the number of cards presented was adjusted until a 50–60% level of correct responding was obtained. This number was then used for the two series of experimental trials, one with the NR2 cards, and one with the R cards, which were run immediately afterwards, in balanced order.

All subjects performed the tasks in the order R, RD, SS, PS, MS, AD.

Results

1. Segmentation of speech

The mean percentage of correct responses for deletion of a syllabic [ʌ] and of [p] followed by a vowel, the tasks for which corrective feedback had been provided through examples, appear in Table 1.

For [p] followed by a vowel, the results replicate almost exactly those of the previous study (19% and 73% of correct responses, on the average, for I and Ex-I subjects, respectively). I subjects were also inferior to Ex-I subjects in the deletion of syllabic [ʌ] ($t = 3.84$, $df = 39$, $p < .005$), but their performance was here substantially higher than on the former task. Eighteen subjects (out of 19 showing a difference) gave a higher number of correct responses in the latter task ($p < .001$ by sign test), showing that illiterates can manipulate vowels better than stop consonants. It can be seen in Figure 1

Table 1. *Segmentation of speech sounds and musical segmentation. Mean percentage of correct responses (SD in brackets) for deletion of the syllabic [ʌ], of [p] followed by vowel, and of musical note*

	Illiterates	Poorer readers	Better readers
Speech segment			
syllabic [ʌ]	55.2 (31.7)	85.0 (9.3)	85.0 (13.8)
[p] followed by vowel	18.6 (26.9)	62.5 (21.2)	83.3 (15.0)
Musical note	26.4 (17.3)	26.5 (18.4)	41.7 (17.1)

Figure 1. *Distributions of percent correct scores for plosive deletion ([p] followed by a vowel), syllabic vowel deletion, rhyme detection and musical note deletion. Above: illiterates. Below: ex-illiterates (poorer readers in black).*

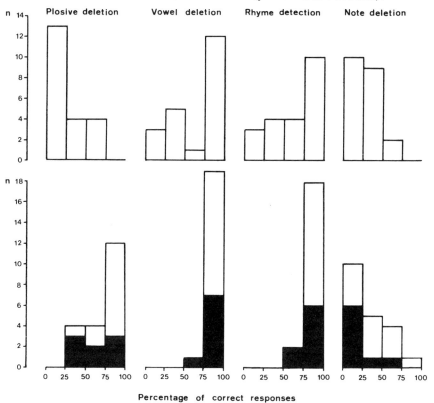

that distributions of the individual scores of the illiterates are very different for the two tasks, one showing the reversed J-shape and the other the J-shape.

Among the Ex-I subjects, better readers scored higher on initial consonant deletion than poorer ones (t = 2.56, df = 18, p < .01), but there is no difference on syllabic vowel deletion, where both subgroups performed at the same high level.

Table 2 shows the types of responses observed most frequently for [ʌ] followed by either [ʃ] or [r] (VCCV-context) and for [p] followed by either [l] or [r] (CCV-context). Given that such stimuli had not been presented during the introductory phase, when corrective feedback was provided, deletion of the initial segment only and of the whole initial cluster are both responses consistent with the information available in the examples. It appears that the choice made by the subjects depends on the identity of the second consonant. When it is [r], there is among both I and Ex-I subjects a preference for deleting the whole cluster. This pattern might be linked partly at least to the particular status of [r] in Portuguese phonology where it never occurs in word-initial position. For utterances starting with [ʌʃ] and with [pl], the two choices are observed, with no strong bias toward either, in both groups of subjects. It would thus seem that the present subjects spontaneously place a syllabic vowel in a category of vowel-initial syllables as well as in a category of vowels, and similarly place an initial consonant in a category which contains also consonantic clusters as well as in a category which contains only consonants.

2. Segmentation of melodies

Performance was not affected by the opportunity to see the hands of the experimenter, hence results were pooled over subgroups with and without such opportunity. Mean percentages correct responses appear in Table 1 and distributions in Figure 1. The difference between I and Ex-I subjects did not reach significance at p = .05 (t = 1.56, df = 39). Performance is, as a matter of fact, poor in both groups. Better readers on the other hand performed significantly better than either poorer ones (t = 1.79, df = 18, p < .05) or illiterates (t = 2.37, df = 31, p < .025).

3. Progressive segmentation of speech

As shown in Table 3, only I subjects gave responses which could not be considered as parts of the presented utterance, such as faster repetitions or paraphrases.

Correct final responses were categorized according to unit size. Responses consisting of a phonetic segment were subdivided according to whether the segment had to be obtained by analysis of a syllable (consonant; non-syllabic vowel) or not (syllabic vowel). A further type of response is the name of a consonant. Since most of the phones provided as responses were vowels, we assumed that conventional names were for these subjects the normal way of

Table 2.   *Segmentation of speech sounds. Percentage of the more frequent types of response in the cluster conditions*

	Illiterates	Poorer readers	Better readers
Initial cluster			
[ʌʃ]			
Deletion of [ʌ]	38.1	35.0	55.0
Deletion of [ʌʃ]	26.7	57.5	40.0
Repetition	13.3	2.5	1.7
Word phonologically related to the stimulus	13.3	5.0	1.7
[ʌr]			
Deletion of [ʌ]	14.3	37.5	20.0
Deletion of [ʌr]	22.9	37.5	58.3
Deletion of [ʌ] + transformation of [r] into [r̄]	2.9	0	6.7
Repetition	37.1	12.5	6.7
Word phonologically related to the stimulus	20.0	12.5	1.7
[pl]			
Deletion of [p]	15.2	40.0	36.7
Deletion of [pl]	12.4	27.5	31.7
Deletion of [p] + misplacement of [l]	5.7	12.5	13.3
Deletion of initial syllable	3.8	7.5	10.0
Repetition	23.8	0	0
Word phonologically related to the stimulus	26.7	2.5	0
[pr]			
Deletion of [p]	0	0	13.3
Deletion of [pr]	29.5	70.0	61.7
Deletion of [p] + transformation of [r] into [r̄]	0	0	6.7
Deletion of initial syllable	4.8	2.5	3.3
Repetition	21.0	0	0
Word phonologically related to the stimulus	29.5	20.0	0

referring to consonants. Sub-syllabic units were produced very rarely by illiterates. Two of them produced one phone (one a vowel, the other the
consonant from a CV syllable) and it is interesting to note that these two
subjects scored 50 and 70% respectively on deletion of [p] followed by a
vowel. Two other illiterates gave a few consonant names. Somewhat unexpec-
tedly, the level of the syllable was not reached very often in this group: 9
subjects only (out of 21) reached it. By contrast, 6 out of the 8 poorer readers
and 11 out of the 12 better ones produced sub-syllabic segments and all of
the Ex-I subjects, with the exception of one poorer reader, reached the level
of the syllable.

4. Detection of speech sounds

There were no erroneous localizations, only correct ones or omissions. Percentage correct responses is for all four targets higher in Ex-I than in I subjects (Table 4). The liquid [r̄] was in both groups of subjects detected much
better than [k] and even slightly better than the syllables. This result is presumably due to the fact that this consonant can, unlike plosives, be pronounced in isolation. Besides, in Portuguese it is pronounced with great
energy. On detection of the other consonant, [k], the illiterates scored much
lower than on the syllables: 14 of these subjects scored better on syllables
while 5 did the reverse ($p = .021$, by sign-test). The difference is observed

Table 3.   *Progressive segmentation of speech. Percentage of final responses of each*
type

	Illiterates	Poorer readers	Better readers
Segmentation			
One phone			
consonant or non-syllabic vowel	0.95	12.5	40.0
syllabic vowel	0.95	12.5	18.3
Name of a consonant	4.8	25.0	16.7
One syllable	24.8	25.0	20.0
One word	17.1	25.0	5.0
Two words or more	8.6	0	0
Incorrect responses			
Faster and/or whispered repetition	26.7	0	0
Paraphrase	7.6	0	0
Others	8.5	0	0

Table 4.   *Detection of speech sounds. Mean percent correct responses (SD in brackets) for each type of target*

	Illiterates	Poorer readers	Better readers
[tá]	57.1 (26.3)	82.5 (16.7)	88.3 (13.4)
[r̄]	67.6 (41.7)	95.0 (14.1)	98.3 (5.8)
[tʌ]	47.6 (33.8)	70.0 (33.8)	85.0 (28.4)
[k]	35.7 (35.9)	84.4 (22.9)	77.1 (31.0)

also at the level of distributions (Figure 2): the distribution for detection of [k] shows the same reversed J-shape as that for deletion of [p] (Figure 1). In the ex-illiterates, there is little difference linked to type of target: as Figure 2 shows, performance approaches ceiling for all targets.

5. Rhyme detection

Table 5 shows the mean percentage of correct responses per type of rhyme (the identical sounds were either the last two syllables, or the ending vowel or diphthong). There is no apparent difference in overall performance level between the two types of target. Distributions of scores, which are shown in Figure 1, are quite similar to those for syllabic vowel deletion.

6. Recall of pictures with rhyming and non-rhyming names

As appears in Table 6, the adjustment procedure which was used during training trials to choose the size of picture sets to be used during experimental trials had the consequence that illiterates worked on the average with smaller sets than the ex-illiterates ($t = 2.07$, $df = 39$, $p < .025$) and gave nevertheless fewer correct responses. Short-term retention is thus slightly poorer in the illiterates. The rhyme effect, measured by the difference between performance on non-rhyming and on rhyming sets, is significant in illiterates ($t = 3.23$, $df = 20$, $p < .005$) and in better readers ($t = 3.57$, $df = 11$, $p < .005$). It approaches significance in poorer readers ($t = 1.47$, $df = 7, p < .10$). Analysis of variance yielded a significant effect of condition ($F = 24.77$, $df = 1.38$, $p < .005$) but no interaction with group ($F = 1.12$, $df = 2.38$).

Figure 2.   *Distributions of percent correct scores for detection of [tʌ], [tá], [r̄] and [k].*
            Above: illiterates. Below: ex-illiterates (poorer readers in black).

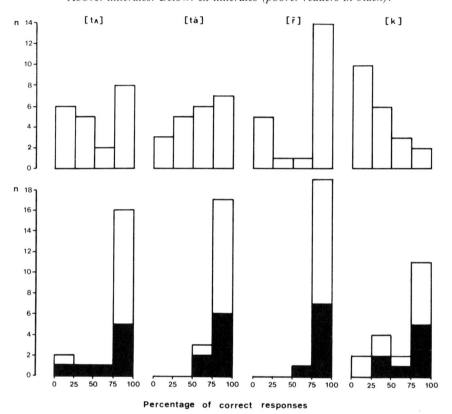

Table 5.   *Detection of rhyme. Mean percent correct re-*
           sponses (SD in brackets) for each type of
           rhyme

	Illiterates	Poorer readers	Better readers
Two syllables			
(n = 17)	63.8 (28.0)	86.8 (15.9)	97.0 (5.4)
Final vowel			
or diphthong			
(n = 8)	70.1 (30.3)	89.1 (20.5)	96.9 (7.8)

Table 6.   *Recall of pictures with rhyming and non-rhyming names. Mean number of items presented and mean percent correct responses (SD in brackets)*

	Illiterates	Poorer readers	Better readers
No. items	4.33 (0.73)	4.75 (0.46)	4.83 (0.83)
% correct responses			
R (rhyming)	41.4 (17.9)	46.3 (13.1)	48.5 (16.3)
NR (non-rhyming)	49.7 (17.9)	57.4 (11.7)	64.5 (14.6)
NR–R	8.3	11.1	16.0

7. Intercorrelations

Availability of scores for a whole battery of tests yielded the opportunity to examine interrelations. In the Ex-I group however, too many distributions were affected by ceiling effects to allow much use of that approach. Exceptions were deletion of [p] followed by a vowel, melody segmentation and rhyme effect: none of the intercorrelations of these three tasks was significant. For the illiterates, the main intercorrelations appear in Table 7. Significant correlations are observed between the two speech segmentation tasks (vowel deletion and consonant deletion), between the different detection tasks, and between syllabic vowel deletion and syllable detection. Two negative results are of particular interest. First, the rhyme effect observed in the picture retention task does not correlate significantly with performance on any of the speech manipulation tasks, nor even with rhyme detection. Second, rhyme detection does not correlate significantly with any speech analysis task: noticing sound similarity and localizing a sound target appear to involve different mechanisms. Further evidence on the latter lack of relation is provided by examination of individual cases. Three out of the four subjects with the lowest scores (less than 30% correct) in rhyme detection obtained high scores (all three 80% correct) in syllabic segmentation. On the other hand, the three subjects with the lowest scores (20% or less) in syllabic segmentation obtained good scores in rhyme detection (96%, 88% and 76%).

In the I group, performance on melody segmentation was unfortunately too low to attach much confidence to the lack of correlation between this task and the deletion of [p] followed by a vowel ($-.13$). It may thus be more interesting to signal some individual patterns of results. Among the four I subjects with the highest scores on the deletion of [p] followed by a vowel (6 or 7 responses out of 10) three gave only one correct response (chance level) in melody segmentation. Of the two I subjects with the highest scores on the latter task (5 correct responses out of 9) one gave a good score on the former

Table 7.   Intercorrelations between syllabic vowel deletion (VDEL), plosive ([p] followed by vowel)
deletion (PDEL), syllable detection (SDET),
plosive detection (PDET), liquid detection
(LDET), rhyme detection (RDET) and RR
(rhyme effect in retention), in the illiterate
group

	PDEL	SDET	PDET	LDET	RDET	RR
VDEL	.48*	.44*	.30	.04	−.11	−.18
PDEL		.14	.28	−.14	.11	.22
SDET			.69**	.72**	.31	.04
PDET				.48*	.42	−.17
LDET					.19	.02
RDET						.11

* $p < .05$; ** $p < .001$.

but the other failed all the items. These results, together with the lack of
significant correlation in the Ex-I group, suggest that phonetic and melodic
segmentation are independent abilities.

Discussion

The basic finding (Morais et al., 1979), that illiterates cannot delete a consonant from the beginning of an utterance while ex-illiterates can, has been
replicated. Moreover, the performance level of the present subjects is strikingly close to that of the original groups, considering the differences in
procedure between the two studies: in the former one, each subject worked
only on one particular task—deletion or addition of the same phone throughout—whereas here the consonant deletion task was preceded by other exercises.

The data from the other tasks make it possible to put that basic finding in
better perspective. The differences in ability for phonetic segmentation are
not due to differences in the general capacity to infer the deletion rule from
examples. In the progressive segmentation task, when explicitly told to analyze speech utterances, illiterates were still largely unable to produce sub-syllabic segments. And in the very explicit detection task, they performed poorly
with the stop consonant target. On the other hand, they showed a much
better ability to infer the rule with other targets, notably with a syllabic

vowel. Finally, if the origin of the ex-illiterates' superiority rested in capacity to infer the rule, it should have showed up also in melody segmentation, where in fact they did not perform better than the illiterates.

The possibility of some contribution to the basic effect of differences in level of general ability or motivation, either consequent on literacy training or pre-existing to, and possibly influencing, enrolment in the literacy course, cannot be ruled out completely on the basis of the present data. The small superiority of the ex-illiterates in picture retention might reflect such a difference. On the other hand, the absence of a significant difference in melody segmentation performance goes against the notion. However, given the low level of performance of both groups, that task is obviously not suited to provide a baseline for comparisons. The problem, however, is not to isolate completely the direct effect of literacy training from contaminating factors— that sort of purity cannot be attained when manipulating institutional variables such as school attendance—but more simply to demonstrate its existence. The main point to consider is thus the degree of specificity of the differences.

The illiterates performed better on syllabic vowel deletion, where more than half of them produced 75% correct responses or more, than on consonant deletion, where none reached that level. A difference in the same direction was observed for syllabic versus stop consonant ([k]) target in the detection task (the case of [r̄] will be considered below). And illiterates performed at a non-negligible level in rhyme detection, where nearly half reached the 75% correct level. The inferior performance of the illiterates is thus more evident in tasks involving phonetic segments than in those which involve syllables, or, like rhyme detection, perhaps only attention to sound properties of the whole utterance rather than of the components.. Pre-school children also appear to reach on syllable segmentation and on rhyme detection levels of performance definitely superior to those obtained on phonetic segmentation (Knafle, 1973, 1974; Lenel & Cantor, 1981).

It is of course necessary to acknowledge the discordant result obtained for detection of the liquid [r̄], which is performed by illiterates as well (in fact slightly better) as syllable detection. Thus, strictly speaking, one cannot conclude that low accessibility in illiterates is typical of all consonants. The case of [r̄] which, as we have noted, is pronounced in Portuguese with strong energy, is however probably exceptional. In the previous study (Morais et al., 1979) equally low performance was obtained for deletion of initial nasal [m] and fricative [ʃ] as of plosive [p].

Although the largest differences linked to literacy were observed in those tasks which involve dealing with phonetic segments, a superiority of ex-illiterates over illiterates showed up also in syllabic tasks (segmentation and detection) and in rhyme detection. And in progressive segmentation, the proportion of subjects reaching the level of the syllable at least once was lower among illiterates. It would thus seem that although some non-negligible sensitivity to sound properties of speech and capacity to analyze it into syllables develops in the absence of reading instruction, a substantial improvement can still be brought by such instruction. This conclusion is consistent with the huge increase observed by Liberman et al. (1974) between kindergarten and Grade 1 in performance on syllable counting, contrasting with the relative stagnation between nursery school and kindergarten. That aspect of their results has on the whole received little attention. In a similar vein, Morais et al. (1984) have found that young dyslexics were inferior to first-graders in a syllable deletion task (68% vs. 95% correct responses).

Thus, the present data appear to support the following picture of the development of speech analysis abilities. Both the capacities to analyze speech into syllable-level units and to appreciate sound similarity can develop in the absence of the specific types of experience linked to formal reading instruction up to some intermediate point, but can still be improved when these become available. On the contrary, analysis into phonetic segments proper is strongly dependent for its emergence on such experience. The resultant improved analytical ability may not transfer to materials outside the linguistic sphere, as the results of the melody segmentation task suggest, but of course the conclusion must remain tentative until a wider range of non-linguistic tasks has been investigated.

Although rhyme detection and syllabic segmentation are influenced by literacy training in the same way, the absence of correlation between the corresponding scores is consistent with the notion that they are not dependent on the same underlying competences. In particular, the finding implies that speech segmentation abilities do not depend on prior development of a more general capacity to attend to the sound aspects of speech. One might thus be able to segment speech into syllables even if one is not able yet to appreciate sound similarity, and vice versa.

The results of the picture retention task deserve separate consideration. Significant rhyme effects have been observed in both illiterates and ex-illiterates. Thus, the availability of phonological codes in retention appears not to be crucially dependent on literacy training nor, as a consequence, on the phonetic segmentation abilities which it promotes. As a matter of fact, no correlation was observed between the rhyme effect and any of our tests of speech segmentation, a result consistent with previous findings by Alegria et al. (1982) (cf. also, Content, Morais, Kolinsky, Bertelson, & Alegria, 1986). These results are definitely not consistent with the notion that phonetic segmentation ability facilitates reading acquisition by making speech-mediated retention possible (for a more extended discussion, see Morais, Cluytens, Alegria, & Content, 1986).

The comparison within the ex-illiterate group of better and poorer readers was not a major objective of the present study. On most tests, better readers scored higher than poorer ones, but there is of course no guarantee that these differences are the effects of higher literacy and not of some common causal factor. In our opinion, the most interesting aspect is that in all the tasks where ex-illiterates score better than illiterates, the difference between poorer and better readers is small compared to that between poorer readers and illiterates. It looks as if the stronger effect of literacy training on speech analysis was associated to some very general, presumably early, acquisition common to the majority of students rather than with later developments that take place only in the better ones.

References

Alegria, J., & Morais, J. (1979). Le développement de l'habileté d'analyse phonétique consciente de la parole et l'apprentissage de la lecture. *Archives de Psychologie, 183,* 251–270.

Alegria, J., & Pignot, E. (1979). Genetic aspects of verbal mediation in memory. *Child Development, 50,* 235–238.

Alegria, J., Pignot, E., & Morais, J. (1982). Phonetic analysis of speech and memory codes in beginning readers. *Memory and Cognition, 10,* 451–456.

Bertelson, P., Morais, J., Alegria, J., & Content, A. (1985). Phonetic analysis capacity and learning to read. *Nature, 313,* 73–74.

Bradley, L., & Bryant, P.E. (1978). Difficulties in auditory organization as a possible cause of reading backwardness. *Nature, 271,* 746–747.

Bradley, L., & Bryant, P.E. (1983). Categorizing sounds and learning to read—a causal connection. *Nature, 301,* 419–421.

Bryant, P.E., & Bradley, L. (1985). *Children's reading problems.* Oxford: Blackwell.

Calfee, R.C., Chapman, R., & Venezky, R. (1972). How a child needs to think to learn to read. In L.W. Gregg (Ed.), *Cognition in learning and memory,* New York: Wiley.

Calfee, R.C., Lindamood, P., & Lindamood, C. (1973). Acoustic-phonetic skills and reading, kindergarten to twelfth grade. *Journal of Educational Psychology, 64,* 293–298.

Conrad, R. (1971). The chronology of the development of covert speech in children. *Developmental Psychology, 5,* 398–405.

Content, A. (1984). L'analyse phonétique explicite de la parole et l'acquisition de la lecture. *L'Année Psychologique, 84,* 555–572.

Content, A., Kolinsky, R., Morais, J., & Bertelson, P. (1986). Phonetic segmentation in prereaders: Effect of corrective information. *Journal of Experimental Child Psychology, 42,* 49–72.

Content, A., Morais, J., Alegria, J., & Bertelson, P. (1982). Accelerating the development of phonetic segmentation skills in kindergartners. *Cahiers de Psychologie Cognitive, 2,* 259–269.

Content, A., Morais, J., Kolinsky, R., Bertelson, P., & Alegria, J. (1986). Explicit speech segmentation ability and susceptibility to phonological similarity in short-term retention: No correlation. *Perceptual and Motor Skills, 63,* 81–82.

Fox, B., & Routh, D.K. (1975). Analyzing spoken language into words, syllables and phonemes: a developmental study. *Journal of Psycholinguistic Research, 4*, 331–342.

Fox, B., & Routh, D.K. (1984). Phonemic analysis and synthesis as word attack skills: Revisited. *Journal of Educational Psychology, 76*, 1059–1064.

Helfgott, J. (1976). Phonemic segmentation and blending skills of kindergarten children: implications for beginning reading acquisition. *Contemporary Educational Psychology, 1*, 157–169.

Jorm, A.F., & Share, D.L. (1983). Phonological recoding and reading acquisition. *Applied Psycholinguistics, 4*, 103–147.

Knafle, J.D. (1973). Auditory perception of rhyming in kindergarten children. *Journal of Speech and Hearing Research, 16*, 482–487.

Knafle, J.D. (1974). Children's discrimination of rhyme. *Journal of Speech and Hearing Research, 17*, 367–372.

Lenel, J.C., & Cantor, J.H. (1981). Rhyme recognition and phonemic perception in young children. *Journal of Psycholinguistic Research, 10*, 57–67.

Liberman, I.Y. (1973). Segmentation of the spoken word and reading acquisition. *Bulletin of the Orton Society, 23*, 65–77.

Liberman, I.Y., Shankweiler, D., Fischer, F.W., & Carter, B. (1974). Explicit syllable and phoneme segmentation in the young child. *Journal of Experimental Child Psychology, 18*, 201–212.

Morais, J., Cary, L., Alegria, J., & Bertelson, P. (1979). Does awareness of speech as a sequence of phones arise spontaneously? *Cognition, 7*, 323–331.

Morais, J., Cluytens, M., & Alegria, J. (1984). Segmentation abilities of dyslexics and normal readers. *Perceptual and Motor Skills, 58*, 221–222.

Morais, J., Cluytens, M., Alegria, J., & Content, A. (1986). Speech-mediated retention in dyslexics. *Perceptual and Motor Skills, 62*, 119–126.

Olofsson, A., & Lundberg, I. (1983). Can phonemic awareness be trained in kindergarten? *Scandinavian Journal of Psychology, 24*, 35–44.

Read, C., Zhang, Y., Nie, H., & Ding, B. (1984). *The ability to manipulate speech sounds depends on knowing alphabetic spelling.* Paper presented at the International Congress of Psychology, Acapulco.

Rosner, J., & Simon, D.P. (1971). The auditory analysis test: an initial report. *Journal of Learning Disabilities, 4*, 384–392.

Treiman, R., & Baron, J. (1981). Segmental analysis ability: development and relation to reading ability. In T.G. Waller and G.E. McKinnon (Eds.), *Reading research: Advances in theory and practice*, vol. 3. New York: Academic Press.

Résumé

De nouveaux groupes d'adultes analphabètes et ex-analphabètes, comparables à ceux de Morais et al. (1979), ont été soumis à des tests destinés à évaluer le degré de spécificité de l'effet de l'alphabétisation sur la segmentation de la parole. Comme lors de l'étude précédente, une différence importante a été constatée entre les deux groupes pour la tâche qui consiste à supprimer la consonne initiale d'un énoncé. Les analphabètes ont montré la même incapacité à utiliser les segments phonétiques dans une tâche de segmentation libre progressive que dans la tâche de détection. Leur performance était meilleure, quoique toujours inférieure à celle des ex-analphabètes dans des tâches de suppression et de détection lorsque l'unité était une syllabe plutôt qu'une consonne, et aussi dans une tâche de détection de rime. Dans une tâche de segmentation de mélodie aucune différence significative n'a été observée entre les deux groupes dont la performance était uniformément médiocre. Le caractère hautement spécifique de ces différences implique qu'elles ne peuvent pas être dues pour l'essentiel à des différences de capacité générale ou de motivation entre les deux groupes. Elles indiquent plutôt que bien que la sensibilité aux rimes et l'analyse en segments syllabiques puissent se développer jusqu'à un certain point en l'absence de l'expérience que constitue l'apprentissage de la lecture, l'analyse en segments phonétiques exige cette expérience. Enfin, dans une tâche de mémorisation d'images, il a été possible de mettre en évidence chez les analphabètes un effet de similitude phonologique, ce qui s'accorde bien avec d'autres résultats qui suggèrent que l'utilisation d'un code phonologique pour la mémorisation à court terme n'exige pas une analyse phonétique explicite.

4

Phonological awareness: The role of reading experience*

VIRGINIA A. MANN

University of California, Irvine and Haskins Laboratories

Abstract

A cross-cultural study of Japanese and American children has examined the development of awareness about syllables and phonemes. Using counting tests and deletion tests, Experiments I and III reveal that in contrast to first graders in America, most of whom tend to be aware of both syllables and phonemes, almost all first graders in Japan are aware of mora (phonological units roughly equivalent to syllables) but relatively few are aware of phonemes. This difference in phonological awareness may be attributed to the fact that Japanese first graders learn to read a syllabary whereas American first graders learn to read an alphabet. For most children at this age, awareness of phonemes may require experience with alphabetic transcription, whereas awareness of syllables may be facilitated by experience with a syllabary, but less dependent upon it. To further clarify the role of knowledge of an alphabet in children's awareness of phonemes, Experiments II and IV administered the same counting and deletion tests to Japanese children in the later elementary grades. Here the data reveal that many Japanese children become aware of phonemes by age whether or not they have received instruction in alphabetic transcription. Discussion of these results focuses on some of the other factors that may promote phonological awareness.

Introduction

The primary language activities of listening and speaking do not require an explicit awareness of the internal phonological structure of words any more

*The research reported in this paper was completed while the author was a Fulbright Fellow and was partially funded by NICHD grant HD21182-01 and by NICHD grant HD01994 to Haskins Laboratories, Inc. This study could not have been completed without the help of Dr. Seishi Hibi, who served as research assistant, and without the very gracious compliance of Ms. Shizuko Fukuda and the children and teachers of the primary school attached to Ochanomizu University. I am also indebted to Dr. M. Sawashima, Dr. Isabelle Liberman, Dr. T. Ueno, and Dr. S. Sasanuma for their advice during many stages of this project. Reprint requests should be addressed to Virginia Mann, Department of Cognitive Sciences, University of California, Irvine, CA 92717, U.S.A.

than they require an explicit awareness of the rules of syntax. Yet a "metalinguistic" awareness that words comprise syllables and phonemes is precisely what is needed when language users turn from the primary language activities of speaking and listening to the secondary language activities of reading, versification and word games (Liberman, 1971; Mattingly, 1972, 1984). While all members of a given community become speakers and hearers, not all become readers, nor do they all play word games or appreciate verse. This difference raises the possibility that the development of phonological awareness might require some special cultivating experience above and beyond that which supports primary language acquisition.

Several different research groups have reported that adults who cannot read an alphabetic orthography are unable to manipulate phonemes (Byrne & Ledez, 1983; Liberman, Rubin, Dugues, & Carlisle, 1986; Morais, Cary, Alegria, & Bertelson, 1979; Read, Zhang, Nie, & Ding, 1984), raising the possibility that knowledge of the alphabet is essential to awareness of phonemes. In further pursuit of the factors which give rise to phonological awareness, the present study has explored the awareness of syllables and phonemes among Japanese children and American children. This particular cross-linguistic comparison is prompted by certain differences between the English and Japanese orthographies, and by certain differences in the word games and versification devices that are available to children in the two language communities.

Children in America learn to read the English orthography, an alphabet which represents spoken language at the level of the phoneme. Many of them also play phoneme-based word games such as "pig-Latin" and "Geography,"[1] and learn to employ versification devices such as alliteration that involve manipulations of phonemes, as well as word games and versification devices that exploit meter and thus operate on syllable-sized units. In contrast, virtually all of the secondary language activities that are available to Japanese children manipulate mora—phonological units that are roughly equivalent to syllables—if they manipulate phonological structure at all. Japanese children learn to read an orthography that comprises two types of transcription: Kanji, a morphology-based system and Kana, a phonology-based system. Kanji is derived from the Chinese logography and represents the roots of words without regard to grammatical inflections, whereas Kana is of native origin and comprises two syllabaries, Hiragana and Katakana, which can represent the

---

[1]"Geography" is a game played by two or more people, which begins with the first player naming a place (a state, city, country, etc.), "Georgia", for example. The next player must then produce another place whose name starts with the same last phoneme (for pre-literate children) or letter (for literate children) as "Georgia" and has not previously been used in the game. He could respond "Argentina", for example. Each subsequent player must respond with the name of a place that begins with the last phoneme of the preceding player's response, with the order of play recycling back to the first player and continuing until a player cannot give a response. That player then drops from the game and play continues until one player is left as the "winner."

root and inflection of any word in terms of their constituent mora. Typically, the two orthographies function together, with Kanji representing most word roots and Kana representing all word inflections and the roots of those words that lack Kanji characters. As for other secondary language activities, Japanese word games such as "Shiritori"[2] (a mora-based equivalent of "Geography") and versification devices such as Haiku manipulate mora.

In short, Japanese secondary language activities do not manipulate language at the level of the phoneme, whereas several English secondary language activities are phoneme-based, most notably the alphabetic orthography. Both Japanese and English afford versification devices and word games which manipulate syllable-sized units, but the Japanese orthography is unique in its inclusion of a syllabary. Given these similarities and differences between the orthographies and other secondary language activities in English and Japanese, it may be reasoned that, if experience with secondary language activities plays a specific role in the development of awareness about syllables and phonemes, Japanese children should be aware of mora (syllables) whereas American children should be aware of both phonemes and syllables. Should the experience of learning to read a given type of orthography play a particularly critical factor, Japanese children should be more aware of syllables than their American counterparts who should be more aware of phonemes. It seems unlikely that the possession of primary language skills is sufficient to make Japanese and American children equivalent in awareness of phonemes, given findings that alphabet-illiterate adults are not aware of phonemes. However it remains possible that children in the two countries will be equivalent in phonological awareness should reading experience or some other form of secondary language experience that draws the child's attention to the phonological structure of language promote the awareness of both syllables and phonemes.

The possibility that reading experience plays a particularly important role in the development of phonological awareness arises from the many studies which reveal an association between phonological awareness and success in learning to read an alphabetic orthography. These reveal that performance on tasks which require manipulations of phonological structure not only distinguishes good and poor readers in the early elementary grades (see, for example, Alegria, Pignot, & Morais, 1982; Fox & Routh, 1976, Katz, 1982; Liberman, 1973; Rosner and Simon, 1971) but also correlates with children's scores on standard reading tests (see, for example, Calfee, Lindamood, & Lindamood, 1973; Fox & Routh, 1976; Perfetti, 1985; Stanovich, Cunning-

---

[2]"Shiritori" is played in a manner analogous to "Geography", except that players must produce a place whose name starts with the same mora (for pre-literate children) or Kana character (for literate children) that ended the previous response. Thus, the first player might respond "Osaka" and the second player might respond "Kamakura".

ham, & Freeman, 1984b; Treiman & Baron, 1983).

In many studies of reading ability and phonological awareness, the question of cause and effect has been broached, but never completely resolved. One of the earliest studies revealed that American children's awareness of phonological structure markedly improves at just that age when they are beginning to read (Liberman, Shankweiler, Fischer, & Carter, 1974): Among a sample of 4-, 5- and 6-year-olds, none of the youngest children could identify the number of phonemes in a spoken word, while half could identify the number of syllables; of the 5-year-olds, 17% could count phonemes while, again, half could count syllables. Most dramatically, 70% of the 6-year-olds could count phonemes and 90% could count syllables. Did the older children become aware of syllables and phonemes because they were learning to read, was the opposite true, or both?

Certain evidence suggests that phonological awareness can precede reading ability or develop independently. First of all, various measures of phoneme awareness and syllable awareness are capable of presaging the success with which preliterate kindergarten children will learn to read the alphabet in the first grade (see, for example, Bradley & Bryant, 1983; Helfgott, 1976; Jusczyk, 1977, Liberman et al. 1974; Lundberg, Olofsson, & Wall, 1980; Mann & Liberman, 1984; Mann, 1984; Stanovich, Cunningham, & Cramer, 1984a). Second, there is evidence that explicit training in the ability to manipulate phonemes can facilitate preliterate children's ability to learn to read (Bradley & Bryant, 1985). Third, the awareness of syllables, in particular, does not appear to depend upon reading experience, as the majority of preliterate children can manipulate syllables by age six without having been instructed in the use of a syllabary or an alphabet (Amano, 1970; Liberman et al., 1974; Mann & Liberman, 1984), and the ability to manipulate syllables is not strongly influenced by the kind of reading instruction, "whole-word" or "phonics", that children receive in the first grade (Alegria, Pignot, & Morais, 1982).

Other evidence, however, has revealed that at least one component of phonological awareness—awareness of phonemes—may depend on knowledge of an alphabet. As noted previously, several different investigators have reported that the ability to manipulate phonemes is markedly deficient in adults who cannot read alphabetic transcription. Awareness of phonemes is deficient among semi-literate American adults (Liberman et al., 1986), reading-disabled Australian adults (Byrne & Ledez, 1973), illiterate Portuguese adults (Morais et al., 1979) and Chinese adults who can read only the Chinese logographic orthography (Read et al., 1984). In addition, the type of reading instruction which children receive can influence the extent of their awareness: first-graders who have been taught to read the alphabet by a "phonics" approach tend to be more aware of phonemes than those who have learned by a "whole-word" method (Alegria, Pignot, & Morais, 1982).

Present evidence, then, suggests that the relationship between phonological awareness and reading ability is a two-way street (Perfetti, 1985) which may depend on the level of awareness being addressed. Awareness of syllables is not very dependent on reading experience and could be a natural cognitive achievement of sorts, whereas awareness of phonemes may depend upon the experience of learning to read the alphabet, in general, and on methods of instruction that draw attention to phonemic structure, in particular. As a test of this view, the present study examined the phoneme and syllable awareness of children in a Japanese elementary school, predicting that these children would be aware of syllables, but would not be aware of phonemes until that point in their education when they receive instruction in the use of alphabetic transcription.

The design of the study involves four experiments which focus on the awareness of syllables (mora) and phonemes among children at different ages. Two different experimental paradigms are employed as a control against any confounding effects of task-specific variables. One paradigm is the counting test developed by Liberman and her colleagues, a test used in several studies of phonological awareness among American children (see, for example, Liberman et al., 1974; Mann & Liberman, 1984). The other is a deletion task, much like that employed by Morais et al. (1979) and Read et al. (1984) in their studies of alphabet-illiterate adults.

Experiment I used the counting test paradigm to study Japanese first graders who had recently mastered the Kana syllabaries. To clarify the impact of knowledge of a syllabary vs. an alphabet, the results are compared with those reported in Liberman et al.'s (1974) study of American first graders. The relation between reading and phonological awareness is also probed by an analysis of the relation between phoneme and syllable counting performance and the ability to read Hiragana, in which case a nonlinguistic counting test guards against the possibility that any correlations might reflect attention capacity, general intelligence, etc. To further clarify the role of knowledge of the alphabet, Experiment II extended use of the counting test paradigm to Japanese children in the third to sixth grades. In Japan, children routinely receive some instruction in alphabetic transcription (Romaji) at the end of the fourth grade. There also exist certain "re-entry" programs for fourth through sixth graders who have spent the first few years of their education abroad and who have learned to read an alphabetic orthography. Comparisons among the re-entering pupils and normal pupils at various grade levels clarifies the relative contribution of alphabetic knowledge vs. knowledge of Kana and Kanji.

Experiment III used the deletion test paradigm to replicate and extend the findings of Experiment I. Aside from the change in procedure, its major innovation was to employ nonsense words as stimuli, constructing them in a fashion to permit parallel testing of first graders in Japan and in America. Analysis of the results concerns performance on each deletion test in relation to reading experience and reading ability. Finally, Experiment IV used the same paradigm in a partial replication of Experiment II, comparing Japanese fourth graders who had not received instruction in Romaji with sixth graders who had been taught about Romaji 1½ years prior to the test session.

Experiment I

Methods

Subjects

The subjects were 40 children attending the first grade of the primary school attached to Ochanomizu University, 20 girls and 20 boys chosen at random from the available population and serving with the permission of their parents and teachers. Mean age was 84.4 months at the time of testing, which was the beginning of the second trimester of the school year. As a measure of Hiragana reading ability, each child rapidly read aloud a list of 30 high-frequency nouns, adjectives and verbs (Sasanuma, 1978), and the total reading time and the number of errors were recorded. Each child was also rated by his or her teacher as above-average, average, or below-average in Kana reading ability.

Materials

The experiment employed three sets of materials designed to measure the ability to count three types of items: mora, phonemes, and 30° angles (a nonlinguistic unit). All three sets were modelled after the materials of Liberman et al. (1974). Each contained four series of training items which offered the child an opportunity to deduce the nature of the unit being counted, followed by a sequence of test items. In the mora counting test and phoneme counting test, all training and test items were common Japanese words which had been judged by four informants (a linguist, a speech scientist, a teacher of Japanese and a librarian) to be readily familiar to young children. In the angle counting test, the items were simple line drawings of abstract designs and common objects. A more complete description of each test follows.

Mora counting test

Mora are rhythmic units of the Japanese language which more-or-less correspond to syllables. Each mora is either an isolated vowel, a vowel preceded by a consonant, an isolated [n], or the first consonant in a geminate cluster. It is a basic difference between mora and English syllables that mora cannot contain consonant clusters, in general, or consonants in final position. It is further the case that a single syllable of English may correspond to two mora of Japanese. This owes to the fact that, in a Japanese word such as "hon", [n] can be a mora, whereas [n] cannot be a syllable of English, and to the fact that differences in vowel duration (one or two mora) and consonant closure duration (normal or an extra mora) distinguish minimal pairs of Japanese words but are not contrastive in English.

In the mora-counting test, each training series contained three words: two-, three- and four-mora in length. Within the first three series, the words formed a progressive sequence, as in "hito" (man), "hitotsu" (one), "hitotsubu" (a grain or drop) but the words of the fourth series bore no such relation to each other (i.e., "ima" (now), "kitte" (stamp), "chiisai" (small)). To introduce some of the complexities of Japanese phonology, the third series included a devoiced vowel, and the fourth included a long vowel and a geminate consonant. To avoid biasing the child's decision as to whether the task was to count the mora in a word (a phonological strategy) or the number of Kana characters needed to spell the word (a spelling strategy), the training items included only those mora which are spelled with a single character. Thus it was left ambiguous whether the task was to count orthographic units, or phonological ones.

The test sequence consisted of 14 two-mora words, 14 three-mora words and 14 four-mora words presented in a fixed random order and they represented common combinations of mora including the nasal mora, geminate vowels, geminate consonants and devoiced vowels. There were four VV words, two CVV words, six CVCV words and two CVC words in the two-mora pool; two VCVV words, two VVCV words, two CVVCV words, three CVCVCV words, two CVCVC words, two CVCCV words and one CVCVV word in the three-mora pool and four VCVCVCV words, two VCCVCV words, one VCVCCV word, four CVCVCVCV words, two CVCVCVV words and one CVCCVCV word in the four-mora pool. As a probe for whether children were counting mora or orthographic units, three of the test items included one of the Japanese mora which are spelled with two characters.

Phoneme counting test

The design was analogous to that for the mora-counting test but items manipulated the number of phonemes instead of the number of mora. The four training series contained a variety of the possible two- three- and four-phoneme sequences of Japanese, including nasal mora, devoiced vowels, long vowels and geminate consonants, and each of the first three contained a progressive sequence of items (i.e., "ho" (sail), "hon" (book), "hone" (bone)) whereas the fourth did not (i.e., "ta" (field), "kau" (buy), "shita" (under)). The test sequence contained 14 two-phoneme words, 14 three-phoneme words and 14 four-phoneme words arranged into a fixed random order, and they comprised a broad sample of the permissible phoneme sequences in Japanese, including nasal mora, geminate consonants and vowels and devoiced vowels, which avoided systematic relationships between the number of phonemes a word contained, and either the number of mora in that word, or the number of Kana needed to spell it. There were four VV words, eight CV words, and two VC words in the two-phoneme pool; two VVV words, four VCV words, four CVV words and four CVC words in the three-phoneme pool, and six CVCV words, two CVVV words, two VCCV words, two VCVV words and two VVCV words in the four-phoneme pool.

Angle counting test

The materials were simple black-and-white line drawings that appeared on 3 in × 5 in cards. From one to three 30° angles were embedded in each drawing and the task was to count the number of these angles. In keeping with the design of the phoneme- and mora-counting tests, there were four series of training trials; in the first three series, the items were a progressive set of simple geometric shapes, but in the fourth they were objects that bore no systematic relationship to each other. The test sequence comprised drawings of objects, seven with one angle, seven with two angles and seven with three angles, arranged in a fixed random sequence.

Procedure

Prior to testing, the children were divided into two groups of 10 girls and 10 boys each. One group received the mora counting test, the other received the phoneme-counting test, and both received the angle-counting test at the onset of the session and the reading test at the end. The procedure for all three counting tests was the same. The instructor (a native speaker of Japanese) took two small hammers and told the child that they would be playing a "counting game". He then demonstrated the first training series in progressive order by saying each word in a normal fashion (or displaying each card) and then tapping the number of mora, phonemes or angles. Next, the demonstration was repeated, with the child copying the instructor (saying each word first), and then items in the series were presented in a fixed random order, and the child responded without benefit of demonstration. If an error was made, the item was repeated and presentation of another randomized series followed. Otherwise, training proceeded to the next series, until, on completion of the fourth training series, the test items were presented and the child was instructed to "count" each item without the benefit of response feedback.

Results and discussion

In evaluating children's responses on the mora and phoneme counting materials, two different scores were computed: the number of correct responses (as in Mann & Liberman, 1984), and a pass/fail score in which the criterion for passing was six consecutive correct responses (as in Liberman et al., 1974). Both appear in Table 1 along with mean age and mean reading scores for children in each group. The children who counted mora were equivalent to those who counted phonemes in terms of mean age, measures of reading ability, and performance on the angle-counting test ($p > .05$). However, whereas scores on the mora-counting test approached ceiling, scores on the phoneme-counting test were considerably lower, $t(38) = 20.20$, $p < .0001$. In addition, all of the children had passed the mora counting test, whereas only 10% had passed the phoneme counting one.

The percentage of Japanese children who passed each test can be compared with the percentage of American first graders who had passed comparable

Table 1. *The ability of Japanese first graders to count mora vs. phonemes*

	Subject group	
	Mora counting	Phoneme counting
Phonological counting		
Mean no. correct	38.1	18.1
(Max. = 42)		
Percentage passing	100.0	10.0
Angle counting		
Mean no. correct	11.9	11.8
(Max. = 21)		
Kana reading ability		
Mean speed	61.1	60.7
(in s)		
Mean errors	1.6	1.8
(Max. = 30)		
Mean teacher rating	1.9	2.0
(Good = 1, avg. = 2, poor = 3)		
Mean age (in months)	83.7	84.1

tests in Liberman et al.'s original study: 90% for syllable counting, and 70% for phoneme counting. Apparently, first-grade children who have been educated in the use of the alphabet tend to perform better on the phoneme counting test than those who have not, and while children who have been educated in a syllabary might do slightly better on the syllable counting test, any difference is less dramatic. At present no strong conclusion can be reached about these differences and their implications: Different test materials were used in the two countries, and children were not told explicitly to focus on the spoken word as opposed to its orthographic representation. Both problems are surmounted in Experiment III, which employed (1) a common set of materials in the testing of Japanese and American first graders, and (2) instructions to manipulate the sound pattern of each item.

Performance on each test gave indications of the influence of knowledge of Kana. In the mora-counting test, children appeared to deduce the task as involving the counting of orthographic units rather than the counting of phonological units. The majority gave an extra "tap" to the three items that contained a mora spelled with two characters instead of one, as if they were counting the number of characters needed to spell the word, instead of the number of mora. Other, much less frequent errors on this test involved words which contained geminate consonants or long vowels, both of which tended to be underestimated and were missed only by the poorest readers of the group.

Analogous adherence to a "spelling strategy" can be found in children's responses to the phoneme counting materials. During a post-hoc interview, some of the children reported that they had tapped the number of Kana characters needed to spell a given a word, and then added one to arrive at the correct response. Use of a "kana plus one" strategy could not allow children to reach the criteria of six consecutive correct responses, but it certainly inflated the number of correct responses. Items ($N = 25$) for which the "Kana-plus-one" strategy yielded the appropriate response were correctly counted by an average of 55% of the children (which is significantly better than chance, $t(24) = 2.62, p < .05$). In contrast, only an average of 38% had been correct on each item ($N = 17$) for which that strategy yielded the incorrect response (which is significantly less than the percentage of children giving correct responses to the strategy-appropriate items, $t(40) = 5.4, p < .001$ and not significantly better than chance $p > .05$).

A final concern of this experiment was the relation between performance on each counting test and the ability to read Kana. For the children, who learned to count mora, the number of correct responses on the mora counting test was significantly related to teacher ratings ($r(20) = .72, p < .0001$), Hiragana reading speed ($r(20) = -.58, p < .003$), and the number of errors

$(r(20) = -.47, p < .02)$, but not to age, sex, or performance on the angle counting test. This is consistent with Amano's (1970) report that mora counting ability is related to the acquisition of the first few Kana characters by pre-school children, and extends his finding to children in the first grade who possess considerably greater knowledge of the Kana syllabary. For the children who learned to count phonemes, the number of correct responses on the phoneme counting test was also significantly related to teacher ratings $(r(20) = .56, p < .005)$, reading speed $(r(20) = -.65, p <. 001)$, and reading errors $(r(29) = -.57, p < .004)$, but not to age, sex, or angle counting performance.

Thus it would appear that performance on the phoneme counting test is related to the ability to read Kana even though Kana does not represent phonemes in any direct way. As both phoneme and syllable counting performance are related to the ability to read Hiragana, just as they are related to the ability to read an alphabet, it is tempting to posit a general capacity for phonological awareness which is related to experience in reading any phonologically-based orthography. This capacity need not be part of general intelligence, given the results of some recent studies of American children (Mann & Liberman, 1984; Stanovich et al., 1984b), and the present finding that there is no significant correlation between measures of reading ability and performance on the angle counting test. It could be a general product of learning to read a phonological orthography rather than the cause of reading success, commensurate with children's reliance on Kana-based strategies. We will return to these issues in the final discussion.

The results of Experiment I are consistent with previous reports that awareness of phonemes depends on the experience of learning to read an alphabet, insofar as the majority of children could not pass the phoneme counting test. Nonetheless, two of the Japanese children did pass the test and our post-hoc interviews of them indicated that they had received no instruction in the alphabet either at home, school or "juku" (i.e., afternoon training programs). Thus, while there may be some facilitating effects of learning a syllabary on awareness of both phonemes and syllables, some other factors may lead to individual variations. As a further test of the view that awareness of phonemes depends on the experience of learning to read an alphabet, we now turn to Experiment II which focused on the phoneme counting ability of Japanese children in the third through sixth grades, comparing children at different grade levels in normal and "re-entering" classrooms.

Experiment II

Method

Subjects

The subjects were children attending the normal third through sixth grade classes and the special "re-entry" class at Ochanomizu University. The "normal class" subjects included 64 children in the third and fourth grades, and 32 children in the fifth and sixth grades. The "re-entry class" subjects included 13 fourth graders, 14 fifth graders and 12 sixth graders, all of whom had learned to read either the English or German alphabet. Approximately equal numbers of boys and girls were included in each group and all served with parental permission, and were tested during the second trimester of school, such that children in the normal fourth-grade classes had not yet received training in the alphabet. Consultation with the teachers, the principal and the children themselves confirmed that none of the subjects in normal classrooms had received instruction in the alphabet at home or "Juku".

Materials and procedure

The materials were the mora- and phoneme-counting materials employed in Experiment I, administered by the same instructor. For convenience, the procedure was adapted for group testing in which case an entire class of children received the basic instructions and practice items with feedback, and learned to "count" each word by drawing slashes through the appropriate number of boxes in a five-box answer grid instead of by tapping the number of syllables/phonemes with a hammer. As in Experiment I, feedback was provided during training, but no feedback was provided during presentation of the test items. To insure the feasibility of group testing, the mora counting materials were administered as a control measure to 32 of the third graders and 32 of the fourth graders. All of the remaining subjects received the phoneme counting materials.

Results and discussion

The data were scored in the manner of Experiment I, by computing both the number of correct responses and a pass/fail score. The results obtained from the mora counting materials indicate the utility of the group testing procedure, as all of the third- and fourth-grade children had passed criterion with mean scores of 38.7 and 39.0, respectively. They also attest to the continuing power of the Kana orthography to mold the Japanese child's concept of language: As was the case in Experiment I, almost all of the children had made errors on the three test words in which the number of kana characters needed to spell the word surpasses the number of mora it contains.

Performance on the phoneme counting test is summarized in Table II, according to the age of the subjects, and whether they were in the normal or re-entry classes. On the basis of previous findings that alphabet-illiterate adults are not aware of phonemes, it might be expected that normal Japanese third and fourth graders would be no more aware of phonemes than the Japanese first graders studied in Experiment I, whereas the normal fifth and sixth graders and all of the re-entry students would be comparable to the American first-graders studied by Liberman et al. (1974). Yet, the data fail to uphold that prediction. First, for children in the normal classrooms, whose data appear in the upper portion of Table 2, the only marked improvement in phoneme counting scores occurs between the third and fourth grades, prior to any instruction in the alphabetic principle. There is also no sharp spurt in the awareness of phonemes between fourth and fifth grades ($p > .05$), such as would be expected if instruction in the alphabet were critical. Second, fourth-graders in the re-entry group performed at the same level as their peers in the normal classrooms ($p > .05$), despite the fact that they alone had learned to read an alphabet. Third, and finally, the proportion of Japanese fourth graders who had passed criterion is comparable to that among the

Table 2. *Phoneme counting ability among Japanese children in the third to sixth grades: Normal vs. re-entering students*

| | Grade | | | |
	Third	Fourth	Fifth	Sixth
Normal students				
Mean no. correct	21.5	30.3	31.2	31.5
(Max. = 42)				
Percentage passing	56.2	73.5	81.3	75.0
Age (in months)	108.5	120.1	131.2	143.7
Re-entering students				
Mean no. correct	—	27.2	28.6	27.7
(Max. = 42)				
Percentage passing	—	60.0	60.0	80.0
Age (in months)	—	118.9	132.7	144.4

American children in Liberman et al.'s (1974) study, despite the fact that the Japanese children had not yet learned to read the Romaji alphabet.

As in Experiment I, the importance of orthographic knowledge is illustrated by the pattern of errors, which suggests that at least some children were relying on the "Kana-plus-one" strategy of counting the number of characters needed to spell the word, and then adding one. Children at all ages tended to be most successful on items for which this strategy yielded the correct response: for strategy-appropriate items the average percent correct was 58%, 80%, 81%, and 82%, for third through sixth graders, respectively, whereas that for the strategy-inappropriate items was 42%, 56%, 64%, 67%, respectively. Here, however, performance on both types of items surpassed the chance level of 33% correct ($p < .05$), suggesting that appreciably many children at each age had been counting phonemes.

A popular organization of the Kana syllabary places the characters in a grid with the vowel mora in a different column to the far right of those containing characters for other mora and this organization had les us to anticipate that some of the subjects in Experiments I and II would use a strategy of giving the vowel mora one count and all other mora two counts. However, in post-hoc interviews of our subjects we found that none of them described such a strategy. Likewise, none of the children reported special treatment of the kana which can receive diacritics to mark the voicing of an initial stop consonant or fricative. Certainly it is possible that knowledge of Kana may have in some other way provoked children to reflect on the internal structure of words and thereby promoted phoneme awareness, but we were unable to determine why, although children master Kana by the very early stages of first grade, the sharpest increase in phoneme counting performance occurs between third and fourth grade. Either increased experience of a very general sort or some maturational factors could be responsible.

In summary, although the findings of Experiment I suggest that both phoneme and syllable counting ability in the first grade might be facilitated by knowledge of an orthography that transcribes language at the level of that unit, the findings of Experiment II suggest that, analogous to the many American children who become aware of syllables by age 6 without having learned to read a syllabary, many Japanese children may become able to count phonemes by age 9 or 10, despite a lack of formal instruction in the alphabet. Moreover, at that age, training in the use of an alphabet does not particularly enhance the ability to count phonemes. This finding stands in contrast to findings that most alphabet-illiterate adults appear to lack an awareness about phonemes.

One possible explanation of the performance differences between alphabet-illiterate adults and Japanese children is that they reflect task differences rather than differences in phonological awareness, per se. Japanese children might appear to be more aware of phonemes because the counting tasks employed in Experiments I and II were not explicit as to whether "sounds" or characters were to be counted, leading to reliance on a Kana-based strategy which inflated the number of correct responses. However, use of such a strategy could not account for changes in the percentage of children who passed the phoneme counting test, which raises the possibility that children passed the test because it provided a less conservative measure of phoneme awareness than the deletion tasks used in studies of adults. The results of at least one study are commensurate with this letter possibility. Performance on counting tasks and deletion tasks emerged as separate factors in a study of the relation between phonological awareness and the reading progress of semi-literate adults enrolled in a remedial reading class (Read & Ruyter, 1985). Another study, however, reveals that task-differences are not of critical importance to the relation between phonological awareness and the future reading success of kindergarten children in America (Stanovich, Cunningham, & Cramer, 1984a). Yet as this latter study did not include counting tests, it remains a possibility that performance on counting tasks involves a more accessible level of phonological awareness than performance on deletion tests, hence the apparently greater awareness of phonemes on the part of Japanese children relative to alphabet-illiterate adults.

If the above explanation is correct, the present findings should not extend to use of an deletion test. On such a test, Japanese children should behave as poorly as alphabet-illiterate adults. With this prediction in mind, we turn to Experiments III and IV which attempted to replicate Experiments I and II with deletion tasks analogous to those employed by Morais et al. (1979) and by Read et al. (1984). Two sets of nonsense-word materials were designed, one for phoneme deletion and one for mora deletion. Nonsense words had been among the most difficult items for the adult subjects and therefore offer a maximally conservative measure of children's performance; they also permit parallel testing of Japanese and American children.

Experiment III

Method

Subjects

The subjects were 40 Japanese first graders and 40 American first graders, equally many girls and boys who served with parental and teacher permission.

The Japanese children were drawn from an available population of children who had not participated in Experiment I. Mean age was 84.4 months at the time of testing, which was midway through the second trimester of the school year. The American children were comparable in age and SES and were attending the Bolles Primary School in Jacksonville, Florida. Mean age was 84.1 months at the time of testing, which was early in the second semester of the school year. Measures of children's reading ability were obtained by having the teachers rate each child as good, average, or poor in reading ability, and by giving each child a test of word decoding skill: the Hiragana reading test described in Experiment I for Japanese children, and the Word Identification and Word Attack Subtests of the Woodcock Reading Mastery Test (Woodcock, 1973) for American children.

Materials

As in Experiment I, two parallel sets of materials were designed, one for assessing syllable deletion ability and one for assessing phoneme deletion ability. The design of each was prompted by the methodology of Morais et al. (1979) and Read et al. (1984): Each set of materials assessed deletion of two different tokens of the segment of interest, with blocked sequences of training items followed by test items. To make the items suitable for use in English and Japanese it was necessary that they contain only those Japanese mora which bear a one-to-one relationship to English syllables. Thus all items contained consonants and vowels shared by the two languages, and none of them contained long vowels, syllabic [n], geminate consonants, diphthongs, consonant clusters, or syllable-final consonants. Each test item, and the item formed by removing its initial mora (or phoneme, as appropriate) was judged to be meaningless in Japanese (by the informants who judged the items of Experiment I) and in English (by comparable English-speaking informants).

Syllable materials

These materials assessed children's ability to remove an initial syllable (mora), [ta] or [u], from a three-syllable/three-mora nonsense word. Twenty items started with [ta] and twenty with [u], the second and third syllable of each word varied freely. For the purpose of testing, the items were blocked with respect to initial syllable, and each block was subdivided into 10 practice items and 10 test items.

Phoneme materials

These materials assessed children's ability to remove an initial phoneme, [ʃ] or [k], from a four- or six-phoneme (i.e. two or three syllables/mora) nonsense word. Twenty items started with [ʃ] and 20 with [k], the second phoneme of each word was always one of the five permissible vowels such that, across the items, each initial phoneme was followed by each vowel once in a four-phoneme word, and once in a six-phoneme word, with the remaining portion of each item varied freely. For the purpose of testing, the items were blocked with respect to initial phoneme, and each block was divided into 10 practice items and 10 test items (such that two- and three-syllable words were equally divided between practice and test items, as were the five vowels which could occur in the second-phoneme position).

Procedure

Children were tested individually by native speakers who used comparable instructions on the two languages. Within each country, half of the children received the syllable deletion test, half received the phoneme deletion test, and all received the reading test at the conclusion of the session. For each deletion test, presentation of practice and test trials was blocked with respect to initial segment (i.e., [ta] or [u], [ʃ] or [k]) with order counterbalanced across subjects. The instructor explained that the task involved repeating a word and then trying to say it without the first sound. He or she then proceeded to demonstrate the first five practice items: saying each word, repeating it and then saying it without the first syllable or phoneme. Next, each of these was repeated and the child was requested to imitate the instructor by repeating the item and then saying it "without the first sound." Then the final five practice items were administered without benefit of demonstration, but with response feedback. Completion of the practice items was followed by the 10 test items which were administered without response feedback. Completion of the first block of trials was followed immediately by presentation of the second block of training and test items.

Results and discussion

Attempts to remove the initial segment from each item were scored as correct or incorrect, and the mean number of correct responses appear in Table 3, separately for the American and Japanese children, according to the type and token of the segment being manipulated. When averaged across tasks and tokens, the scores of American children are slightly superior ($F(1,76) = 7.31$, $p < .009$). With regard to the type of segment being deleted, children in both countries found the phoneme deletion task more difficult than the syllable (mora) deletion one, ($F(1,76) = 87.64, p < .0001$). However, the extent of the

Table 3.   *Mora (syllable) elision ability vs. phoneme ability: A comparison of first graders in Japan and America*

	Mora elision		Phoneme elision	
	[u]	[ta]	[ʃ]	[k]
Japanese children				
Mora group				
Mean no. correct:	9.15	9.55		
(Max. = 10, Age = 83.8 mo.)				
Phoneme group				
Mean no. correct:			1.75	3.10
(Max. = 10, Age = 85.1 mo.)				
American children				
Syllable group				
Mean no. correct:	8.90	8.80		
(Max. = 10, Age = 83.5 mo.)				
Phoneme group				
Mean no. correct:			5.72	5.61
(Max. = 10, Age = 84.8 mo.)				

difference between scores on the two tasks was greater for the Japanese children, $(F(1,76) = 13.01, p < .0006)$. As compared to the American children, the Japanese children received higher scores on the syllable deletion task $(t(38) = 2.73, p < .05)$, but lower scores on the phoneme deletion task $(t(38) = 4.09, p < .01)$. There were no significant effects of token differences, nor interactions between this manipulation and other factors.

A further analysis considered the relations between phoneme and syllable deletion performance (summed across tokens) and reading ability in each country. As anticipated by the results of Experiment I, the mora deletion performance of the Japanese children was related to the speed $(r(20) = -.69, p < .001)$ and number of errors made on the Hiragana test $(r(20) = -.72, p < .001)$, and also to the teacher's ratings of reading ability $(r(20) = .54, p < .005)$. Likewise, their phoneme deletion ability also proved to be related to speed $(r(20) = -.37, p < .05)$, and errors on the Hiragana test $(r(20) = -.38, p < .05)$, and to teacher ratings $(r(20) = .47, p < .02)$. For the American children, phoneme deletion ability was related to the sum of raw scores on the Woodcock tests $(r(20) = .61, p < .005)$ and to the teacher's ratings $(r(20) = .57, p < .008)$, but syllable deletion ability was not related to either measure of reading ability. In neither language community was the age or sex of the first graders related to reading ability, mora deletion ability or phoneme deletion ability ($p > .1$). The relative superiority of the American children in the case of the phoneme deletion task corroborates previous indications that awareness about phonemes is facilitated by the learning of an alphabetic orthography. The analogous finding that Japanese children perform at a superior level on the syllable deletion task suggests that awareness about syllables may be likewise facilitated by learning to read a syllabary. Nonetheless, the finding that both Japanese and American children achieved higher levels of performance on the syllable deletion test than on the phoneme deletion test suggests that the ability to read a syllabary is less critical to awareness about syllables than the ability to read an alphabet is to awareness about phonemes. We now turn to Experiment IV which attempted to replicate the findings of Experiment II regarding the contribution of orthographic knowledge to the phoneme deletion performance of Japanese children in normal fourth and sixth grade classrooms.

Experiment IV

Method

Subjects

The subjects were 20 fourth graders and 20 sixth graders attending the normal classes of the Ochanomizu Elementary School, equally many boys and girls at each age chosen at random from among the available pool of children who had not participated in Experiment II (i.e., those whose only experience with alphabetic instruction had occurred in school) and serving with teacher and parental permission. Testing was conducted during the first trimester of the school year such that only the sixth graders had been educated in the use of an alphabetic orthography. Mean ages for each group were 117.1 and 142.5 months, respectively.

Materials and procedure

The materials and procedure for Experiment IV were the phoneme deletion materials employed in Experiment III, the only innovation being that, at the completion of the test session, each subject was given two of the test items to which he or she had responded correctly and was asked to explain how the correct response had been derived. This provided a test of whether subjects had relied on either a Kana-based or a Romaji-based spelling strategy.

Results

The mean number of correct responses appears in Table 4, separated according to grade level and the phoneme token ([ʃ] or [k]) being manipulated. It can be seen that the performance of the sixth graders surpassed that of the fourth graders ($F(1,38) = 18.49$, $p < .0001$), consistent with the fact that only the sixth graders had learned to use alphabetic transcription. When the present results were compared with those obtained in Experiment III (and shown in Table 3), it was found that both the Japanese fourth and sixth graders had surpassed the Japanese first graders in mean performance on the phoneme deletion task ($t(38) = 4.08$, $p < .01$ for fourth graders, $t(38) = 4.53$, $p < .01$ for sixth graders). The Japanese fourth graders performed at the same level as the American first graders ($p > .1$), and the Japanese sixth graders had actually surpassed them ($t(38) = 5.11$, $p < .01$).

To gain some appreciation of the Japanese children's knowledge of Romaji, we conducted an informal post-hoc interview with the five children who performed best at each grade level. We found that none of the fourth graders could read the nonsense test materials written in Romaji, whereas three of the sixth graders could do so. In contrast, although we had not asked the American children to try to read the test materials, they had been able to read an appreciable number of nonsense words on the Woodcock word-attack test. It may be remembered that the Japanese fourth graders had not received any instruction in Romaji, whereas the sixth graders had received approximately 4 weeks of instruction a full year and a half prior to the test session. The American first graders, on the other hand, had been receiving intensive phonics-based instruction in the use of the English alphabet for

Table 4.   *Phoneme elision performance among older Japanese children*

	Phoneme elision	
	[ʃ]	[k]
Grade in school		
Fourth grade		
Mean no. correct:	4.82	7.55
(Max. = 10, Age = 117.1 mo.)		
Sixth grade		
Mean no. correct:	8.33	10.00
(Max. = 10, Age = 142.5 mo.)		

more than 6 months immediately prior to the test session.

A further analysis reveals an effect of token variations: Both fourth and sixth graders tended to give more correct responses to items which began with [k] than to those which began with [ʃ], ($F(1,38) = 20.73$, $p < .0001$). This may be explained by hypothesizing a "character-substitution" strategy based on the previously mentioned grid for representing the Kana syllabary as a matrix of rows and columns in which mora which share a vowel lie in the same row, and those which share a consonant lie in the same column. Within that matrix, the character for [a] is to the immediate right of that for [ka], [i] is to the immediate right of [ki], [u] to [ku], etc., and children might be tempted to spell a word, replace the first character with the character which lies to its immediate right on the matrix. Use of this strategy could cause [k] to be easier to delete than [ʃ] because characters containing [k] are immediately adjacent to those for isolated vowels, whereas most which contain [ʃ] are spelled with digraphs composed of the character for [ʃi] with a subscripted character for [ya], [ye], [yu] or [yo] (according to the identity of the vowel), and these lie at the opposite end of the grid from the vowel characters making it less obvious how to derive the character for the relevant vowel from that which represents the CV.

In this regard, we had actually asked children to explain how they had been able to arrive at a correct response. Of the fourth graders, seven were unable to describe their strategy at all, nine gave evidence of using the "character substitution strategy," and four subjects described a "phonological" strategy which more or less amounted to doubling the vowel of the first syllable in a word and then removing the initial consonant-vowel portion (i.e., making [ki-pi] into [ki-i-pi], and then deleting [ki] to yield [i-pi]. The children who reported the "phonological strategy" had achieved some of the best scores in their age group, and they tended to be equally accurate in their responses to items containing [k] and [ʃ]. As for the sixth graders, all of whom had been exposed to the alphabet, only four appeared to have employed the "character substitution strategy", and they achieved some of the lowest scores in their age group especially for items which began with [ʃ]. Fifteen of the remaining children reported some version of the "phonological strategy", and only a single child reported a strategy of using Romaji.

General discussion

The present study asked whether Japanese children's awareness of syllables and phonemes differs from that of American children, as a consequence of their having learned to read a syllabary instead of an alphabet. The results clearly showed that Japanese children's approach to phonological counting and deletions tests is influenced by their reading experience. Knowledge of the Kana syllabary tended to confound performance on tasks which attempted to assess the ability to manipulate phonological units, whether they involved the counting or deletion of phonemes or syllables, and whether instructions were ambiguous or explicit as to whether orthographic or sound units were being counted. Younger children in particular tended to manipulate the characters which spell a word rather than the phonological units which the characters transcribe. This tendency has previously been observed among American children (Ehri & Wilce, 1980) and has been one form of evidence that knowledge of an alphabet is responsible for phoneme awareness.

The results further reveal performance differences between first graders in Japan and America and these illustrate that knowledge of a syllabary/logography as opposed to an alphabet can have a very specific effect on phonological awareness. Relative to first graders in Japan, first graders in America can more accurately count the number of phonemes in words and can more accurately remove the initial phonemes from nonsense words. Thus the experience of learning to read an alphabet must facilitate children's awareness of phonemes at this age. The analogous finding that Japanese children can perform slightly better than American children on tasks that call for syllable manipulation likewise reveals that experience with a syllabary can facilitate the awareness of syllables. However, children, in general, find syllable manipulation an easier task than phoneme manipulation which suggests that the experience of learning to read a syllabary vs. an alphabet is not the sole determinant of phonological awareness.

What might the other determinants be? First of all, the development of phonological awareness may be a multi-faceted process that depends on the abstractness of the unit at issue. Syllables, as compared to phonemes, are isolable acoustic segments; they are more superficial, less encoded components of the speech signal. Thus it is reasonable that syllable awareness should be an easier to achieve, more natural achievement of such factors as cognitive maturation and primary language development, requiring less special cultivating experience than awareness of phonemes. The results of previous research favor this view (Liberman et al., 1974; Alegria et al., 1982; Read et al., 1984). While awareness of syllables may be a precursor of awareness of phonemes it is not sufficient, given that some individuals can manipulate syllables but not phonemes. Previous research had suggested that the ability to manipulate phonemes depends on knowledge of an alphabet (Byrne & Ledez, 1983; Liberman et al., 1986; Morais et al., 1979; Read et al., 1984), but the present study suggests that other factors can also play a role.

The findings of Experiments II and IV emphasize the role of factors other than knowledge of the alphabet in the development of phoneme awareness, by revealing that, whereas most Japanese first graders could manipulate syllables but not phonemes, the majority of Japanese children were able to manipulate both syllables and phonemes by the fourth grade, whether or not they had been instructed in the use of an alphabet. Thus, with increasing age and educational experience Japanese children may become more and more capable of manipulating phonemes whether or not they are alphabet-literate.

This finding stands in contrast to previous reports that adults who do not know how to read an alphabet are not aware of phonemes, and some explanation is required. We may disregard the possibility that the differences between Japanese children and the alphabet-illiterate adults are due to task differences rather than differences in phonological awareness, per se. A concern with this possibility prompted Experiments III and IV which employed deletion tasks analogous to those used in previous studies of illiterate adults, and the results obtained in these experiments are much the same as those obtained with the counting tasks employed in Experiments I and II. This accords with some other observations that the task-unique cognitive demands posed by different tests of phonological awareness do not appreciably confound conclusions about young children's phonological awareness and its role in reading acquisition (Stanovich et al., 1984a).

Perhaps a more reasonable interpretation is to accept the differences between the present findings and those obtained with alphabet-illiterate adults as differences in phonological awareness. We might then explore the possibility that other types of secondary language activity are responsible for the superior phonological awareness of the older Japanese children. One clear likelihood is that awareness of both syllables and phonemes is promoted by the experience of learning Kana, owing to the fact that it is a phonological orthography. This accords with the fact that many of the adults who proved deficient in phoneme awareness were functional illiterates (i.e., the American and Portuguese adults). It would also accord with the correlations between Kana reading ability and both syllable and phoneme awareness, observed in Experiments I and III (although the correlation leaves causality ambiguous). It might seem inconsistent with certain findings (i.e., Experiment III and Mann, 1984) that syllable awareness fails to correlate with the ability to read the alphabet, but ceiling effects are a possible confounding factor, and other studies have reported a correlation between syllable awareness and reading ability (see, for example, Mann & Liberman, 1984; Alegria et al., 1982).

A more serious problem with the view that knowledge of a phonological orthography promotes all aspects of phonological awareness concerns the lack of phoneme awareness among adult readers of the Chinese orthography

(Read et al., 1984). As noted by Gelb (1963), Chinese, the most logographic of all the writing systems, is not a pure logographic system because from the earliest times certain characters have represented not words but phonological units. Many Chinese characters, the "phonetic compounds," are digraphs—compounds composed of a radical and a phonetic—each of which otherwise represents a word of the language. As noted by Leong (in press), since 600 A.D. the "fanqui" principal has been employed for decoding phonetic compounds, a strategy which calls for blending the first part (initial consonant) and the tone of the word represented by the phonetic with the final part (syllable rime) of the word represented by the radical. Thus a compound composed of the radicals representing "t'u" and "l'iau" decodes as "t'iau." Several Chinese colleagues inform me that classical methods of education in the Chinese logography have explicitly called the reader's attention to the phonetic radicals. Moreover, although historical changes have necessarily altered the relationship between phonetic compounds and the words they represent, one recent study reveals that the adult readers of Chinese make use of the phonetic insofar as they name low-frequency (but not high-frequency) characters which involve phonetic compounds faster than non-phonetic compound characters (Seidenberg, 1985). Likewise, adult readers of Chinese can use phonetic radicals productively (Fong, Horn, & Tzeng, in press), to give consistent pronunciations for nonsense logographs composed of phonetics and radicals that do not usually co-occur. Given these findings, it is somewhat puzzling that exposure to phonetic compounds did not promote phonological awareness among Read et al.'s subjects, if exposure to any phonological orthography facilitates phoneme awareness.

Placing aside the role of reading experience, it is possible that phoneme awareness is facilitated by some other secondary language experience that is available to Japanese children but not to the adults studied in Portugal and China. For Japanese children, the appropriate experience might involve learning to analyze or manipulate the phonological structure of spoken words while playing word games like "Shiritori" or while learning about Haiku. That the experience facilitating phonological awareness need not be limited to reading is evident from previous findings about the utility of explicit training in phonemic analysis (see Treiman & Baron, 1983, for example). Exposure to nursery rhymes and other poetry, for example, could help to explain why many American children are aware of syllables, before they learn to read. But it would have to be argued that experience with such secondary language activities facilitates the development of all aspects of phonological awareness, in a very general way, else how are we to explain the fact that Japanese children became able to manipulate phonemes despite a lack of experience with games and versification devices which directly manipulate phoneme-sized units? Even if it is postulated that any secondary language experience which manipulates phonological structure can give rise to awareness of both syllables and phonemes, there remains a problem insofar as meter and rhyme are exploited by both Chinese and Portuguese verse, song lyrics, etc. and would probably have been available to the illiterate adults who nonetheless lacked phoneme awareness. A further problem arises from the fact that, in the present study, all of the children were familar with the Kana syllabary and the same types of word games and versification devices, yet only a small minority of the first graders (10%) were able to count phonemes whereas the majority of fourth graders could do so.

A similar argument can be made against the view that Japanese children knew about phonemes because they had seen signs, labels, etc. written in the Romaji alphabet. Any explanation that passive exposure to the Romaji alphabet is responsible for the phoneme awareness of Japanese children would have to account for the fact that all children are exposed to Romaji signs and logos, yet only those aged 9 and older had profited from that exposure. It would also have to account for the fact that passive exposure to alphabetically-written material failed to promote phoneme awareness among the Portuguese adults studied by Morais et al. (1979).

One final explanation of the differences between the present results and those obtained with alphabet-illiterate adults remains. The ability to manipulate both syllable and phoneme-sized units could be a natural concomitant of primary language development which is exploited by many secondary language activities such as reading, versification and word games. But if this capacity is a natural concomitant of primary language, how can it be deficient in alphabet-illiterate adults? Perhaps the ability to manipulate phonemes tends to atrophy unless maintained by appropriate reading experience. It has often been speculated that children acquire their primary language with the aid of a language acquisition device that is not present in adults. That the capacity for manipulating phonemes could be part and parcel of a language acquisition device follows from a suggestion made by Mattingly (1984), in answer to the question of why readers might be able to gain access to the otherwise reflexive processes that support the processing of phonological structure in spoken language. He suggests that an ability to analyze the phonological structure of spoken words might serve to increase the language learner's stock of lexical entries, and this, together with some other evidence that children have a privileged ability to acquire new lexical entries (Carey, 1978), could lead to the speculation that children have a privileged ability to manipulate phonological structure which somehow facilitates their ability to engage in secondary language activities that involve manipulations of phonological units. The prevalence of this capacity in childhood could promote children's acquisition of phonological orthographies during their elementary school years and by postulating that this capacity atrophies in the absence of appropriate orthographic knowledge, one might explain the lack of phoneme awareness observed among alphabet-illiterate adults. However, this view is not without its problems, one being the fact that Japanese children could not do well on either the counting or elision tasks until relatively late in their childhood. Here, the cognitive demands of tests that are used to measure phoneme awareness and the confounding role of orthographic knowledge cannot be disregarded. Ongoing research with a broader battery of tests and a broader range of ages may further elucidate the basis of phonological awareness in the interplay between cognitive skills, primary language skills and experience with secondary language activities such as reading.

References

Alegria, J., Pignot, E., & Morais, J. (1982). Phonetic analysis of speech and memory codes in beginning readers. *Memory and Cognition, 10*, 451–456.

Amano, K. (1970). Formation of the act of analyzing phonemic structure of words and its relation to learning Japanese syllabic characters. *Japanese Journal of Education, 18*, 12–25.

Bradley, L., & Bryant, P.E. (1983). Difficulties in auditory organization as a possible cause of reading backwards. *Nature, 271*, 746–747.

Bradley, L., & Bryant, P. (1985). *Rhyme and reason in reading and spelling.* Ann Arbor: University of Michigan Press.

Byrne, B., & Ledez, J. (1983). Phonological awareness in reading-disabled adults. *Australian Journal of Psychology, 35*, 185–197.

Calfee, R.C., Lindamood, P.O., & Lindamood, C. (1973), Acoustic-phonetic skills and reading—kindergarten through twelfth grade. *Journal of Educational Psychology, 64*, 293–298.

Carey, S. (1978). The child as words learner. In M. Halle, J. Bresnan, & G.A. Miller (Eds.), *Linguistic theory and psychological reality* (pp. 264–293). Cambridge, MA: MIT Press.

Ehri, L.C., & Wilce, L.S. (1980). The influence of orthography on readers' conceptualization of the phonemic structure of words. *Applied Psycholinguistics, 1*, 371–385.

Fong, S.P., Horn, R.Y., & Tzeng, O.J. (1986). Consistency effects in Chinese character and pseudo-character naming tests. In S.R. Kao & R. Hoosain (Eds.), *Linguistics, psychology and the Chinese language.* Hong Kong: University of Hong Kong Press.

Fox, B., & Routh, D.K. (1976). Phonemic analysis and synthesis as word-attack skills. *Journal of Educational Psychology, 69*, 70–74.

Gelb, I.J. (1963). *A Study of Writing.* Chicago: University of Chicago Press.

Helfgott, J. (1976). Phonemic segmentation and blending skills of kindergarten children: Implications for beginning reading acquisition. *Contemporary Educational Psychology, 1*, 157–169.

Jusczyk, P. (1977). Rhymes and reasons: Some aspects of children's appreciation of poetic form. *Developmental Psychology, 13*, 599–607.

Katz, R. (1982). *Phonological deficiencies in children with reading deficiencies: Evidence from an object naming task.* Doctoral Dissertation, Department of Psychology, University of Connecticut, Storrs, CT.

Leong, C.K. (in press). What does accessing a morphophonemic script tell us about reading and reading disorders in alphabetic scripts. *Bulletin of the Orton Society.*

Liberman, I.Y. (1971). Basic research in speech and the lateralization of language: Some implications for reading. *Bulletin of the Orton Society, 21*, 71–87.

Liberman, I.Y. (1973). Segmentation of the spoken word and reading acquisition. *Bulletin of the Orton Society, 23*, 65–77.

Liberman, I.Y., Rubin, H., Dugues, S., & Carlisle, J. (1986). Linguistic skills and spelling proficiency in kindergarteners and adult poor spellers. In D.B. Gray & J.F. Kavanagh (Eds.), *Biobehavioral measures of dyslexia*. Parkton, MD: York Press.

Liberman, I.Y., Shankweiler, D., Fischer, F.W., & Carter, B. (1974). Explicit syllable and phoneme segmentation in the young child. *Journal of Experimental Child Psychology, 18*, 201–212.

Lundberg, I., Olofsson, A., & Wall, S. (1980). Reading and spelling skills in the first school years predicted from phonemic awareness skills in kindergarten. *Scandinavian Journal of Psychology, 21*, 159–173.

Mann, V.A. (1984). Longitudinal prediction and prevention of reading difficulty. *Annals of Dyslexia, 34*, 117–137.

Mann, V.A., & Liberman, I.Y. (1984). Phonological awareness and verbal short-term memory. *Journal of Learning Disabilities, 17*, 592–598.

Mattingly, I.G. (1972). Reading, the linguistic process and linguistic awareness. In J.F. Kavanagh & I.G. Mattingly (Eds.), *Language by Ear and by Eye: The Relationship between Speech and Reading*. Cambridge, MA: MIT Press.

Mattingly, I.G. (1984). Reading, linguistic awareness and language acquisition. In J. Downing & R. Valtin (Eds.), *Linguistic awareness and learning to read* (pp. 9–25). New York: Springer-Verlag.

Morais, J., Cary, L., Alegria, J., & Bertelson, P. (1979). Does awareness of speech as a sequence of phones arise spontaneously? *Cognition, 7*, 323–331.

Perfetti, C.A. (1985). *Reading ability*. New York: Oxford University Press.

Read, C., Zhang, Y., Nie, H., & Ding, B. (1984). The ability to manipulate speech sounds depends on knowing alphabetic transcription. Paper presented at the 23rd International Congress of Psychology, Acapulco, September, 1984.

Read, C., & Ruyter, L. (1985). Reading and spelling skills in adults of low literacy. *Remedial and Special Education, 6*, 43–52.

Rosner, J., & Simon, D.P. (1971). The auditory analysis test: An initial report. *Journal of Learning Disabilities, 4*, 384–392.

Sasanuma, S. (1978). *Token Test of Differential Diagnosis of Aphasia*. Tokyo: Yaesu Rehabilitation Center.

Seidenberg, M.S. (1985). The time course of phonological code activation in two writing systems. *Cognition, 19*, 1–30.

Stanovich, K.E., Cunningham, A.E., & Cramer, B.B. (1984a). Assessing phonological awareness in kindergarten children: Issues of task comparability. *Journal of Experimental Child Psychology, 38*, 175–190.

Stanovich, K.E., Cunningham, A.E., & Freeman, D.J. (1984b). Intelligence, cognitive skills and early reading progress. *Reading Research Quarterly, 14*, 278–303.

Treiman, R., & Baron, J. (1983). Phonemic-analysis training helps children benefit from spelling-sound rules. *Memory and Cognition, 11*, 382–389.

Woodcock, R.W. (1973). *Woodcock Reading Mastery Test*. Circle Pines, MN: American Guidance Services.

Résumé

Lors d'une étude trans-culturelle sur des enfants japonais et américains nous avons examiné le développement de la conscience des syllabes et des phonèmes. Les expériences I et III, qui utilisent des tests de comptage et d'effacement, montrent que, à la différence des élèves américains de première année d'école primaire, qui ont en général conscience à la fois des phonèmes et des syllabes, presque tous les élèves en première année d'école primaire au Japon ont conscience d'unités phonologiques de l'ordre de la syllabe alors qu'assez peu ont conscience des phonèmes. Cette différence est attribuable au fait que les élèves japonais apprennent à lire un syllabaire alors que les élèves américains apprennent à lire un alphabet. Pour la plupart des enfants de cet âge, la conscience des phonèmes nécessite l'expérience d'une transcription alphabétique, alors que la conscience des syllabes peut être facilitée par l'expérience d'un syllabaire, sans en dépendre aussi fortement. Pour éclaircir davantage le rôle de la connaissance d'un alphabet sur la conscience des phonèmes chez les enfants, nous avons fait effectuer des tâches de comptage et d'effacement (expériences II et IV) à des enfants japonais en fin d'école primaire. Les résultats montrent que beaucoup d'enfants japonais prennent conscience des phonèmes vers dix ans d'âge, qu'ils aient ou non appris une transcription alphabétique. La discussion de ces résultats porte sur certains autres facteurs qui peuvent produire la conscience phonologique.

5

Word recognition in early reading: A review of the direct and indirect access hypotheses*

RODERICK W. BARRON

University of Guelph

Abstract

Research on the development of word recognition, like that on fluent word recognition, has been strongly influenced by the dual-route model. One route is non-lexical and indirect because access to lexical meaning is mediated by pre-lexical phonological representations assembled through the application of grapheme-to-phoneme correspondence (GPC) rules. The other route, which is independent of the first, is regarded as lexical and direct because orthographic representations of whole words are used to retrieve lexical meanings or post-lexical phonological representations. Evidence is reviewed for two opposing developmental hypotheses based on the dual-route model: fluent readers use both direct and indirect access to lexical meaning, while beginning readers use (1) only indirect access or (2) only direct access. It was concluded that neither mode of access predominates in early reading. A review of other evidence suggests two reasons why the dual-route model fails to provide a satisfactory account of the development of early word recognition. First, it does not offer an adequate characterization of the orthographic units represented in early lexicons. Second, the independence of the two routes prevents lexical information from being acquired through the application of GPC rules. Finally, alternatives to the dual-route model are discussed. One of the most promising is a single process lexical model in which it is proposed that acquisition and performance in word recognition can be accounted for by interactions among orthographic and phonological units of various sizes in the lexicon.

The relationship between speech and reading has enjoyed a prominent place in research on reading since the turn of the century. Huey devoted several

*The writing of this paper was supported, in part, by a grant from the Natural Sciences and Engineering Research Council of Canada (A9782). The author gratefully acknowledges comments by Derek Besner, Len Haines, Maureen Lovett, John Mitterer and Keith Stanovich on earlier versions of this paper. Correspondence and requests for reprints should be addressed to Roderick W. Barron, Department of Psychology, University of Guelph, Guelph, Ontario, N1G 2W1, Canada.

chapters to this issue in his classic 1908 book and Crowder (1982) recently suggested that it may be the biggest theoretical issue in the psychology of reading. A major question is how fluent readers obtain access to the meanings of printed words. One possibility is direct access in which the letter identities corresponding to a printed word are used to access the orthographic representation for that word in the mental lexicon. This whole word orthographic representation is then used to access the word's semantic representation. The phonological representation for the word can be accessed through its orthographic or its semantic representation (e.g., it is necessary to determine the meaning of homographs like *lead* before a pronunciation can be generated). This phonological representation is regarded as being post-lexical because it is activated along with other lexical information after the lexical orthographic representation has been activated. In the direct access procedure, post-lexical phonological representations are not necessary for obtaining access to lexical meaning. A second possibility is indirect access in which the string of letter identities corresponding to a word or nonword is first segmented into graphemes which are letters or letter clusters (e.g., *oa, th, gh*) corresponding to phonemes. A phonological representation is then assembled by applying context sensitive grapheme-to-phoneme correspondence (GPC) rules, such as those described by Venezky (1970) and Wijk (1966). Finally, a semantic representation in the lexicon is accessed through this assembled phonological representation. GPC assembled phonological representations are referred to as pre-lexical because their construction does not involve the use of lexical information (i.e., specific known words). In the indirect access procedure, pre-lexical phonological representations are necessary for obtaining access to the lexicon and to lexical meaning. A third possibility involves both direct and indirect access. Although they may operate simultaneously, these two procedures for accessing lexical meaning are independent.

There are several reasons why the third possibility tends to be favored by a number of investigators. First, the ability to use both direct and indirect access procedures may be particularly useful for reading English because historical and linguistic factors have conspired to make it difficult to rely exclusively on indirect access, and the visual complexity and number of words in written English makes it difficult to rely exclusively on direct access (e.g., Barron, 1985; Henderson, 1982). Second, the phonological knowledge and processes employed by the direct and indirect access procedures are equivalent to those used by the lexical and non-lexical routes, respectively, of the dual-route model of word recognition (e.g. Coltheart, 1978, 1980, 1981; Meyer, Schvaneveldt, & Ruddy, 1974; Morton & Patterson, 1980), at least in the strong version of that model (Humphreys & Evett, 1985). The lexical route is equivalent to direct access because both use a whole word orthographic representation in the lexicon to retrieve the post-lexical phonological representation of a word. The non-lexical route is equivalent to indirect access because in both cases GPC rules function without any lexical involvement in assembling a pre-lexical phonological representation. Like the direct and indirect access procedures, the lexical and non-lexical routes are regarded as being strictly independent. Third, conditions have been identified whereby one access procedure is more likely to be used than another (e.g., Barron, 1978; McCusker, Hillinger, & Bias, 1981; Seidenberg, 1985a). For example, pre-lexical, phonologically mediated access to meaning is regarded as being optional and more likely to be employed when direct access is slow, as can occur with low frequency words (Seidenberg, 1985b, Seidenberg, Waters, Barnes, & Tanenhaus, 1984).

The ability to use both direct and indirect access procedures is often associated with fluent reading skill whereas reliance on only one procedure tends to be associated with a level of reading skill that is lower on the developmental continuum (e.g., see reviews by Barron, 1981a; Jorm & Share, 1983). As a result, one major developmental issue is whether reading skill begins with direct access or with indirect access. This issue is particularly controversial because different instructional methods, such as phonics and look-say (whole word), involve different assumptions about how lexical meaning is accessed (e.g., Mathews, 1966). Phonics instruction is often justified on the grounds that it provides beginning readers with a set of general procedures (GPC rules) for making contact with previously acquired linguistic representations (phonological) that are associated with word meanings. On the other hand, look-say instruction is often portrayed as being more consistent with the primary purpose of reading—extraction of meaning from print—because subjects learn to associate letter strings with word meanings rather than learn rules for producing word pronunciations.

Two basic hypotheses have been proposed about how access to word meaning develops during the course of learning to read. According to the first, word meaning access in beginning reading is indirect because it is always mediated by a pre-lexical phonological representation that is assembled by GPC rules. As fluency is acquired, however, direct access gradually, though not completely, replaces indirect access. According to the second hypothesis, word meaning access in beginning reading is direct because the semantic representation of a word is always accessed through its whole word orthographic representation in the lexicon. Indirect access through GPC rules is regarded as being a product of formal instruction in reading and, as fluency is acquired, it begins to function as an additional procedure for accessing meaning. It is important to note that these two hypotheses are quite similar. Both propose that beginning readers have only one procedure for accessing word meaning (indirect or direct) and that they acquire a second, independent procedure during the course of developing reading skill. The hypotheses differ only in the order in which the procedures appear during development.

The purpose of this paper is to review some of the main evidence for these two developmental hypotheses. This will be followed by a reevaluation of the hypotheses with regard to several considerations including recent theoretical challenges to dual-route models of fluent adult reading and some problems that such models have in accounting for the development of an orthographic lexicon. Finally, some alternatives to dual-route models will be discussed along with their implications for the development of early reading skill.

Indirect-to-direct meaning access

The first hypothesis, indirect-to-direct meaning access, is the most prominent and widely accepted of the two hypotheses. It is attractive because reading is a language skill and children should be able to capitalize upon their knowledge of oral language in learning to read (e.g., Gleitman & Rozin, 1975; Liberman, 1982). Specifically, they should be able to use the phonological representation of the words they have acquired through experience with oral language to access the meanings of those words in their printed form. GPC rules might be used to translate printed words into phonological representations and phonics instruction might be used to teach those rules. The observation that beginning readers are often more heavily dependent upon subvocalization when reading silently than older, more fluent readers is frequently cited as evidence that beginning readers are more likely than fluent readers to translate print into sound in order to access meaning (e.g., Gibson & Levin, 1975).

There are also several experiments which have been interpreted as being consistent with a developmental shift from indirect to direct word meaning access. One of the most influential was reported by Doctor and Coltheart (1980). They showed that beginning readers (6 years of age) made more erroneous *yes* responses in evaluating the meaningfulness of sentences such as "We walk in the would," which sound but do not look meaningful, than on sentences which neither sound nor look meaningful, such as "We walk in the won." They also made more *yes* errors on sentences containing nonwords, which sound but are not spelled like English words (We walk in the woud), than on sentences containing nonwords which neither sound nor are spelled like English words (We walk in the wun). Consistent with the indirect-to-direct hypothesis, the difference in the frequency of errors between the *would* and *won* and between the *woud* and *wun* sentences decreased with an increase in the age of the children.

Doctor and Coltheart (1980) were able to eliminate graphic similarity as the basis of the beginning readers' errors by showing that the erroneous *yes* responses to the homophones (*would*) and pseudohomophones (*woud*) did not arise because these items looked more similar to the "correct" item (*wood*) than did the control items (*won* and *wun*). They were not, however, able to eliminate the possibility that the phonological representations for the homophones were derived post-lexically rather than pre-lexically as required by the indirect component of the indirect-to-direct hypothesis. This criticism does not apply to their nonword data because phonological representations for pseudohomophones cannot be retrieved directly since they do not have whole word orthographic entries in the internal lexicon; instead, they must be assembled pre-lexically by applying GPC rules. Unfortunately, Doctor and Coltheart (1980) failed to offer any direct evidence that the procedures their subjects used for reading nonwords were the same as those for reading words. As a result, their evidence for the indirect-to-direct hypothesis is limited as it is confined to items (nonwords) that do not have lexical meanings.

Although the task of reading single words aloud does not necessarily involve access to lexical meaning, subjects' performance in this task can provide information about developmental changes in the phonological representations involved in obtaining access to lexical semantics. Backman, Bruck, Hebert and Seidenberg (1984) found that older (9- and 17-year-old) readers read aloud exception words, which violate GPC rules (e.g., *have*), as accurately as regular words, which are consistent with those rules (e.g., *made*). Younger (7- and 8-year-old) readers, however, made more errors on exception than regular words and their errors on the exception words tended to be "regularized" pronunciations (e.g., mispronouncing the exception word *come* so that it sounds like *comb*). They also tended to regularize the pronunciation of nonwords that were generated from exception words (pronouncing *naid* so that it rhymes with *raid* rather than *said*). These results suggest that younger children may initially use GPC rules to assemble pre-lexically the phonological representations of both words and nonwords. Later, they shift to using the orthographic representations of words in the lexicon to retrieve post-lexically phonological representations. The younger children did not, however, rely exclusively on pre-lexical phonology as prescribed by the indirect component of the indirect-to-direct hypothesis. They were able to pronounce correctly over 75% of the exception words and about one-third of the errors on inconsistent regular words like *wave*, which share orthographic neighborhoods with exception words (i.e., *have*), involved an exception pronunciation of the overlapping spelling pattern (i.e., *-ave*). Similarly, Marcel (1980) has pointed out that many of the errors children make in misreading are not just incorrect applications of GPC rules; instead, these errors appear to originate from the orthographic overlap between the target word and specific words in their lexicons (e.g., pronouncing *gaol* as *goal*).

Finally, Reitsma (1984) has also obtained evidence for the indirect-to-direct access hypothesis. Dutch speaking children (ages 7 to 12) were presented with a proposition auditorially, such as "This is an animal." The proposition was followed by a speech sound which corresponded to the beginning or end of a subsequently presented target word that was displayed visually. If, for example, the target word was "bunny," then it would be preceded by the sound /bu/ or /ni/ and the subjects would be required to decide whether or not the proposition was confirmed by the target word. Reitsma (1984) found that prior presentation of either a similar beginning or end sound decreased the youngest subjects' response times to the target word compared to a dissimilar sound (e.g., /ga/) or a humming sound control condition. In addition, the size of this sound priming effect decreased with an increase in the age of the readers suggesting that older readers became increasingly less reliant on a phonological code in word meaning access. One difficulty in interpreting Reitsma's (1984) results is that the /ga/ control condition was not slower than the humming control condition. This is unexpected because facilitation should arise from the match between the specific speech sounds produced by the application of GPC rules and those produced by the priming stimulus and interference should arise from a mismatch between specific speech sounds. Since humming is not speech, it should not produce specific interference or facilitation effects and subjects' performance in this control condition should fall between the similar and dissimilar speech sound conditions. The fact that humming did not provide an adequate baseline against which to evaluate the facilitating and interfering effects of the two types of speech sounds suggests an alternative interpretation of Reitsma's (1984) results. It is possible that priming by similar speech sounds does not facilitate printed word decoding; instead, it may produce results which do not differ from a condition in which sound priming stimuli are deleted altogether, a control that Reitsma (1984) did not employ.

Direct-to-indirect meaning access

Despite the plausibility of the indirect-to-direct access hypothesis, it is possible to make a case for the second hypothesis: direct-to-indirect word meaning access. First, children are frequently able to read some words before they have acquired any knowledge of GPC rules (Ehri & Wilce, 1985; Goswami, 1985; Mason, 1980, 1984; Masonheimer, 1982; Seymour & Elder, in press).

Second, GPC rules cannot be applied successfully to words which are exceptions (e.g., words like *of* and *have*) to those rules, yet readers learn to pronounce many of those words quite early in the course of learning to read (Backman et al., 1984; Baron, 1979). Third, look-say methods of instruction explicitly promote the learning of associations between printed words as unsegmented units and their corresponding pronunciations and meanings. Consequently, the meanings of words learned by this method may be initially accessed directly in the sense that a graphic feature of a word (e.g., shape) may be associated with its pronunciation. Finally, there are also several experiments which have been interpreted as being consistent with the direct-to-indirect access hypothesis.

Barron and Baron (1977) required children in grades one through eight (ages 6 to 13) to decide whether or not pairs of pictures and words were similar in meaning or in sound. Repeating the word *double* concurrently with performing the decisions interfered with the sound task, but not the meaning task across all of the grades suggesting that even the youngest readers were using direct access in the meaning task. It is possible, however, that concurrent articulation produced interference only in the rhyme task because judgments about rhyming involve a different speech-based representation than judgments about meaning. Besner, Davies and Daniels (1981), Besner and Davelaar (1982) and Perfetti and McCutchen (1982) have proposed that several speech-based representations may be involved in reading and Alegria, Pignot and Morais (1982) have suggested that the representation employed in rhyming may be articulatory. Barron and Baron's (1977) rhyme task requires subjects to segment a word into an initial consonant(s) plus a vowel-consonant group forming the rhyme. This explicit phonemic segmentation is not, however, required in the meaning task. The segmentation requirements associated with rhyming may contribute to the formation of an articulatory representation, possibly because such a representation makes it easier to remember and match the segments.

Bryant and Bradley (1982) investigated the effects of concurrent articulation on segmentation in an experiment that was very similar to Barron and Baron (1977). In one task, 6- and 7-year-olds were required to respond yes if a letter was in the word that named a corresponding picture (e.g., picture of a cat—C**) and no if the letter was not in the word (e.g., picture of a cat—**P). This picture-letter task requires explicit segmentation and Bryant and Bradley (1982) showed that concurrent articulation reduced children's accuracy. Concurrent articulation did not, however, reduce the same children's accuracy in a picture–word meaning task similar to that used by Barron and Baron (1977). Taken together, the evidence suggests that segmentation processes, articulatory representations and/or memory may be subject to interference from concurrent articulation in Barron and Baron's (1977) rhyming task and in Bryant and Bradley's (1982) picture-letter task. If this is the case, then it is possible that either an orthographic representation or a speech-based representation that is not influenced by concurrent articulation was employed in Barron and Baron's (1977) and Bryant and Bradley's (1982) meaning task. The speech-based representation might be post-lexical or even pre-lexical on the grounds that the segmentation processes involved in applying GPCs to single words involves different units, representations and/or demands on memory than are involved in explicit segmentation tasks. Unfortunately, these alternatives cannot be distinguished in their experiments.

The second experiment consistent with the direct-to-indirect access hypothesis was reported by Condry, McMahon-Rideout and Levy (1979). Subjects in grades two, five and university were presented with a target word and two choice words. They were required to decide which one of the choice words was graphemically (looks task) or phonemically (rhymes task) or semantically (means task) similar to the target word. Within a task, the distractor words were either dissimilar to the target word (control condition) or they were similar to the target on each of the dimensions that was not relevant for performance in that particular task. In the means task, for example, when the target word was *boat* and the correct choice was *ship*, the distractor could be *wrote* (phonemically similar) or *boot* (graphemically similar) or *dish* (not similar on any dimension—control). Of greatest relevance to the direct-to-indirect access hypothesis, Condry et al. (1979) found that the means task decisions of the grade two children were slowed (compared to the control) by the graphemic but not the phonemic distractors, while the two older groups of subjects were slowed by both types of distractors. These results are consistent with the direct-to-indirect access hypothesis because they suggest that the younger readers were less able than the older readers to access a phonological code quickly enough for it to influence semantic decisions in the means task. It is difficult, however, to tell from the Condry et al. (1979) experiment whether the phonological code used by the older subjects was pre-lexical or post-lexical. If it was post-lexical, then it cannot be argued that it is actually necessary to assemble a phonological representation in order for word meaning access to take place.

Towards new hypotheses of the development of word meaning access

This survey of the experimental evidence does not indicate overwhelming support for either the indirect-to-direct or the direct-to-indirect access hypotheses. Barron and Baron's (1977) evidence for direct access in beginning readers is limited because the results only indicate that the representation used to access semantic information in their meaning task is not influenced by concurrent articulation. What remains unclear is whether or not that representation is actually orthographic. Age related changes in the magnitude of phonological priming in Reitsma's (1984) experiment are difficult to evaluate without additional information on baseline performance. Most importantly, some of the evidence indicates that both direct and indirect access are involved in beginning as well as in fluent reading. For example, beginning readers appear to use direct access with homophones (Doctor & Coltheart, 1980) and correctly pronounced exception words (Backman et al., 1984), but they appear to use indirect access with pseudohomophones (Doctor & Coltheart, 1980), exception words given regularized pronunciations and nonwords (Backman et al., 1984). As a result, one possible conclusion from the available evidence is that the procedures of word meaning access (i.e., direct and indirect) and the types of phonological representations they employ (post-lexical and pre-lexical, respectively) do not change with development. The problem with accepting this conclusion is that there do seem to be real developmental changes in how meaning is accessed because some experiments show a shift from using primarily, though not exclusively, one of the procedures to using both procedures (e.g., indirect-to-direct access—Backman et al., 1984; Doctor & Coltheart, 1980; direct-to-indirect access—Condry et al., 1979).

Jorm and Share (1983) have suggested a possible solution to this problem by proposing that both beginning and fluent readers use both direct and indirect access, but that the probabilities attached to the use of the two procedures may be unequal and change across age. Unfortunately, their hypothesis may be as limited as the two hypotheses it proposes to replace because, like the indirect-to-direct and the direct-to-indirect hypotheses, Jorm and Share's (1983) hypothesis also assumes the basic theoretical tenets of the dual-route model of word recognition. The dual-route model was developed to account for the performance of fluent readers. Although it continues to be influential, the model has been recently criticized on several grounds, particularly the strong or "standard" version (e.g., Glushko, 1979; Henderson, 1982, 1985; Humphreys & Evett, 1985; Marcel, 1980; Seidenberg, 1985a, b). Accordingly, the merits of those criticisms and their implications for development will be evaluated before considering further Jorm and Share's (1983) revised hypothesis of the development of word meaning access.

The major limitation of the standard version of the dual-route model is that assembled phonological representations can only be assembled by GPC rules and those rules explicitly deny any role for lexical knowledge in the assembly process. The only role for lexical knowledge in the dual-route model is in the process of retrieving whole word phonological and semantic representations. There is, however, substantial evidence for the use of lexical knowledge in assembling phonological representations. Syntactic (Campbell & Besner, 1981), semantic (Rosson, 1983) and lexical (Kay & Marcel, 1981) context can influence nonword pronunciation through priming. Glushko (1979) has shown that the pronunciation of inconsistent regular words (e.g., *pave*) is influenced by their exception word orthographic neighbors (e.g., *have*), at least when the words are low frequency (Seidenberg et al., 1984). Using nonwords, Glushko (1979) and Kay and Lesser (1985) found that although subjects often regularized the pronunciation of nonwords, they occasionally assigned exception pronunciations when the nonwords were derived from exception words (e.g., pronouncing *gead* so that it rhymes with *head* rather than *bead*). Finally, Henderson (1982) has shown that many of the GPC rules proposed by Venezky (1970) and Wijk (1966) are actually lexical because knowledge of specific words can influence how they are applied (e.g., lexical knowledge is involved in the decision to segment the *ph* in *shepherd* and not to segment it in *morpheme*).

This and other evidence has prompted a reconsideration of the standard version of the dual-route model. One alternative model involves retaining the distinction between lexical and non-lexical routes, but expanding the scope of the non-lexical route so that the assembly of a phonological representation is not limited to orthographic units that map onto phonemes. Patterson and Morton (1985), for example, have recently proposed a dual-route model in which one route employs an orthography-to-phonology correspondence (OPC) system that uses large orthographic units called bodies (vowel plus terminal consonant segments of single syllable words; e.g. *-ave, -ook*) as well as small orthographic units (i.e., graphemes). They regard the OPC system as being non-lexical because it employs rules to assemble a phonological representation out of sub-word units, regardless of their size. The lexical route deals with whole word orthographic representations. The lexical and non-lexical routes interact during the process of transforming the phonological representations generated by the two routes into a single representation that can serve as the basis of a response. Any interference between the lexical and non-lexical representations is handled by a lexical check system. Patterson and Morton's (1985) modified dual-route model, and other models which postulate separate lexical and non-lexical routes while allowing crosstalk between them (e.g., Carr & Pollatsek, 1985), do a better job of characterizing the complexity of the word recognition process and can account for much more of the evidence than the standard version. A modified dual-route model may be limited, however, by an absence of constraints on the number of processes, knowledge sources and pathways that can be postulated (e.g.,

Henderson, 1982; Humphreys & Evett, 1985; Seidenberg, 1985a, b). Also, the fact that there are lexical influences on non-lexical processing at various levels tends to weaken the modified model by violating the critical assumption of independent routes (e.g., Henderson, 1982, 1985).

Another alternative to the standard dual-route model involves doing away with independent lexical and non-lexical routes altogether and replacing them with a single, lexically based process for assembling phonology. According to such a lexical model, the basic evidence for the use of phonological representations in word recognition can be accounted for by the activation of orthographic segments in the lexicon ranging from single letters and other, larger subword units (e.g., Shallice, Warrington & McCarthy, 1983) to morphemes or whole words (e.g., Henderson, 1982; Marcel, 1980). These lexical units would activate similar orthographic segments (orthographic neighbors) and their corresponding phonological representations. Instead of rules, the assembly of a phonological representation might be based upon the relative strengths of the activated units and their compatibility with units that were larger and smaller. Presumably, the distinction between pre-lexical and post-lexical phonological representations would be unnecessary because all phonological representations would be lexical, regardless of whether they were based on whole words, morphemes or assembled from large or small subword units.

Within the framework of a lexical model, the question of whether or not word meaning access is mediated by a phonological representation might depend on when such a representation was activated in the lexicon relative to a semantic representation (Barron, 1981b; Perfetti, 1985; Seidenberg, 1985a, b). The time course of these activations would depend on a number of factors including the readers' task, decision criteria, familiarity with the materials and level of skill (Waters, Seidenberg & Bruck, 1984; Waters & Seidenberg, 1985). Accordingly, one interpretation of the evidence for "direct access" to lexical meaning might be that the orthographic representation of a word activates its semantic representation before its phonological representation can be activated and influence semantic access. The opposite order of events might be consistent with the evidence for "indirect access" to lexical meaning—a word's orthographic representation activates its phonological representation before its semantic representation, thus allowing the phonological representation time to influence semantic access. Although a lexical model is appealing, it has not been worked out in detail except with regard to some basic graphemic and orthographic processes in word recognition (e.g., McClelland & Rumelhart, 1981; Paap, Newsome, McDonald, & Schvaneveldt, 1982). Complex questions remain to be answered about how various levels of lexical units are activated, selected and combined in assembling a phonological representation as well as about the extent to which such a model can actually be distinguished from a modified dual-route model (see Shallice & McCarthy, 1985, for an initial attempt to deal with these questions).

If these criticisms of the standard dual-route model can be extended to the developmental case, then the model and the hypotheses derived from it, including Jorm and Share's (1983) modified hypothesis, may have limited value in accounting for the development of word meaning access and the development of word recognition in general. When considered from a developmental perspective, the standard dual-route model appears to have two major problems. First, the model provides beginning readers with only two options for recognizing words: (1) they can learn and apply associations between orthographic representations and phonological (also semantic) representations at the whole word level or (2) they can learn GPC rules and apply them to decode words which are consistent with those rules. Although these two procedures appear to cover all of the words that children might encounter (e.g., regular, exception, nonword), the model does not really offer an adequate characterization of the knowledge or the processes that children employ in attempting to read words during the transition period between being a nonreader and being a reader. The evidence reviewed below will suggest that the orthographic units children use in early reading, particularly before they are given much formal instruction, may be different from those identified with either route of the dual-route model. Second, the fact that the lexical and non-lexical processes function independently in the dual-route model makes it difficult to see how beginning readers could make much progress in acquiring an orthographic lexicon because changes in the efficiency of the non-lexical route are only associated with the acquisition and execution of GPC rules; this route can not acquire and use any lexical knowledge (Henderson, 1982, 1985). Consequently, any progress would be associated with the lexical route, which operates only on whole word orthographic units. Evidence reviewed below will suggest that lexical knowledge may also be acquired during the course of learning and using GPC rules.

Units of orthographic knowledge in the developing lexicon

Whole word units

Ehri and Wilce (1985) and Mason (1980, 1984) have proposed that the onset of reading, at least in an alphabetic orthography, is signalled by attempts to use letter-sound (or letter-name) associations in recognizing words. For example, children may preserve the initial and/or final letter-sound in an otherwise incorrectly read word or exhibit evidence of noticing that some letters in words, particularly boundary consonants, tend to correspond to letter-sounds that they know. The ability to decode words accurately is argued to be a later acquisition because it requires relatively complete letter-sound knowledge (vowels as well as consonants), plus the ability to sound out particular letter-sound and letter cluster-sound combinations according to a set of context sensitive spelling-to-sound rules (e.g., GPC rules). They also propose that the ability to associate a pronunciation with the features of a whole word as a graphic configuration (e.g., a visually distinctive letter or letter cluster, word shape, type font or graphic context) does not constitute evidence of the onset of reading. Masonheimer (1982; see also Masonheimer, Drum & Ehri, 1984) reported evidence which pertains to the second proposal. Two groups of preschoolers (3 to 5 years of age) were identified, both of whom could read aloud at least eight out of ten printed environmental words (e.g., McDonald's, Star Wars, K-Mart, Stop, Pepsi) when those words occurred in their familiar and distinctive graphic contexts. One group was designated as prereaders because they could read less than 2% of words taken from a list of simple, preprimer words (e.g., *go, run, in, big*). The other group, which was quite small (eight children), was designated as readers because they could read well over 90% of the preprimer words, plus some of the words on the Slosson Oral Reading Test. The prereaders' accuracy declined when they were required to read the environmental words minus some of the supporting graphic context, and it plunged close to zero when they were required to read the words in standard, manuscript type. The readers, on the other hand, maintained a uniformly high level of performance (90%+) with and without the supporting graphic context. In addition, the readers noticed first and last letter changes in the environmental words (e.g., XEPSI or PEPSO for PEPSI) whereas the prereaders did not, even after some coaching. Instead, the prereaders appeared to label the graphic context rather than actually read the print.

Masonheimer's (1982) study suggests that learning associations between pronunciations and the graphic contextual features of environmental print is not very important for making the transition from prereading to reading. The possibility that letter-name and letter-sound knowledge may be more important in this transition was investigated by Ehri and Wilce (1985). They identified three groups of children (5 years of age) on the basis of their ability to read a list of 40 preprimer and primer words (e.g., *up, go, we, book, see, school, blue*): prereaders (2% correct), novices (11% correct) and veterans (44% correct). Although all three groups knew at least 75% of the letter-names, the prereaders knew considerably fewer of the letter-sounds (26%) than the novices and veterans (77% and 83%, respectively). A paired-associate learning task was administered in which the sounds associated with each of the letters in a nonword response term roughly corresponded to the sounds making up the name of the picture used for the stimulus term. The sequence of letter-sounds making up the responses JRF and SZRS, for example, sound somewhat similar to the sequence of component sounds making up the names of the stimulus pictures giraffe and scissors, respectively. The prereaders, who were limited in their letter-sound knowledge, were less accurate on this task than on another paired-associate task in which the spellings making up the response terms were characterized by their graphic rather than their phonetic distinctiveness (e.g., picture of a pair of scissors–qDjK). The novices and veterans, on the other hand, were more accurate on the letter-sound task than on the graphic distinctiveness task. These two groups had better (and equivalent) recall of the phonetic spellings than the prereaders, while recall of the graphic spellings was uniformly low across the three groups. Furthermore, the boundary letters of phonetic spellings were much more likely to be recalled than the boundary letters of graphic spellings even when degree of learning was equated between the two types of spellings.

Ehri and Wilce's (1985) results suggest that some children (i.e., novices) know letter-sound associations and can use that knowledge to learn and remember nonwords made up of letters that represent those associations even when they otherwise have very meager reading skills. Children who do not possess letter-sound knowledge (i.e., prereaders), but who are at approximately the same beginning level of word reading skill, seem to use distinctive graphic information in the printed configuration of the word to acquire print-pronunciation associations. These associations appear similar to the graphic context-pronunciation associations learned by the prereaders in Masonheimer's (1982) study (see also Mason, 1980). Although children do not appear to have much difficulty learning associations between a pronunciation and features of the printed word as a graphic configuration, and may even acquire them quite naturally (e.g., Gough & Hillinger, 1980), this ability does not appear to be a precursor to reading.

The lexical route of the dual-route model can be regarded as a mechanism for beginning readers to build their orthographic lexicons by learning associations between whole words and their whole word phonological representations. This mechanism is designed to acquire word-specific knowledge and it has the potential of being quite useful in learning exception words (e.g., broad) and words with unusual orthographic patterns (e.g., yacht). It has limited value, however, in accounting for the performance of beginning readers because of their tendency to treat the word as a graphic configuration and associate whole word pronunciations with features of that configuration (e.g., Ehri & Wilce, 1985; Masonheimer, 1982) rather than with the sequence of letters making up the word. Furthermore, children may be at a disadvantage in learning the essentials of the alphabetic code when formal reading instruction is specifically designed to employ the whole word mechanism (e.g., as in look-say or whole word instruction). Information about the alphabetic code is more likely to be acquired when instruction requires words to be segmented into letter-sound or letter cluster-sound units than when instruction encourages words to be treated as unsegmented wholes. Alegria, Pignot and Morais (1982), for example, found that children (6 years old) given look-say instruction were less able to reverse two phonemes in an utterance (e.g., to say *os* for *so*) than children given phonics instruction. The two groups of children produced an equivalent level of performance on a word and a syllable reversal task. These results indicate that look-say instruction is not as effective as phonics instruction in heightening children's ability to analyze spoken language at the phonemic level, an ability which appears to be important in learning to read (e.g., Bradley & Bryant, 1983, 1985; Treiman & Baron, 1983). Barr (1974–75) found that children given look-say instruction were less likely to make errors which were nonwords and which preserved the sound and/or spelling of a mispronounced word than children given phonics instruction. Instead, look-say instructed children made many errors that were words and these erroneous responses tended to come from the sample of taught words (see also similar results by Seymour & Elder, 1986). Barr (1974–75) suggests that phonics-instructed children tend to segment words and treat the letter as the unit of print while look-say instructed children do not segment words and tend to treat the whole word as the unit of print. Finally, Chall (1967), Williams (1979) and others (e.g., Evans & Carr, 1985) have shown that children are more successful in learning the basic skills of reading with an instructional method based upon phonics than upon look-say.

Taken together, these results suggest that the lexical route of the dual-route model may not provide a very adequate characterization of the knowledge represented in early orthographic lexicons or how that knowledge is acquired. One qualification to this general conclusion, however, is that whole word learning may make a contribution to the orthographic lexicon later in development when children learn enough about letter-sound and letter cluster-sound relations that they are less susceptible to treating whole words as graphic configurations. Also, look-say may be as successful as phonics instruction with some types of words (e.g., exception) and with some groups of readers (e.g., disabled), in part, because look-say instruction often involves extensive practice on individual words. In phonics instruction, individual words tend to be treated as illustrations of general rules, thus they are not practiced as extensively (Lovett, Ransby & Barron, 1984).

Letter-sound/name units

Ehri (e.g., 1978, 1980, 1984, 1985; see also Ehri & Wilce, 1985) has a model of reading development which specifically identifies a role for letter-sound knowledge in the acquisition of early reading skill. Ehri proposes that letters function as symbols for their corresponding sounds in memory. Before any progress can be made on reading, it is necessary for children to make a start on learning the alphabetic principle by acquiring some letter-sound associations. Once a preliminary set of associations has been learned (e.g., consonant letter-sounds), it is hypothesized that children can use this knowledge to determine how words are pronounced, at least partially, by recognizing the correspondence between what they hear when a word is pronounced (e.g., initial and/or final consonant sounds) and the letter-sound associations that they know. This recognition process has the potential of providing children with a mechanism for beginning an orthographic lexicon, and for making the transition from prereader to reader, because it gives them procedures for segmenting printed words into units (e.g., the initial letter-sound or final letter-sound can be distinguished from the remaining letters and sounds in the word) and for representing those units as part of the lexical entry for a word. Importantly, the mechanism can function without GPC rules or forming associations at the whole word level. The experiment by Ehri and Wilce (1985) on learning phonetic versus visual spellings provides some evidence for this letter-sound recognition process because it showed that manipulations in the opportunity for employing letter-sound knowledge can influence subjects' memory for letter sequences in paired-associate learning. Similarly, sound-letter associations offer children a mechanism for initiating the process of spelling as they can apply this knowledge to generate letters that are associated with the sounds they hear in spoken words. The evidence for preschoolers' invented spellings reported by Read (1971) and Chomsky (1977) is consistent with this possibility (e.g. spelling *prd* for pretty, *wtr* for water, *bk* for back).

   Central to Ehri's model is the notion that letter-sound knowledge causes children to move from being prereaders to being readers, yet Ehri and Wilce's (1985) experiment does not provide evidence for causation. Their prereaders, for example, were relatively deficient in letter-sound knowledge yet they knew a substantial number of letter-names, and many of those contained letter-sounds (approximately 75% of the consonants contain their essential sound either at the beginning or end of their letter name). It is unclear why this knowledge was not used in learning phonetic spellings. Deliberately instructing children in letter-names and/or in letter-sounds may offer a more direct way of answering the question of causation than Ehri and Wilce's

(1985) multiple group design. Although knowledge of letter-names is highly correlated with initial success in learning to read (e.g., Chall, 1967), experimental attempts to facilitate reading acquisition by providing specific instruction in letter-names has not been very successful (e.g., Jenkins, Bausell, & Jenkins, 1972; Ohnmacht, 1969; Samuels, 1972; Silberberg, Silberberg, & Iversen, 1972). Ehri (1983), however, has pointed out that these experimental studies may be inconclusive because of factors like incomplete training, use of artificial letters and inadequate opportunity to demonstrate transfer.

Training letter-sounds has produced some success in facilitating learning to read when it was combined with training in letter-names (Ohnmacht, 1969) or involved children who already knew some letter-names (Jenkins et al., 1972). Bradley and Bryant (1983, 1985) included letter-sound training in an experiment on phonemic analysis in which they trained 6-year-olds, who knew their letter-names, to categorize spoken words on the basis of common beginning (e.g., *hen, hat*), middle (e.g., *hen, pet*) or end (e.g., *hen, man*) sounds. This sound categorization training facilitated learning to read and spell, relative to a control condition requiring conceptual categorization, only when it was augmented by training in how the sounds were represented by letters of the alphabet. Hohn and Ehri (1983) identified three groups of children who were equivalent in letter-name knowledge and gave two of the groups training in phonemic segmentation: one with letter tokens, allowing letter-sound associations to be formed, and one with tokens that were not letters and did not have any features which distinguished them. Posttest performance indicated that the two trained groups learned to segment novel consonant-vowel items better than the control condition and that the letter token group was better than the other training group as well as the control in segmenting items on which they had practiced. It is not clear, however, whether the letter group's superior performance on the practiced items was due to training on the letters per se, possibly allowing them to use their letter-name knowledge, or due to the advantage of being able to form associations between distinctive visual patterns and sounds. The groups did not differ on posttest measures of decoding skill indicating that neither type of training influenced word reading.

In summary, while there is some suggestion from the current evidence that letter-sound, and possibly letter-name, knowledge may play some role in analyzing the component sounds of spoken words and in learning to read, there is no evidence that these factors play a causal role. It might be possible to address the question of causation more directly by using the combined training and longitudinal design advocated by Bradley and Bryant (1983, 1985) and Bryant and Bradley (1985). Ideally, such a study would involve training and longitudinal assessment of phonemic analysis as well as letter-name/sound knowledge in order to determine if such knowledge facilitates reading and spelling directly (e.g., Ehri & Wilce, 1985) or indirectly, by facilitating phonemic analysis (e.g., Bradley & Bryant, 1983; Hohn & Ehri, 1983). Another possibility is that only phonemic analysis training facilitates reading and spelling (e.g., Treiman & Baron, 1983) and that knowledge of letters as symbols for sounds does not have a direct or indirect causal effect on the acquisition of literacy.

Letter cluster-sound units in analogy

Unfortunately, letter-sound knowledge may not allow beginning readers to form complete orthographic representations of printed words in their lexicons. Children need to acquire considerably more information about printed words including morphemic units, the multi-letter units corresponding to phonemes that are associated with the application of GPC rules (e.g., *th, tch, ng*), frequent (e.g., *-ade, -ill*) and infrequent letter clusters (e.g., *acht* in *yacht*), and letter clusters containing letter-sounds that are exceptions in some orthographic neighborhoods (e.g., *-ave* in *have*). Analogies provide one possible mechanism for acquiring some of this knowledge. Recently, Goswami (1985) showed that beginning readers can learn new words by capitalizing on the sound and spelling similarity between known and unknown words (e.g., the -ood in *good* could be used to read *wood*). Contrary to claims that reading by analogy is a relatively late arriving skill (Marsh & Desberg, 1983) and that it requires instruction (Baron, 1977, 1979), Goswami (1985) showed that children (6 years old) who could not read (they did not score on the Schonell reading test) were able to use analogies in a priming task. Subjects were shown a priming word and heard it pronounced, then a target word was displayed which the children were required to read aloud (pretesting indicated that, prior to the experiment, the children could not read aloud either the prime or the target words when the words were presented individually). Subjects were more accurate when the target words (e.g., *peak*) shared a final spelling pattern with the priming words (e.g., *beak*) than in a control condition in which the target words only shared letters with the priming word (e.g., *bank*). More experienced readers showed priming effects based on common initial (e.g., *beak, bean*) as well as final spelling patterns. The fact that the youngest children were better on the common final than the common initial items is consistent with Treiman's (1985) recent finding that it is easier for children to segment both spoken and written syllables into an initial consonant or consonant cluster (onset) and a vowel plus any following consonants (rime) than other possible segmentations (e.g., those suggested by GPC rules).

Grapheme-to-phoneme (GPC) rules and the developing lexicon

The evidence presented above suggests that children begin to make the transition from nonreaders to readers by acquiring rudimentary letter-sound/name knowledge and knowledge obtained from applying analogies. These two sources of knowledge result in printed words being segmented into two basic types of orthographic units: (1) letter-sound units (most likely consonants) which are constrained by position (initial, final) and (2) letter cluster-sound units corresponding to the terminal portion of a syllable, respectively. Although letter-sound units may correspond to some of the orthographic units segmented in the application of GPC rules, the letter cluster-sound units used in analogy do not have any such correspondence. Furthermore, children's tendency to treat the whole word as a graphic configuration, rather than a string of letters, reduces the contribution of whole word orthographic representations in the transition to being a reader. Considered together, the evidence suggests that neither the non-lexical route nor the lexical route of the standard dual-route model provide a very satisfactory characterization of the units that appear to be initially represented in the orthographic lexicons of beginning readers.

In addition, the non-lexical route faces another difficulty in accounting for the development of orthographic knowledge because GPC rules do not include mechanisms for acquiring and using lexical information (Henderson, 1982, 1985). They are merely devices for translating print into sound and any advance in the efficiency of word recognition can only be attributed to an increase in the number and sophistication of the rules and/or the speed with which they can be executed. It cannot be due to increasing lexical knowledge. Consequently, Backman et al.'s (1984) finding, described earlier, that older children can read exception words as accurately as regular words, is not easily explained by greater efficiency in the use of GPC rules because exception words cannot be read by GPC rules. In the context of the dual-route model, the only explanation for this result is that the lexical route completely replaced the non-lexical route during development, resulting in all words being retrieved as whole units rather than assembled by GPC rules. Unfortunately, this explanation of Backman et al.'s (1984) results places the major burden of reading acquisition upon the lexical route despite the evidence reviewed above indicating that successful acquisition of reading skill is not associated with informal or formal attempts to employ that route in learning to read.

Although inconsistent with the dual-route model, it is possible that the lexical and non-lexical routes do not function independently. If this is the case, then the Backman et al. (1984) results might be accounted for by a GPC-based system that can acquire and use lexical knowledge in assembling phonological representations. Evidence consistent with lexical influences on non-lexical processing comes from two experiments. First, Waters, Seidenberg and Bruck (1984) showed that children (grade three) read aloud high frequency regular words more accurately than low frequency regular words even though many of the same GPC rules apply to both categories of words. These results suggest that the children acquired word-specific, orthographic knowledge as a function of the number of times they applied GPC rules to particular words. It is unlikely that this frequency effect can be attributed entirely to the lexical route because they made fewer errors on regular than exception words (with both low and high frequency words). The Waters et al. (1984) findings suggest that the children used GPC rules and that the lexical mechanism had not replaced the non-lexical mechanism.

Second, Reitsma (1983) investigated the acquisition of word specific knowledge in a training study involving Dutch orthography. He found that beginning readers (7 years old) learned to read more rapidly nonwords (e.g., *sneik*), on which they were given specific training, than control nonwords which were spelled differently but had exactly the same pronunciation (e.g., *snijk*). Although Reitsma (1983) did not explicitly require the children to learn and apply GPC rules, he showed that they did not simply learn an association between the pronunciation and the word as a graphic configuration. He found that the size of the effect was the same regardless of the type of graphemic difference between the nonword given specific training and the identically pronounced control nonword. Reitsma's (1983) results provide additional evidence for the possibility that word-specific, orthographic information can be learned by repeatedly applying GPC rules. In summary, the results of both experiments show that the non-lexical route can be influenced by lexical knowledge. This evidence is inconsistent with the independent lexical and non-lexical routes postulated in the standard dual-route model.

Summary and conclusions

It has been proposed that two independent procedures are involved in obtaining access to the meanings of printed words by fluent readers. One is non-lexical and employs context sensitive GPC rules in assembling a pre-lexical phonological representation. Access to lexical meaning is indirect in this procedure because it is necessarily mediated by a pre-lexical phonological representation. The other procedure is lexical and is referred to as direct access because the orthographic representation of a whole word is used to access its lexical meaning or to retrieve its (post-lexical) phonological representation. The post-lexical phonological representation is not necessary for accessing lexical meaning. Two hypotheses have been proposed about the development of access to lexical meaning: (1) access is initially indirect, and (2) access is initially direct. A review of the basic evidence for these two hypotheses indicated that neither was strongly supported. Instead, the evidence suggested that both indirect and direct access may be used in early reading, with the relative contribution of each procedure changing during the course of development (Jorm & Share, 1983). This conclusion was questioned, however, on the grounds that the direct and indirect access procedures assume the basic theoretical tenets of the standard (i.e., strong) version of the dual-route model of word recognition.

The standard dual-route model has been criticized in the adult literature, particularly the assumption that lexical information is not involved in the assembly of a phonological representation. Evidence was presented indicating that such information is indeed involved. A single process lexical model as well as a modified dual-route model were discussed as alternatives to the standard dual-route model. The standard model was also criticized from a developmental perspective because it fails to provide an adequate characterization of the orthographic units that are initially represented in the lexicons of beginning readers. These units include letter-sound/name knowledge (primarily consonants in the initial or final positions of a word) and letter cluster-sound knowledge derived from rhyme analogies. Only the letter-sound units have any correspondence with the units that are segmented during the application of GPC rules in the non-lexical route. Whole word orthographic units, which are used by the lexical route, were not regarded as being very influential in the development of early lexicons. Young children have a tendency to treat whole words as graphic configurations rather than strings of letters and to associate whole word pronunciations with features of those configurations. Instructional procedures which encourage the use of the whole word route, such as look-say, tend to be ineffective in promoting orthographic segmentation, phonemic analysis skills and success in learning the basic skills of reading. It should also be noted that there is little evidence for development proceeding from small to large or from large to small orthographic units because small (letter-sound) as well as relatively large units (derived from analogy) appear to be represented in early orthographic lexicons.

Another criticism of the standard dual-route model from a developmental perspective is that the independence of the lexical and non-lexical routes prevents any lexical knowledge being acquired through the non-lexical route. As a result, the model cannot account for the fact that essentially the same GPC rules can be applied more efficiently to frequent than infrequent regular words. In order to avoid the conclusion that all words are acquired by the lexical route, it is necessary to assume that lexical information can influence the non-lexical, GPC rule based route. This modification violates the independence assumption and eliminates the primary reason for postulating two separate routes.

The theoretical and empirical considerations described above offer a basis for rejecting the standard dual-route model and its associated developmental hypotheses of direct and indirect access. It is not clear, however, what sort of model should replace the dual-route model. A lexical model is attractive from a developmental perspective because it encourages the view that learning to read words entails the acquisition of an orthographic lexicon with multiple levels of interacting units rather than a set of GPC rules and some isolated whole word representations. Furthermore, it does not ignore the alphabetic principle because, unlike the whole word lexical process associated with the dual-route model, it allows lexical orthographic units to range in size from letters to whole words (e.g., Henderson, 1982; Marcel, 1980; Shallice, Warrington, & McCarthy, 1983; Shallice & McCarthy, 1985). One disadvantage of a lexical model, however, is that it tends to discount any role for GPC rules. Although it may be possible to account for fluent adult reading without appealing to GPC rules (but see Rosson, 1985, for an objection to this possibility), it is more difficult to account for the development of reading skill without them. One reason for including GPC rules in a developmental model is that they are explicitly taught in phonics based instruction programs and such programs are quite successful. Furthermore, children are often heavily reliant upon GPC rules in the early stages of formal instruction (e.g., Backman et al., 1984; Doctor & Coltheart, 1980), possibly because they provide them with general procedures for pronouncing unknown as well as known words—the rules can function as mechanisms for self-instruction (Jorm & Share, 1983). Unfortunately, children are unlikely to have acquired very much rule knowledge until they have had some formal instruction. Even partial knowledge of GPC rules, however, might be very useful to beginning readers in building an orthographic lexicon. The rules could provide them with additional procedures for forming grapheme-phoneme associations, particularly associations involving vowels and digraphs, and for correctly selecting and sequencing those associations. In addition, Gough and Hillinger (1980) and Henderson (1977) have suggested that the process of learning GPC rules may be valuable for beginning readers because it encourages them to attend to information about letters and letter sequences in a word rather than information characterizing a word as a graphic configuration.

Finally, although GPC rules are accommodated within both a standard and a modified dual-route model, they might also be accommodated within a lexical model in the following way: each time GPC rules are applied to a word, the letter string is segmented into grapheme-phoneme units which are stored as part of the lexical entry for that word. On subsequent occasions, those specific units, or closely related units (e.g., orthographic neighbors), may be activated as part of the process of recognizing the word. Unlike their role in dual-route models, GPC rules would not participate in the actual construction of a phonological representation; instead, they would contribute a set of procedures for segmenting, sequencing and retaining one level of orthographic units within an interactive system of developing lexical knowledge. Other procedures (e.g., analogies) might contribute different levels of units (e.g., bodies). Consistent with this conception of GPC rules, investigators have argued that it is possible to account for rule based performance solely through interactions among stimulus specific instances (e.g., Brooks, 1978; Jacoby & Brooks, 1984) such as orthographic units in the lexicon (e.g., Glushko, 1979; Henderson, 1982; McClelland & Rumelhart, 1981; Marcel, 1980; Shallice & McCarthy, 1985).

References

Alegria, J., Pignot, E., & Morais, J. (1982). Phonetic analysis of speech and memory codes in beginning readers. *Memory and Cognition, 10*, 451–456.

Backman, J., Bruck, M., Hebert, M., & Seidenberg, M.S. (1984). Acquisition and use of spelling-sound correspondences in reading. *Journal of Experimental Child Psychology, 38*, 114–133.

Baron, J. (1977). Mechanisms for pronouncing printed words: use and acquisition. In D. LaBerge & S.J. Samuels (Eds.), *Basic processes in reading* (pp. 175–216). Hillsdale, NJ: Erlbaum.

Baron, J. (1979). Orthographic and word specific mechanisms in children's reading of words. *Child Development, 50*, 587–594.

Barr, R. (1974–75). The effect of instruction on pupil reading strategies. *Reading Research Quarterly, 4*, 555–582.

Barron, R.W. (1978). Access to the meanings of printed words: some implications for reading and learning to read. In F.B. Murray (Ed.), *The recognition of words: IRA series on the development of the reading process* (pp. 34–56). Newark, DE: International Reading Association.

Barron, R.W. (1981a). The development of visual word recognition: A review. In G.E. MacKinnon & T.G. Waller (Eds.), *Reading research: advances in theory and practice* Vol. 3 (pp. 119–158). New York: Academic Press.

Barron, R.W. (1981b). Reading skill and reading strategies. In A.M. Lesgold & C.A. Perfetti (Eds.), *Interactive processes in reading* (pp. 299–327). Hillsdale, NJ: Erlbaum.

Barron, R.W. (1985). Interactions between spelling and sound in literacy. In D.R. Olson, N. Torrance & A. Hildyard (Eds.), *Literacy, language and learning: The nature and consequences of reading and writing* (pp. 368–388). New York: Cambridge University Press.

Barron, R.W. & Baron, J. (1977). How children get meaning from printed words. *Child Development, 48*, 587–594.

Besner, D. & Davelaar, E. (1982). Basic processes in reading: Two phonological codes. *Canadian Journal of Psychology, 36*, 701–709.

Besner, D., Davies, J. & Daniels, S. (1981). Reading for meaning: The effects of concurrent articulation. *Quarterly Journal of Experimental Psychology, 33A*, 415–437.

Bradley, L. & Bryant, P.E. (1983). Categorizing sounds and learning to read—a causal connection. *Nature*, *310*, 419–421.

Bradley, L. & Bryant, P.E. (1985). *Rhyme and reason in reading and spelling*. Ann Arbor: University of Michigan Press.

Brooks, L.R. (1978). Nonanalytic concept formation and memory for instances. In E. Rosch & B.B. Lloyd (Eds.), *Cognition and categorization*. Hillsdale, NJ: Erlbaum.

Bryant, P.E. & Bradley, L. (1982). Psychological strategies and the development of reading and writing. In M. Martlew (Ed.), *The psychology of written language* (pp. 163–178). Chichester: John Wiley.

Bryant, P.E. & Bradley, L. (1985). *Children's reading problems*. Oxford: Basil Blackwell.

Campbell, R. & Besner, D. (1981). This and Thap—constraints on the pronunciation of new written words. *Quarterly Journal of Experimental Psychology, 33A*, 375–396.

Carr, T.H. & Pollatsek, A. (1985). Recognizing printed words: a look at current models. In D. Besner, T.G. Waller, & G.E. MacKinnon (Eds.), *Reading research: Advances in theory and practice* Vol. 5 (pp. 1–82). New York: Academic Press.

Chall, J. (1967). *Learning to read: The great debate*. New York: McGraw-Hill.

Chomsky, C. (1977). Approaching reading through invented spelling. In L.B. Resnick & P.A. Weaver (Eds.), *Theory and practice of early reading* Vol. 2 (pp. 43–65). Hillsdale, NJ: Erlbaum.

Coltheart, M. (1978). Lexical access in simple reading tasks. In G. Underwood (Ed.), *Strategies of information processing* (pp. 151–216). London: Academic Press.

Coltheart, M. (1980). Reading, phonological coding and deep dyslexia. In M. Coltheart, K.E. Patterson, & J.C. Marshall (Eds.), *Deep dyslexia* (pp. 197–226). London: Routledge and Kegan Paul.

Coltheart, M. (1981). Disorders of reading and their implications for models of normal reading. *Visible Language, 15*, 245–286.

Condry, S.M., McMahon-Rideout, M. & Levy, A.A. (1979). A developmental investigation of selective attention to graphic, phonetic, and semantic information in words. *Perception and Psychophysics, 25*, 88–94.

Crowder, R.G. (1982). *The psychology of reading: An introduction*. New York: Oxford University Press.

Doctor, E.A. & Coltheart, M. (1980). Children's use of phonological encoding when reading for meaning. *Memory and Cognition, 8*, 195–209.

Ehri, L.C. (1978). Beginning reading from a psycholinguistic perspective: Amalgamation of word identities. In F.B. Murray (Ed.), *The recognition of words: IRA series on the development of the reading process* (pp. 1–33). Newark, DE: International Reading Association.

Ehri, L.C. (1980). The development of orthographic images. In U. Frith (Ed.), *Cognitive processes in spelling* (pp. 311–338). London: Academic Press.

Ehri, L.C. (1983). A critique of five studies related to letter-name knowledge and learning to read. In L. Gentile, M. Kamil & J. Blanchard (Eds.), *Reading research revisited* (pp. 143–153). Columbus, Ohio: C.E. Merrill.

Ehri, L.C. (1984). How orthography alters spoken language competencies in children learning to read and spell. In J. Downing & R. Valtin (Eds.), *Language awareness and learning to read* (pp. 119–147). New York: Springer-Verlag.

Ehri, L.C. (1985). Effects of printed language acquisition on speech. In D.R. Olson, N. Torrance & A. Hildyard (Eds.), *Literacy, language and learning: The nature and consequences of reading and writing* (pp. 333–367). New York: Cambridge University Press.

Ehri, L.C. &Wilce, L.S. (1985). Movement into reading: Is the first stage of printed word learning visual or phonetic? *Reading Research Quarterly, 20*, 163–179.

Evans, M.A. & Carr, T.H. (1985). Cognitive abilities, conditions of learning, and the early development of reading skill. *Reading Research Quarterly, 20*, 327–350.

Gibson, E.J. & Levin, H. (1975). *The psychology of reading*. Cambridge, MA: MIT Press.

Gleitman, L.R. & Rozin, P. (1975). The structure and acquisition of reading I.: Relations between orthographies and the structure of language. In A.S. Reber & D.L. Scarborough (Eds.), *Toward a psychology of reading* (pp. 1–53). Hillsdale, NJ: Erlbaum.

Glushko, R.J. (1979). The organization and activation of orthographic knowledge in reading aloud. *Journal of Experimental Psychology: Human Perception and Performance, 5*, 674–691.

Goswami, U.C. (1985). The role of analogy in early reading development. Paper presented at the meeting of the Society for Research in Child Development, Toronto, Ontario, Canada.

Gough, P.B. & Hillinger, M.L. (1980). Learning to read: An unnatural act. *Annals of Dyslexia, 30*, 179–206.

Henderson, L. (1977). Word recognition. In N.S. Sutherland (Ed.), *Tutorial essays in psychology* Vol. 1 (pp. 35–74). Hillsdale, NJ: Erlbaum.

Henderson, L. (1982). *Orthography and word recognition in reading*. London: Academic Press.

Henderson, L. (1985). Issues in the modelling of pronunciation assembly in normal reading. In K.E. Patterson, J.C. Marshall & M. Coltheart (Eds.), *Surface dyslexia*. London: Erlbaum.

Hohn, W.E. & Ehri, L.C. (1983). Do alphabetic letters help prereaders acquire phonemic segmentation skill?. *Journal of Educational Psychology, 75*, 752–762.

Huey, E.B. (1908). *The psychology and pedagogy of reading*. New York: Macmillan (republished Cambridge: MIT Press, 1968).

Humphreys, G.W. & Evett, L.J. (1985). Are there independent lexical and nonlexical routes in word processing? An evaluation of the dual-route theory of reading. *The Behavioral and Brain Sciences, 8*, 689–705.

Jacoby, L.L. & Brooks, L.R. (1984). Nonanalytic cognition: Memory, perception and concept learning. In G.H. Bower (Ed.), *The psychology of learning and motivation: Advances in research and theory* Vol. 18 (1–47). New York: Academic Press.

Jenkins, J.R., Bausell, R.B. & Jenkins, L.M. (1972). Comparison of letter name and letter sound training as transfer variables. *American Educational Research Journal, 9*, 75–86.

Jorm, A.F. & Share, D.L. (1983). Phonological recoding and reading acquisition. *Applied Psycholinguistics, 4*, 103–147.

Kay, J. & Lesser, R. (1985). The nature of phonological processing in oral reading: Evidence from surface dyslexia. *Quarterly Journal of Experimental Psychology, 37A*, 39–81.

Kay, J. & Marcel, A.J. (1983). One process, not two, in reading aloud: Lexical analogies do the work of nonlexical rules. *Quarterly Journal of Experimental Psychology, 33A*, 397–414.

Liberman, I.Y. (1982). A language-oriented view of reading and its disabilities. In H. Myklebust (Ed.), *Progress in learning disabilities* Vol. 5 (pp. 81–101). New York: Grune & Stratton.

Lovett, M.W., Ransby, M.J. & Barron, R.W. (1984). Word type and subtype effects in dyslexic children's response to remedial treatment. Paper presented at the meeting of the International Neuropsychological Society, Houston, Texas.

McClelland, J.L. & Rumelhart, D.E. (1981). An interactive activation model of the effect of context on perception. Part 1: An account of basic findings. *Psychological Review, 88*, 375–407.

McCusker, L.X., Hillinger, M.L. & Bias, R.G. (1981). Phonological recoding and reading. *Psychological Bulletin, 89*, 217–245.

Marcel, A.J. (1980). Surface dyslexia and beginning reading: a revised hypothesis of the pronunciation of print and its impairments. In M. Coltheart, K.E. Patterson & J.C. Marshall (Eds.), *Deep dyslexia* (pp. 227–258). London: Routledge and Kegan Paul.

Marsh, G. & Desberg, P. (1983). The development of strategies in the acquisition of symbolic skills. In D.R. Rogers & J.A. Sloboda (Eds.), *The acquisition of symbolic skills* (pp. 149–154). New York: Plenum Publishing Corporation.

Mason, J. (1980). When do children begin to read: An exploration of four-year-old children's letter and word reading competencies. *Reading Research Quarterly, 15*, 203–227.

Mason, J. (1984). Early reading from a developmental perspective. In P.D. Pearson (Ed.), *Handbook of reading research* (pp. 505–543). New York: Longmans.

Masonheimer, P.E. (1982). Environmental print identification by preschool children. Unpublished doctoral dissertation, University of California, Santa Barbara.

Masonheimer, P.E., Drum, P.A. & Ehri, L.C. (1984). Does environmental print identification lead children into word reading? *Journal of Reading Behavior, 16*, 257–271.

Mathews, M.M. (1966). *Teaching to read historically considered*. Chicago: University of Chicago Press.

Meyer, D.E., Schvaneveldt, R.W. & Ruddy, M.G. (1974). Functions of graphemic and phonemic codes in visual word recognition. *Memory and Cognition, 2*, 309–321.

Morton, J. & Patterson, K.E. (1980). A new attempt at an interpretation, or, an attempt at a new interpretation. In M. Coltheart, K.E. Patterson & J.C. Marshall (Eds.), *Deep dyslexia* (pp. 91–118). London: Routledge and Kegan Paul.

Ohnmacht, D.C. (1969). The effect of letter knowledge on achievement in reading in the first grade. Paper presented at the meeting of the American Educational Research Association, Los Angeles.

Paap, K.R., Newsome, S.L., McDonald, J.E. & Schvaneveldt, R.W. (1982). An activation-verification model for letter and word recognition: The word superiority effect. *Psychological Review, 89*, 573–594.

Patterson, K.E. & Morton, J. (1985). From orthography to phonology: An attempt at an old interpretation. In K.E. Patterson, J.C. Marshall & M. Coltheart (Eds.), *Surface dyslexia* (pp. 335–359). London: Erlbaum.

Perfetti, C.A. (1985). *Reading ability*. New York: Oxford University Press.

Perfetti, C.A. & McCutchen, D. (1982). Speech processes in reading. In N. Lass (Ed.), *Speech and language: advances in basic research and practice* Vol. 7 (pp. 237–269). New York: Academic Press.

Read, C. (1971). Pre-school children's knowledge of English orthography. *Harvard Educational Review, 41*, 1–34.

Reitsma, P. (1983). Printed word learning in beginning reading. *Journal of Experimental Child Psychology, 36*, 321–339.

Reitsma, P. (1984). Sound priming in beginning reading. *Child Development, 55*, 406–423.

Rosson, M.B. (1983). From SOFA to LOUCH: Lexical contributions to pseudoword pronunciation. *Memory and Cognition, 11*, 152–160.

Rosson, M.B. (1985). The interaction of pronunciation rules and lexical representations in reading aloud. *Memory and Cognition, 13*, 90–99.

Samuels, S.J. (1972). The effect of letter-name knowledge on learning to read. *American Educational Research Journal, 9*, 65–74.

Seidenberg, M.S. (1985a). The time course of information activation and utilization in visual word recognition. In D. Besner, T.G. Waller & G.E. MacKinnon (Eds.), *Reading research: advances in theory and practice* Vol. 5 (pp. 199–252). New York: Academic Press.

Seidenberg, M.S. (1985b). The time course of phonological code activation in two writing systems. *Cognition, 19*, 1–30.

Seidenberg, M.S., Waters, G.S., Barnes, M.A. & Tanenhaus, M.K. (1984). When does spelling or pronunciation influence word recognition? *Journal of Verbal Learning and Verbal Behavior, 23*, 383–404.

Seymour, P.H.K. & Elder, L. (in press). Beginning reading without phonology. *Cognitive Neuropsychology*.

Shallice, T. & McCarthy, R. (1985). Phonological reading: From patterns of impairment to possible procedures. In K.E. Patterson, J.C. Marshall & M. Coltheart (Eds.), *Surface dyslexia* (pp. 361–397). London: Erlbaum.

Shallice, T., Warrington, E.K. & McCarthy, R. (1983). Reading without semantics. *Quarterly Journal of Experimental Psychology, 35A*, 111–138.

Silberberg, N.E., Silberberg, M.C. & Iversen, I.A. (1972). The effect of kindergarten instruction in alphabet and numbers on first grade reading. *Journal of Learning Disabilities, 5*, 254–261.

Treiman, R. (1985). Onsets and rimes as units of spoken syllables. *Journal of Experimental Child Psychology, 39*, 161–181.

Treiman, R. & Baron, J. (1983). Phonemic-analysis training helps children benefit from spelling-sound rules. *Memory and Cognition, 11*, 383–389.

Venezky, R.L. (1970). *The structure of English orthography*. The Hague: Mouton.

Waters, G.S. & Seidenberg, M.S. (1985). Spelling-sound effects in reading: Time-course and decision criteria. *Memory and Cognition, 13*, 557–572.

Waters, G.S., Seidenberg, M.S. & Bruck, M. (1984). Children's and adult's use of spelling-sound information in three reading tasks. *Memory and Cognition, 12*, 293–305.

Wijk, A. (1966). *Rules of pronunciation for the English language*. London: Oxford University Press.

Williams, J. (1979). Reading instruction today. *American Psychologist, 34*, 917–922.

Résumé

La recherche sur le développement de la reconnaissance des mots, comme celle sur la reconnaissance des mots par le lecteur avancé, a été fortement influencée par le modèle des deux voies. Une voie est non-lexicale et indirecte parce que l'accès à la signification lexicale passe par des représentations phonologiques pré-lexicales qui sont assemblées par application de règles de correspondance entre graphèmes et phonèmes (CGP). L'autre voie, qui est indépendante de la première, est lexicale et directe, parce que des représentations orthographiques des mots complets sont utilisées pour accéder à la signification lexicale ou aux représentations phonologiques post-lexicales. Nous passons en revue les données concernant deux hypothèses au sujet du développement fondées toutes deux sur le modèle des deux voies: les lecteurs avancés utilisent à la fois l'accès direct et l'accès indirect à la signification lexicale, alors que les lecteurs débutants utilisent soit 1) exclusivement l'accès indirect, soit 2) exclusivement l'accès direct. La conclusion est que aucun des deux modes d'accès ne prédomine chez les débutants. D'autres données suggèrent deux raisons pour lesquelles le modèle à deux voies ne fournit pas une explication satisfaisante du développement de la reconnaissance des mots. En premier lieu, il n'offre pas une caractérisation adéquate des unités orthographiques représentées dans le lexique des débutants. En deuxième lieu, l'indépendance des deux voies interdit que l'information lexicale soit acquise par application de règles CGP. Enfin, nous discutons des alternatives au modèle à deux voies. La plus prometteuse semble être un modèle lexical à processus unique dans lequel l'acquisition et la performance dans la reconnaissance des mots peut être expliquée par des interactions entre unités orthographiques et phonologiques de différentes tailles dans le lexique.

6

The similarities between normal readers and developmental and acquired dyslexics

PETER BRYANT*
LAWRENCE IMPEY**
University of Oxford

Abstract

Recently several people have suggested strong similarities between the symptoms of acquired and developmental dyslexia. It is an interesting suggestion because it offers us a new way of looking at differences among dyslexic children (always a thorny problem) and also a possible explanation for these children's difficulties. However, the symptoms in question could only be used as a basis for such an explanation if they really were distinctive, that is, did not crop up in normal children at the same reading level. We take two attempts to connect acquired with developmental dyslexia, each involving an adolescent girl who read roughly at the level of a 10-year-old child. One of these two girls (Temple & Marshall, 1983) read in a rather similar way to that of a typical phonological dyslexic. The other (Coltheart et al. 1983) resembled a typical surface dyslexic. Neither study included any comparison with normal children, and so one cannot be certain that there was anything unusual about either girl's reading patterns. We gave the tests used in the two reports just mentioned to 16 normal readers, all reading at the 10-year-level, and we found evidence for all the symptoms described in those reports in normal children as well. The symptoms were not abnormal and cannot be used to explain the two dyslexic children's difficulties. We also found strong and systematic individual differences in our normal group along a "phonological to surface" continuum. So our study does two things. One is show that the reading patterns reported by Temple and Marshall and of Coltheart et al. do not provide an explanation of the causes of these children's reading difficulties. The other is to provide a new way of looking at qualitative differences among normal readers.

*Reprint requests should be addressed to P.E. Bryant, Department of Experimental Psychology, University of Oxford, South Parks Road, Oxford OX1 3UD, United Kingdom.
**Now at The Middlesex Hospital, Mortimer Street, London W1, United Kingdom.

Introduction

The claim has often been made that there are different types of developmental dyslexia. Several psychologists, among them Boder (1973), Mattis, French and Rapin (1975) and Mitterer (1982), have argued that different kinds of difficulty afflict different dyslexic children. These claims were all based on studies of groups of children with reading problems.

Recently the argument for differences among such children has taken a new turn. Several people have drawn analogies between "acquired" and "developmental" dyslexia. Acquired dyslexics are people who, as a result of some damage to their brain, begin to have great difficulty in reading and often in writing as well. There can be no doubt at all that there are recognisably different kinds of acquired dyslexia. Different patients do display radically different symptoms. The point of analogies between developmental and acquired dyslexia is the possibility that the differences among developmental dyslexics may correspond fairly closely to those found among acquired dyslexics.

Most of the people who have made this connection have done so on the basis of intensive case studies of individual developmental dyslexics who, when given the sort of tests usually administered to acquired dyslexics, make mistakes which are characteristic of one or other type of acquired dyslexia. The most notable examples are to be found in two recent papers by Temple and Marshall (1983) and by Coltheart, Masterson, Prior, and Byng (1983). The first of these describes a teenage dyslexic girl whose pattern of reading closely resembled that of a phonological (acquired) dyslexic. The second deals with another teenage girl who, in contrast, made the same sort of mistakes as a surface (acquired) dyslexic.

The reading problems of phonological and surface dyslexics are quite different in character. The phonological dyslexic seems to have particular difficulty with letter-sound correspondences. Nonsense words and long unfamiliar regular words, like "herpetology", are particularly difficult for him, and this is a fairly certain sign that his problem is a phonological one, since reading both these types of word probably depends to some extent on knowing how to convert letters into sounds. Many of the phonological dyslexic's reading errors take the form of visual paralexias (e.g., reading "camp" as "cape" which sounds very different from, but looks quite like, the right word) and of derivational errors (e.g., "weigh" read as "weight"). Both types of mistake seem to show that the phonological dyslexic is forced to depend on the visual appearance of words which he is trying to read, and cannot use the letter-sound relationships much to help him decipher these words.

A surface dyslexic, on the other hand, seems to be able to use the phonological rules without much difficulty, but to have little idea of the visual appearance of the words that he reads. If he reads in this way he should read nonsense words reasonably well but find irregular words like "gauge" particularly difficult, and a great deal harder than regular words (e.g., "pivot"). Regular and nonsense words can be read on the basis of relationships: irregular words cannot. This pattern—of being "better at reading regular words and non-words than irregular words" (Coltheart, 1982)—has been widely adopted as the criterion for surface dyslexia. The surface dyslexic's dependence on letter-sound relationships is also shown by the fact that he often reads irregular words phonetically: he makes regularisation errors (e.g., "brode" for "broad" and "steek" for "steak") and stress errors which consist of stressing the wrong syllable.

The girl studied by Temple and Marshall, a 17-year-old girl with a reading age of around 10 years, produced all the characteristic symptoms (difficulty with nonsense words and long regular words, visual paralexias and derivational errors, no difference between regular and irregular words) of phonological dyslexia. The case reported by Coltheart et al. (also a 17-year-old girl with a reading age of around 10 years) produced, with one exception, all the symptoms of surface dyslexia. She had difficulty with irregular words and made several regularisation and stress errors. The exception, not explained by the authors, was a considerable difficulty on her part with nonsense words.

Together these studies make a powerful case for a direct correspondence between types of acquired and types of developmental dyslexia. The most important thing about this connection is that it might throw new light on the underlying causes of developmental dyslexia. Marshall (1984) and Ellis (1984) have claimed as much. To quote Marshall: "The syndromes of developmental dyslexia will accordingly be interpreted as *consequent upon* [our emphasis] the selective failure of a particular adult component (or components) to develop appropriately, with relatively intact, normal (adult) functioning of the remaining components".

If the causes of a child's reading difficulties are to be traced back to his or her peculiar reading patterns, as Marshall is claiming here, then these patterns must be different from those of other children whose progress in reading is quite normal. That is a minimum and essential requirement for this kind of causal theory. It could not be the case *both* that a particular way of reading is the reason why certain children become dyslexic *and* that this same way of reading is to be found among children who read quite normally for their age. So anyone trying to prove a theory such as Marshall's would have to show that the dyslexic children concerned did read in radically different ways from normal children. Yet neither of these two studies makes any comparison with normal readers. This is a serious omission, and it means that the data presented in the two papers cannot be used to explain either of the two children's reading problems until such a comparison is made.

To whom should the two dyslexics be compared? The answer quite clearly is to normal children at the same reading level. Suppose that we found that one or both these girls read in exactly the same way as some typical 10-year-old children do. In that case we should know more about the way 10-year-old children read, but nothing about the causes of developmental dyslexia. The results would simply confirm that the dyslexic girl in question reads at a 10-year-old level, which we knew anyway. But if she responded to the various tests in one way and normal 10-year-olds in quite another way, we could conclude that we had found something to do with the reason why her progress in reading is not normal and theirs is.

On the face of it it seems likely that the performance of at least one of the two girls in question should be unlike that of a typical 10-year-old, since the two are very different from each other. However there are differences too among children who read quite normally (Baron & Treiman, 1980; Treiman, 1984). So there might be nothing unusual about either of the two dyslexic children apart from their general backwardness in reading.

That sounds like a possible negative result. But it would, from the point of view of the study of the way normal children learn to read, be of very great interest. We need to know about differences between normal children too if we are to understand the nature of learning to read.

Methods

The children

We tested 16 children, selected on the basis of their reading age as assessed by the Schonell reading test from a larger sample of 45. The RAs (reading ages) of the children fell between 9 y 6 month and 10 y 6 m with a mean of 10 y 1 m. Their mean CA (calendar age) was 8 y 9 m (range 6 y 3 m to 11 y 9 m). They were also given the British Picture Vocabulary Test (the British version of the PPVT) on which their mean score was 103 (range 95–144—100 is the "average" for the population).

Procedure

We gave the children a number of tests, most of which were also given by Temple and Marshall or by Coltheart et al.

I. Regular/irregular words

Each child was asked to read 39 regular and 39 irregular words (listed in Coltheart, Besner, Jonasson, & Davelaar, 1979) and also 50 regular and 50 irregular words collected by Stanovich and Bauer (1978).

II. Long regular words

We asked the children to read a list of 20 long regular words of decreasing frequency, devised by Nelson (Nelson & O'Connell, 1978) and used by Temple and Marshall.

III. Homophone matching task

The children had to judge whether pairs of words, typed on cards, had identical pronunciations, that is, were homophones. This task was devised by Coltheart et al. In half the pairs the two words looked similar and sounded the same ("hair", "hare"): in the other half they looked the same but sounded different ("hair", "hard"). This was done with two sets, in one of which the words were regular and in the other irregular.

IV. Homophone comprehension/confusion task

We gave the child a list of 19 words to read, all of which had homophones (e.g., "hair"). The child was asked to look at the word, to say what it meant, to read it aloud and then to spell it letter by letter. This task was used by Coltheart et al.

V. Words vs. non-words

(a) We gave the children 25 words and 25 non-words to read. Each non-word was matched with one of the real words, in that the two differed by one letter (e.g., "room", "foom"). The list was devised by Coltheart in 1981 and used by Temple and Marshall (1983).

(b) We also gave them 40 more non-words, 20 of which were homophones of real words (e.g. "bair") and 20 not (e.g. "korp"). The list was used by Temple and Marshall.

(c) We gave the children another list of non-words, also used by Temple and Marshall, of which half were homophones to real words and half not. Half of the homophones were visually similar to their homophone (e.g. "scowt") and half not.

VI. *The derivational list*

This was a list, used by Temple and Marshall, of 100 real words, many of which could in principle produce derivational errors.

Results

Our question was whether the patterns of reading reported by Temple and Marshall and by Coltheart could also be found among normal children at the same reading level as the two dyslexics concerned.

There are three ways of looking at this question. One is to compare the performance of the two dyslexic girls to our group's mean scores. Another is to look at patterns of the different scores among the normal group. The third is to look at the individuals in our group of normal readers to see if any of them is like either of the two dyslexics.

Comparisons with the normal group's means

A. *Symptoms of surface dyslexia*

Regular/Irregular comparison

CD, the girl put forward by Coltheart et al. as a developmental surface dyslexic, read 35/39 regular and 26/39 irregular words correctly—a irregular:regular ratio of 0.74. On average the equivalent mean scores in our group were 36.1 (S.D. 1.83) and 29.7 (S.D. 3.07) ($t = 7.31, p < .001$), giving a ratio of 0.82. So normal children too find irregular words harder. The irregular:regular ratio was actually below 0.74 (i.e., a greater difference than CD) for three of our children.

In the other regular/irregular comparison—the Stanovich and Bauer list (not given by Coltheart et al.)—our children read 45.9/50 (S.D. 2.62) of the regular words and 37.2/50 (S.D. 3.35) of the irregular ones correctly.

Thus normal children also have difficulty with irregular words and some of them more difficulty even than CD.

Regularisation and stress errors

Coltheart et al. do not put a figure to the number of regularisation and stress errors made by CD, but they do give all her responses to the 39 irregular words and we calculate that she made 4 regularisation errors with them.

Our children on average made 3.1 (S.D. 2.26) regularisation errors to the same 39 words. Six of our children made more than 4 regularisation errors (i.e., more than CD) to these words.

We also looked at all the regularisation errors made to all 178 real words which we gave the children to read and found that 35% (S.D. 16.98) took the form of regularisation errors. So, again there is nothing at all unusual in these errors and nothing abnormal about CD making them.

Our children often made stress errors. Every child made at least one. But we could make no direct comparison with CD because no figures are available.

Neologisms

Coltheart et al. report that CD produced neologisms, but do not say how many. However from a rather similar study of a "surface" developmental dyslexic by Temple (1984) we calculated that 64% of all errors made were neologisms. The mean figure for our group was 63.2% (S.D. 11. 67) (many neologisms were also regularisation errors). No sign of any abnormality here.

Reading comprehension

Coltheart et al. gave CD a list of words which she had previously misread. She had misread many of these as words meaning another word with a similar sound pattern, for example, "beer" for "bear". She was now asked about these words' meanings and also to read each word letter by letter. Of the 46 words falling into this category her definition of the meaning of the word coincided with the word she produced when she originally misread it.

The same was true of our children. Their definition almost without exception coincided with their misreading.

Homophones

CD was much better at spotting that pairs of words were homophones when they were regular words (44/50) than when they were irregular (34/50)—an irregular:regular ratio of 0.77.

We had to use different pairs of words, because Coltheart et al. did not give details of theirs. However our mean results were much the same as CD's: 17.75/18 (S.D. 0.58) for regular pairs and 25.0/30 (S.D. 1.9) for irregular ones—a irregular:regular success ratio of 0.84.

In the homophone confusion test our children defined the word as having the same meaning as its homophone (e.g., "beer" for "bear") on an average of 3.5 (S.D. 2.38) out of 19 words. Coltheart et al. give no equivalent figure, but since this is a characteristic surface symptom we can conclude that here is another example of a purported abnormality being quite normal at this level of reading.

B. Symptoms of phonological dyslexia

Non-words

HM, the girl studied by Temple and Marshall and put forward by them as a developmental, phonological dyslexic, read all 25 words correctly and only 9/25 non-words in the matched word/non-word list.

On average our children read all 25 real words and 19.3 (S.D. 3.50) of the non-words correctly. The lowest individual score on the non-words in our group was 12. So we found the same difference between words and non-words. But it was not so pronounced.

Turning to the homophonic and non homophonic non-words, in the first list HM read 7/40 homophonic ones and 2/40 non homophonic ones—a non homophonic:homophonic ratio of 0.29. The equivalent mean scores in our group were 31.0/40 (S.D. 6.06) and 29.2/40 (S.D. 7.79)—giving a ratio of 0.94. However in the second list we did find a sizeable difference between the two kinds of non-words. In this case the ratio figure for HM was 0.58, while for our group it was 0.75. Thus here once again we get the same overall pattern, but in not so pronounced a form.

In this second list, half of the 48 homophonic non-words looked rather like their homophone, while the other half did not. Temple and Marshall found no difference in HM's success with these two categories (6 correct in each case) and concluded that here HM took no account of the visual appearance of the words (this, it should be noted, goes against their hypothesis which is that she was unusually dependent on the visual appearance of words). This inconsistency notwithstanding, our evidence shows that there was nothing unusual here. On average our children read 10.1/12 (S.D. 1.51) of the first and 10.5/12 (S.D. 1.18) of the second category.

In all, HM was given 88 non-words and we have calculated that she read 34 of them correctly. The lowest score in our group was 42. Thus our results show that HM was worse than normal children with non-words—a result which is consistent with the earlier studies by Frith and Snowling (1983) and by Baddeley, Ellis, Miles, and Lewis (1982) who showed groups of dyslexic children to be worse at reading non-words than are normal children at the same reading level.

Coltheart et al. also gave CD two lists of non-words. She read 12/50 monosyllabic and 28/120 three syllable non-words correctly. These are low scores for someone whose phonological processes are meant to be intact, and they appear to be considerably lower than those of our normal children. (We cannot make a direct comparison, because we did not use Coltheart et al.'s non-words, which are not given in their paper.) So a difficulty with non-words may be a general characteristic of dyslexic children, whatever their other problems.

Visual paralexias and derivational errors

Fifty percent of HM's errors with real words took the form of visual para-lexias. The average figure in our group was 28.8% (S.D. 9.31). However one of our children's figures was 52% and another's 44%. HM made 6/100 deri-vational errors to the words in the derivational list. The average for our children was 2.1 (S.D. 1.3), and the highest figure was 4.

So there is nothing abnormal about either type of error, and there are children who make around as many errors of the visual paralexia type as HM. On the other hand HM made more derivational errors than any of our child-ren.

Long regular words

HM got 7/20 correct. She read 7 of the first 10, more common, words correctly, and none of the 10 less frequent words. The overall average for our children was 11.5/20 (S.D. 3.17), with 7.4 (S.D. 1.77) correct among the commoner and 4.1 (S.D. 1.74) among the less common words.

Two of our children scored lower than 7/20—that is, lower than HM.

C. Other responses

Letter errors—omissions, additions, alterations and position errors

Coltheart et al. report that CD made a few errors which involved leaving out or adding or changing letters in words or changing the order of letters in words when reading. They do not make it clear whether they think of these as a characteristic surface symptom. We found that all our children made mistakes of this category. We cannot make a direct comparison with CD because no figures are given. We reckoned that on average 23.8% (S.D. 8.8) of all errors took this form. There was also considerable variation. The maxi-mum percentage was 48, and the minimum was 17.

We shall show later that these errors were strongly related to the symptoms of phonological dyslexia.

Summary of comparisons with mean scores

None of the "surface" symptoms claimed for CD turned out to be in any way abnormal. They were all shared at least as strongly by some of the children in our normal group. The same was true of some of the "phonological" symptoms (e.g., visual paralexias) claimed for HM. However HM did show other symptoms, such as difficulty with non-words, (a difficulty rather embarrassingly shared by CD) more strongly than any of our children. This particular difficulty has already been reported in a number of studies of groups of dyslexic children.

Are there subgroups of normal children with "phonological" and "surface" symptoms?

Our group as a whole showed all the symptoms reported in CD and HM and these symptoms were stronger in some children than in others. In most cases there were individuals whose scores either approached or actually exceeded those of CD or HM. One possible reason for our mean scores being less extreme than those of the two dyslexics is that there were some in our group who were like CD and others like HM, and that the average fell somewhere in between these two extremes. There are two ways of looking to see whether this is what happened. One is to work out the relationships between the different scores, and the other is to pick out individuals who show distinctive patterns of reading.

We concentrated on the more frequent types of error and left out stress and derivational errors because these were relatively uncommon. (It is worth noting straightaway that the letter errors proved to be strongly related to phonological symptoms: we shall treat it henceforth as a symptom of that type.) Table 1 gives the correlation matrix and shows two things. One is that the phonological symptoms are strongly related to each other. (Please note that some of these positive relationships are shown by a negative correlation, as for example in the negative correlation between visual paralexias and success in reading non-words.)

The second point is that the relationships *between* the two symptoms were negative ones. For example, the more visual paralexias the children made, the lower was the number of regularisation errors ($r = -0.75$).

We carried out a factor analysis of these variables. It yielded one large common factor which accounted for 67.9% of the variance. As Table 2 shows this sharply discriminates the two types of symptoms. The phonological symptoms were strongly negatively loaded, and the surface symptoms just as

Table 1. *Correlations (RA and CA partialled out)*

	Reg. errors[a]	Visual paralexias	Letter errors	Non-words (correct)	Long regular words (correct)
Reg. errors	1.00	−0.75	−0.55	0.50	0.67
Visual paralexias		1.00	0.53	−0.41	−0.47
Letter errors			1.00	−0.32	−0.62
Non-words				1.00	0.71
Long regular words					1.00

[a]Regularisation errors

Table 2. *Loadings in the factor analysis*

Variable	Loadings	Significance
Regularisation errors	0.86	$p < .001$
Non-word reading	0.64	$p < .001$
Long regular words	0.84	$p < .001$
Visual paralexias	−0.52	$p < .001$
Letter errors	−0.43	$p < .001$

strongly positively loaded, on this factor. This demonstrates a marked difference between the two symptoms, and one that must be of immense significance in children's reading, since it accounts for so much of the variance. It is strong support for our idea that the difference between the two dyslexic children is a difference which is present among normal readers and therefore cannot in itself be a reason for the two dyslexic children's difficulties.

We turned to canonical correlations to see how significant the difference between the two types of reading is. Our canonical correlation compared the phonological symptoms on the one hand with the surface symptoms on the other. It showed that the two sets of symptoms were negatively related ($p = .032$). The number of visual paralexias (coefficient of canonical variable = 0.79) on the one hand, and the number of regularisation errors on the other (coefficient = −0.91) contributed most to the negative relationship between the two sets of symptoms. Here then is strong evidence for striking qualitative differences among normal readers.

Are there individuals who have the same patterns of responses as the two dyslexics?

The correlations, factor analysis and the canonical correlation demonstrate that there are some children who conform to the surface pattern and others to the phonological pattern. We decided to see if there were extreme cases in our normal group who were at all like the two dyslexics. We already know that there were individual children who produced more extreme scores on particular tests than HM or CD. But we have not yet established whether there was a pattern here. Did the two children who produced more visual paralexias than HM also do particularly badly on non-words (another phonological symptom), and did they also show little sign of any surface symptom such as regularisation errors?

We found two children who showed strong signs of phonological symptoms (CM and SC) and one (KS) who showed a strong surface pattern. (It is as well to remember that, though we talk of symptoms, we are dealing here with children who are not backward in reading.) Table 3 gives the ordinal positions of these three children over the main tests. It shows that these extreme individuals were either phonological-like or surface-like. CM and SC produced the most visual paralexias and were near the worst on non-words. They also made the fewest regularisation errors and the smallest number of mistakes with irregular words.

In contrast, KS made a large number of regularisation errors (many more than CD), found irregular words very difficult to read, but produced very few visual paralexias and was among the best at reading non-words. In fact KS was a great deal more surface-like than CD, since KS could read non-

Table 3.   *Individual "extreme" normal readers. Ordinal positions on the different tests*

Child	RA		NW[a]	VP[b]	Irreg.[c]	R'gation[d]	Leterr[e]
CM	10 y 2 m	Ordinal position[f]	3	1	15	15	1
SC	9 y 9 m	Ordinal position	2	2	16	16	4
KS	10 y 3 m	Ordinal position	14	16	4	1	15

[a]No. of mistakes on non-words; [b]No. of visual paralexias; [c]No. of mistakes on irregular words; [d]No. of regularisation errors; [e]No. of letter errors; [f]Ordinal position 1 means the highest, and 16 the lowest, score in the group.

words well and CD managed them very badly.

Despite such strong biases CM, SC and KS, we must repeat, were not backward in reading.

Discussion

Our discussion will make two points: (1) that our results indicate that the patterns of reading found by Coltheart et al. and by Temple and Marshall tell us nothing definite about the causes of reading problems and may be nothing to do with these causes, and (2) that our experiment produces new and significant information about differences among normal readers.

The first point is now clear. None of the symptoms is unique to dyslexics. Both "phonological" and "surface" patterns are characteristic features of normal reading in children whose reading ability is the same as CD's and HM's. Many of the symptoms can be found in equal strength in children at the same level of reading. Indeed many of the normal children showed "surface" symptoms even more strongly than CD did.

HM, on the other hand, did make more derivational errors and did have more difficulty with non-words than any of our children. We cannot say yet whether this is a genuine dyslexic–normal reader difference or whether a larger sample of normal readers than ours would have produced examples as extreme as HM. HM's difficulties with non-words may indeed reflect a characteristic weakness of dyslexic children. Their relative difficulty with non-words has already been shown in group studies of dyslexic children by Frith and Snowling (1983) and by Baddeley et al. (1982) and supports the idea of these and of other authors (Bradley & Bryant, 1978; Bryant & Bradley, 1980) of a general phonological difficulty among dyslexic children. So some of HM's mistakes may help to confirm the conclusions drawn from earlier work on groups of dyslexic children of a common phonological difficulty among dyslexics. CD, as well as HM, had greater difficulty than our children did with non-words. This is hard to reconcile with the idea that she is a surface dyslexic who has no particular phonological weakness.

On the remaining measures the children in our group showed the various symptoms which were found in CD and HM as strongly as they themselves did. Furthermore we showed that the differences between CD and HM are not at all unusual. Exactly the same differences exist among normal children too.

We were able to produce "extreme" cases in our normal group who were very like HM and CD. But of course most of our group were not so extreme and fell somewhere in the middle. It seems quite likely to us that it is just the same with dyslexics and that a randomly selected group of dyslexic children at the same reading level as CD and HM would consist of some cases like them and others who fell between them. This would be further reason for doubting Marshall's claim that the selective failure of some "adult component" causes developmental dyslexia. It would indicate that terms like "surface" and "phonological" are misleading because they imply discontinuities where there is a continuum.

It seems possible to us that developmental dyslexics rely on different strategies in reading for the same reasons as normal children do, and that some non-specific factor which does not affect the operation of one strategy more than another holds them back, though we cannot yet say what this factor is. Whatever the factor is, it is probably independent of the reading pattern which they show. This is a possibility which can only be tested by comparing the differences among a group of developmental dyslexics with the same differences among a group of normal children at the same reading level. Our prediction is that this sort of comparison would show identical patterns of differences in the two groups.

We conclude that the patterns reported in the studies by Coltheart et al. and by Temple and Marshall (with the possible exception of the difficulty, shared by HM and CD, with non-words) tell us nothing about the causes of the two dyslexics' reading problems. The claim that the dyslexic syndromes are "consequent upon the selective failure of an adult component" must be discarded. The same patterns and the same biases are to be found in perfectly normal children and do not hold their reading back. Our study shows that it is futile to do studies of individual dyslexic children without at the same time comparing them to children who have no particular problem with reading.

The notion of Temple and Marshall (1983) that dyslexics are held back because their "functional architecture" is different, must be wrong. We have found the same functional architecture in normal children. We disagree, too, with the rather similar arguments developed by Coltheart et al. They couch their analysis of CD's symptoms in terms of a damaged system (p. 489) and argue that she suffers from a "defect" in the "input logogen system" (pp. 469, 490). Now that we have shown that these "symptoms" exist as strikingly in many of our normal children, this claim is surely untenable. Towards the end of their paper (p. 486) Coltheart et al. do acknowledge the possibility that CD's symptoms might also occur among normal children at the same reading level (though not the possibility of strong individual differences among normal children). They argue that such a result would indicate "delay" rather than "deviance" and so our results, in their terms, do demonstrate a delay in CD. However we think that the distinction can be made more strongly. The pattern of reading shown by CD was typical for the reading level which she happened to be at. Her performance in these tests, therefore, does not tell us anything about the reasons for her extreme backwardness in reading and provides no evidence at all for any specific defect or damage. The "defect" is in her general reading level, which is well behind her mental age, and not in the reading pattern itself.

The nearest thing that we can find to the kind of direct comparison of individual differences between dyslexic and normal children which we advocate is the recent work of Seymour and his colleagues. In one study Seymour and McGregor (1984) looked intensively at a small and strikingly heterogeneous group of developmental dyslexics, and made the occasional comparison between individual dyslexics and a group of normal children at roughly the same stage of reading. However the authors are more interested in differences between the dyslexic children and the comparisons with the normal group are scanty. Seymour and McGregor give no details of individual differences among their normal children. In another study Seymour (1986) did look at individual differences among competent readers as well as among less competent readers. However the reading levels of these different groups were different. This means that any difference in patterns between the groups might be a normal developmental change (and no less important for that) and have nothing to do with the fact that one group is having more difficulty with the business of learning to read than the other.

Our second point concerns the differences among normal children. Our data support and extend the hypothesis put forward by Baron (1979) and by Treiman (1984) that children can be classified as "Chinese" or as "Phoenician" readers. The Chinese group does not use phonological codes much and is said to depend heavily on the visual appearance of the words that it reads. The Phoenician group on the other hand uses phonological codes heavily and does not rely on visual cues. These categories correspond almost exactly to the distinction between phonological (Chinese) and surface (Phoenician) dyslexia, and our discovery that the phonological/surface distinction applies as much to normal children as to developmental dyslexics is thus completely consistent with the Baron/Treiman scheme. Their main evidence for the scheme is correlational. They gave various groups of children lists of matched regular, irregular and nonsense words, and correlated the children's success on reading (and spelling) the different lists. They found a greater correlation between regular and nonsense words than between irregular and nonsense words and interpreted this as evidence for a Phoenician strategy, on the argument that regular and nonsense words can be read phonetically. They also found a greater correlation between regular and irregular words than between regular and nonsense words and, since both regular and irregular words can in principle be read as wholes, they argued that this was evidence for the Chinese strategy. These seem to us to be convincing arguments for the two strategies. But the pattern of correlations does not in our opinion provide a way of identifying which children rely on the different strategies.

Our evidence does show that different children adopt different strategies and thus extends the support for the distinction made by Baron and Treiman. We have shown too that it is possible to identify the strategies used by individual children, with the help of the techniques used by Temple and Marshall and by Coltheart et al. We also found that there is a negative relationship between the two strategies even in quite a small group of children. The more a child uses one strategy the less likely he is to resort to the other. Of course all children will use a combination of both strategies but our discovery of a negative relationship suggests a considerable amount of specialisation in one strategy at the expense of the other.

This is a conclusion of some educational as well as theoretical significance. Different types of children might well benefit from different kinds of teaching. Presumably teachers should capitalise on the strategy which the child does use most strongly and at the same time try to encourage her to use and to see the value of other approaches to reading. This is a topic that needs to be studied.

If, in the end, the main effect of intensive studies of dyslexic children is to alert us to differences among normal children, we can only be happy that such studies have been done. But we must take care to place their results firmly within the framework of theories about the normal development of reading as Frith (1985) and Ellis (1984, 1985) have done, and of theories about individual differences among normal children as we have begun to do in this paper.

References

Baddeley, A.D., Ellis, N.C., Miles, T.R., & Lewis, V.J. (1982). Developmental and acquired dyslexia: A comparison. *Cognition, 11*, 185–199.

Baron, J. (1979). Orthographic and word specific mechanisms in children's reading of words. *Child Development, 50*, 60–72.

Baron, J., & Treiman, R. (1980). Some problems in the study of differences in cognitive processes. *Memory and Cognition, 8*, 313–321.

Boder, E. (1973). Developmental dyslexia: A diagnostic approach based on three atypical reading-spelling patterns. *Developmental Medicine and Child Neurology, 15*, 663–687.

Bradley, L., & Bryant, P.E. (1978). Difficulties in auditory organisation as a possible cause of reading backwardness. *Nature, 271*, 746–747.

Bryant, P.E., &Bradley, L. (1980). Why children sometimes write words which they cannot read. In U. Frith (Ed.), *Cognitive processes in spelling*. London: Academic Press.

Coltheart, M. (1982). The psycholinguistic analysis of acquired dyslexias: Some illustrations. In D.E. Broadbent & L. Weiskrantz (Eds.), *The neuropsychology of cognitive function.* London: The Royal Society.

Coltheart, M., Besner, D., Jonasson, J.T., & Davelaar, E. (1979). Phonological coding in the lexical decision task. *Quarterly Journal of Experimental Psychology, 31*, 489–508.

Coltheart, M., Masterson, J., Byng, S., Prior, M., & Riddoch, J. (1983). Surface dyslexia. *Quarterly Journal of Experimental Psychology, 35*, 469–495.

Ellis, A. (1984). *Reading, writing and dyslexia.* London: Erlbaum.

Ellis, A.W. (1985). The cognitive neuropsychology of developmental (and acquired) dyslexia: A critical survey. *Cognitive Neuropsychology, 2*, 169–205.

Frith, U. (1985). Beneath the surface of Surface Dyslexia. In K. Patterson, J.R. Marshall, & M. Coltheart (Eds.), *Surface dyslexia.* London: Erlbaum.

Frith, U., & Snowling, M. (1983). Reading for meaning and reading for sound in dyslexic and normal children. *British Journal of Developmental Psychology, 1*, 329–342.

Marshall, J.C. (1984). Towards a rational taxonomy of developmental dyslexia. In R.N. Malatesha & H.A. Whitaker (Eds.), *Dyslexia: A global issue.* The Hague: Nijhoff.

Mattis, S., French, J.H., & Rapin, I. (1975). Dyslexia in children and young adults; Three independent neuropsychological syndromes. *Developmental Medicine and Child Neurology, 17*, 150–163.

Mitterer J.O. (1982). There are at least two kinds of poor readers: Whole word poor readers and recoding poor readers. *Canadian Journal of Psychology, 36*, 445–461.

Nelson, H.E., & O'Connell A. (1978). Dementia: The estimation of premorbid intelligence levels using the new adult reading test. *Cortex, 14*, 234–244.

Seymour, P.H.K. (1986). Individual cognitive analysis of competent and impaired reading. Unpublished manuscript.

Seymour, P.H.K., & MacGregor, C.J. (1984). Developmental dyslexia: A cognitive experimental analysis of phonological, morphemic and visual impairments. *Cognitive Neuropsychology, 1*, 43–82.

Stanovich, K.E., & Bauer, D.W. (1978). Experiments on the spelling-to-sound regularity effect in word recognition. *Memory and Cognition, 6*, 410–415.

Temple, C. (1984). Unpublished D.Phil thesis, Oxford University.

Temple, C., & Marshall, J. (1983). A case study of developmental phonological dyslexia. *British Journal of Psychology, 74*, 517–533.

Treiman, R. (1984). Individual differences among children in reading and spelling styles. *Journal of Experimental Child Psychology, 37*, 463–477.

Résumé

Dernièrement, plusieurs personnes ont suggéré qu'il existait de fortes similitudes entre les symptomes de la dyslexie acquise et ceux de la dyslexie de développement. Cette suggestion est intéressant car elle nous offre une nouvelle manière d'envisager les différences entre enfants dyslexiques (problème toujours difficile) et aussi une explication possible des troubles que connaissent ces enfants. Cependant, les symptomes en question ne peuvent servir à une telle explication que s'ils sont véritablement distinctifs, c'est-à-dire si on ne les retrouve pas chez des enfants normaux du même niveau de lecture. Nous considérons deux tentatives de relier dyslexie acquise et dyslexie de développement, qui concernent chacune une adolescente qui lisait à peu près comme un enfant de dix ans. L'une de ces deux filles (Temple & Marshall, 1983) lisait comme un dyslexique phonologique typique; l'autre (Coltheart et al., 1983), comme un dyslexique de surface typique. Aucune de ces études ne comportait une comparaison avec des enfants normaux, et on ne peut donc pas être certain que la lecture des deux adolescentes était véritablement anormale. Nous avons fait passer les tests utilisés dans les deux études à 16 lecteurs normaux du niveau de dix ans, et nous avons constaté tous les symptomes décrits dans ces deux études chez des enfants normaux. Ces symptomes n'étaient pas anormaux et ne peuvent donc servir à expliquer les difficultés des deux adolescentes dyslexiques. Nous avons aussi constaté d'importantes différences individuelles systématiques dans le groupe normal, selon un continuum "phonologie-surface". Notre étude démontre donc deux choses. L'une est que les résultats rapportés par Temple et Marshall et Coltheart et al. ne constituent pas une explication des difficultés de lecture de ces adolescentes. L'autre est de fournir une nouvelle manière d'envisager les différences qualitatives entre lecteurs normaux.

7

Language mechanisms and reading disorder: A modular approach*

DONALD SHANKWEILER
STEPHEN CRAIN
University of Connecticut and Haskins
Laboratories

Abstract

In this paper we consider a complex of language-related problems that research has identified in children with reading disorder and we attempt to understand this complex in relation to proposals about the language processing mechanism. The perspective gained by considering reading problems from the standpoint of language structure and language acquisition allows us to pose specific hypotheses about the causes of reading disorder. The hypotheses are then examined from the standpoint of an analysis of the demands of the reading task and a consideration of the state of the unsuccessful reader in meeting these demands. The remainder of the paper pursues one proposal about the source of reading problems, in which the working memory system plays a central part. This proposal is evaluated in the light of empirical research which has attempted to tease apart structural knowledge and memory capacity both in normal children and in children with notable reading deficiencies.

1. Introduction

There is a growing consensus among researchers on reading that the deficiencies of most children who develop reading problems reflect limitations in the language area, not general cognitive limitations or limitations of visual per-

*Portions of this research were supported by NSF Grant BNS 84-18537, and by a Program Project Grant to Haskins Laboratories from the National Institute of Child Health and Human Development (HD-01994). We would like to thank Brian Byrne, Robert Crowder, Alvin Liberman, Virginia Mann, Ignatius Mattingly and three anonymous reviewers for their comments on earlier drafts. The order of the authors' names was decided by a coin toss. Reprint requests should be addressed to either author, Haskins Laboratories, 270 Crown Street, New Haven, CT 06510, U.S.A.

ception. In this paper we take this for granted.[1] Our concern is with analysis of the language deficiencies research has identified in poor readers, and with how these deficiencies affect the reading process. Our main goal is to determine whether or not the complex of deficits commonly found in poor readers forms some kind of unity. In order to proceed we will make use of two central ideas. One is the idea of modular organization and the other is the distinction between structure and process.

To begin, our conception of reading and its special problems grows out of a biological perspective on language and cognition in which language processes and abilities are taken to be distinct from other cognitive systems. On this perspective, which has long guided research on speech at Haskins Laboratories, the language apparatus forms a biologically-coherent system—in Fodor's terms, a module (1983)—which is distinguished from other parts of the cognitive apparatus by special brain structures and by other anatomical specializations. An extension of the modularity hypothesis supposes that the language faculty is itself composed of several autonomous subsystems, the phonology, lexicon, syntax and semantics. These systems, together with a processing system, working memory, constitute the relevant cognitive apparatus. When a person learns to read, this apparatus, which nature created for speech, must be adapted to the requirements of reading.

A modular view of the language mechanism raises the possibility that any number of components of the system might be the source of reading difficulties. At the same time, the fact that these components are related in a hierarchical fashion creates the possibility that a complex of symptoms of reading disorder may derive from a *single* affected component. Just such a proposal has been offered by M.-L. Kean (1977, 1980) in interpreting the symptom picture in Broca-type aphasia. Kean attributes the agrammatic features in the productions of these aphasics to an underlying deficit at the phonological level. Beyond that, the specific pattern of syntactic errors is predictable from the characteristics of the putative phonological deficit. It is not our intention to defend this particular application of the modularity principle or to assess its empirical adequacy. We mention it as an example of a strategy that can help us to understand the possible connections among the elements of the total symptom picture in poor readers. In later sections, we develop an explanation along similar lines: we interpret the apparent failures of poor readers in syntactic comprehension as manifestations of a low-level deficiency that masquerades as a set of problems extending throughout language. Our ac-

---

[1]Some of the evidence for this position is sketched in succeeding pages, but space does not allow us to make the complete case here. The interested reader should consult Gough and Hillinger (1980), Liberman (1983), Perfetti (1985) and Vellutino (1979).

count builds also on earlier empirical findings and interpretive discussion of researchers at Haskins Laboratories and on the work of Perfetti and his associates at Pittsburgh.[2]

The second idea that plays an important role in our analysis of reading problems is the distinction between structure and process. By a linguistic structure we mean a stored mental representation of rules and principles corresponding to a formally autonomous level of linguistic knowledge (see N. Chomsky, 1975). We assume that the language apparatus consists of several structures, hierarchically related, each supported by innately specified brain mechanisms. A processor, crudely put, is a device that brings linguistic input into contact with linguistic structures. The special purpose parsers, which access rules and resolve ambiguities that arise at each structural level of representation—phonologic, syntactic, semantic, lexical— are considered to be linguistic processors. The processor on which much of our discussion focuses is working memory (see Hamburger & Crain, 1984, for related discussion of language processing).

Since reading builds on earlier language acquisition, it is appropriate to begin discussion by considering why the link from the orthography to preexisting language structures and processes should be so difficult for many children to establish. Then we consider the state of the would-be reader who is unsuccessful in meeting the demands of the reading task. The remainder (and largest part) of the paper deals with analysis of poor reader's problems in language comprehension and considers how higher-level problems are related to their difficulties at the level of the word. We review studies that were specifically designed to tease apart deficits in structural knowledge from deficiencies in the working memory system that accesses and manipulates this knowledge. On the basis of the research findings, we reach the tentative conclusion that a major source of reading difficulties is in working memory processing and in the metalinguistic abilities required to interface the orthography with the existing language subsystems, not a deficit in basic language structures. Throughout this discussion, we emphasize the formative stages of reading, because it is here that the difficulties are most pronounced.

---

[2]References to the work of investigators at Haskins Laboratories and at Pittsburgh are made throughout the paper. We should also note similarities between the position we have developed on reading disorder and the conclusions of studies of children's cognitive development that indicate a dissociation of language-based skills and nonlinguistic abilities (see, for example, Keil, 1980; Kohn & Dennis, 1974; Netley & Rovet, 1983).

2. Reading acquisition: Demands of the task

At first cut, we can roughly identify two levels of processing in reading: (i) deciphering the individual words of the text from their orthographic representations and (ii) processing sentences and other higher-level units of the text. Corresponding to the two levels are two critical kinds of language abilities. The first have to do with forming strategies for identifying the printed word. These may very in kind with the specific demands posed by different languages and orthographies. Alphabetic orthographies place especially heavy demands on the beginning reader. To gain mastery, the reader must discover how to analyze the internal structure of the printed word and the internal structure of the spoken word, and must discover how the two sets of representations are related. For successful reading in an alphabetic system, the phonemic segmentation of words must become accessible to conscious manipulation, engaging a level of structure of which the *listener*, qua *listener*, need never be aware. Explicit conscious awareness of phonemic structure depends on metalinguistic abilities that do not come free with the acquisition of language (Bradley & Bryant, 1983; Liberman, Shankweiler, Fisher, & Carter, 1974; Mattingly, 1972; 1984; Morais, Cary, Alegria, & Bertelson, 1979). The speech processing routines give automatic rapid access to many lexical entries. During the course of learning to read, the orthographic representations of words also become capable of activating this lexical knowledge. But mastery of the orthographic route to the lexicon ordinarily requires a great deal of instruction and practice.

A second set of abilities relate to the syntactic and semantic components of the language apparatus. These abilities take the would-be reader beyond the individual words to get at the meanings of sentences and the larger structures of text. Since reading is compositional, there is an obvious need for some kind of memory in which to integrate spans of words with preceding and succeeding material. The need applies to all languages and orthographies (Liberman, Liberman, Mattingly, & Shankweiler, 1980). Although this is a requirement that reading shares with the perception of spoken sentences, we will argue that reading may make especially severe demands on working memory. Research reviewed in the next section makes it clear that beginning readers are often unable to meet these demands.

3. The state of the poor reader

This section draws upon research based on children who have encountered more than the average degree of difficulty in learning to read. Further, since not all of the possible causes of reading failure concern us here (for example, reading problems caused by sensory loss or severe retardation), we have generally required average IQ and a disparity (at least six months for a second-grade child) between the child's measured reading level and the expected level based on test norms. We do not assume that by such means we obtain a tightly homogeneous group. But use of an IQ cutoff and a disparity measure serves to distinguish the child with a relatively specific problem from the child who is generally backward in school subjects, including reading. The research to which we refer has observed these criteria in selecting the affected subjects. For convenience, we will call them simply "poor readers." Research of the past two decades has identified the following areas of performance in which poor readers characteristically fail or perform at a lower level than appropriately matched good readers.

1. Poor conscious access to sublexical segmentation and poorly developed metalinguistic abilities for manipulation of segments. Beginning readers and older people who have never learned to read do not readily penetrate the internal structure of the word to recover its phonemic structure. Research from several laboratories has shown that weakness or absence of phonemic segmentation ability is characteristic of poor readers and illiterates of all ages (for reviews, see Liberman & Shankweiler, 1985; Morais et al., 1979; Stanovich, 1982; Treiman & Baron, 1981).

2. Difficulties in naming objects. Poor readers frequently have difficulties finding the most appropriate names for objects in speaking (Denckla & Rudel, 1976; Wolf, 1981). They are less accurate than good readers and, under some conditions, also slower. By testing subjects' recognition of the object when the name is given, and by questioning them about the objects they misname, it has been discovered that when the poor reader misnames an object, the problem is less often a semantic confusion than a problem with the name itself. Thus the failure seems to involve the phonological level in some way (Katz, 1986).

3. Special limitations in phonetic perception. Although poor readers usually pass for normal in ordinary perception of spoken language, tests of phonetic perception under difficult listening conditions find them to be less accurate than good readers. For example, it has been found that poor readers were significantly worse than good readers at identifying speech stimuli degraded by noise (Brady, Shankweiler, & Mann, 1983). Since the investigation also found that the poor readers did as well as the good readers in perceiving environmental sounds masked by noise, it is unlikely that a general auditory defect can account for the findings with degraded speech.

4. Deficiencies in verbal working memory. Evidence from several laboratories indicates that children who are poor readers have limitations in verbal working memory that extend beyond the normal constraints (Liberman, Shankweiler, Liberman, Fowler, & Fischer, 1977; Mann & Liberman, 1984; Olson, Davidson, Kliegl, & Davies, 1984; Perfetti & Goldman, 1976; Vellutino, 1979). It should be emphasized that these deficiencies are to a large extent limited to the language domain. Other kinds of materials, such as nonsense designs and faces, can often be retained without deficit by poor readers (Katz, Shankweiler, & Liberman, 1981; Liberman, Mann, Shankweiler, & Werfelman, 1982).

Research of the past 20 years offers much evidence that the verbal working memory system exploits phonological structures. It has been shown many times, for example, that the recall performance of normal subjects is adversely affected by making all the items in each set rhyme with one another (Conrad, 1964, 1972; Baddeley, 1966). The strength of the rhyme effect is one indication of the importance of phonological codes for working memory. This prompted members of the reading group at Haskins Laboratories to study children who were good and poor readers on memory tasks while manipulating the phonetic similarity (i.e., confusability) of the stimulus materials (Liberman, Shankweiler, Liberman, Fowler, & Fischer, 1977; Mann, Liberman, & Shankweiler, 1980; Shankweiler, Liberman, Mark, Fowler, & Fischer, 1979). This research has had two major outcomes: first, regardless of whether the stimulus items were presented in printed form or in spoken form, poor readers are consistently worse than good readers in recall of nonconfusable (nonrhyming) items. Second, performance of good readers, like normal adults, is strongly and adversely affected by rhyme; poor readers, on the other hand, typically display only a small relative decrement on the rhyme condition of the recall test.

5. Difficulties in understanding spoken sentences. Failure to comprehend sentences in print that could readily be grasped in spoken form is diagnostic of specific reading disability. Recently, however, it has been found that, under some circumstances, poor readers are less able than good readers even to understand spoken sentences. Special tests employing complex structures are required to bring the difficulties to light (Byrne, 1981; Mann, Shankweiler, & Smith, 1984; Stein, Cairns, & Zurif, 1984; Vogel, 1975). Poor readers have been found to make errors on several syntactic constructions including relative clauses and sentences like *John is easy to please*, which were contrasted with sentences like *John is eager to please* (see Section 6).

Having briefly surveyed the performance characteristics of poor readers, we see that their problems are dispersed throughout language. However, it is important to appreciate that the five problem areas are not independent. Although not every one may be demonstrable in all poor readers, the deficits clearly tend to co-occur. There is much evidence, moreover, that difficulties at the level of the word are a common denominator; word recognition measures of reading account for a large portion of the variance in comprehension-related measures of reading (Perfetti & Hogaboam, 1975; Shankweiler & Liberman, 1972). Thus the problems at higher levels would appear to be associated with problems at lower levels.

Researchers at Haskins Laboratories have argued that underlying this diversity in symptoms may be a common problem at the level of the phonology. It is clear that problems (1)–(3) can be seen as manifestations of poor readers' failure to use phonologic structures properly. On the face of it, a different kind of explanation might seem to be required for problems in working memory (4) and in understanding complex spoken sentences (5). However, it has also long been supposed that the verbal working memory system, which is deficient in poor readers, is a faculty that is phonologically-grounded (Conrad, 1964; 1972). Moreover, it has been suggested, in keeping with this view, that poor readers' problems in sentence processing may reflect working memory limitations, and, by extension, phonological limitations (Liberman & Shankweiler, 1985; Mann et al., 1980, 1984).

In what follows we pursue the possibility that all the "symptoms" noted in the preceding section are reflections of a unitary underlying deficit. Our goal is to explain why poor readers sometimes fail to comprehend even spoken language as well as good readers, by asking to what extent problems at the sentence level may be related to problems at the level of the word. It should be emphasized that failure to comprehend a sentence correctly does not necessarily indicate an absence of critical syntactic structures. Understanding a sentence is a complex task in which both structures and processors are engaged. Examples of their interdependence can be found in recent research findings in language acquisition in which young children failed to comprehend complex sentences in some tests, yet were shown (under favorable test conditions) to have the necessary structures. Thus, errors which on the surface might appear to be syntactic have been found, on a closer analysis, to be a result of processing limitations. Later, we discuss some of this research and we show that the same problems of interpretation arise when we encounter failures of sentence understanding in older children who are poor readers.

4. Two hypotheses about the source of reading difficulties

In order to bring the research on poor readers into sharper focus, we distinguish what we take to be the major alternative positions concerning the relationships between language acquisition and reading. Broadly, two positions can be distinguished: one hypothesis proposes delays in the availability of critical structures; the alternative hypothesis emphasizes processing limitations. Since both are idealized positions, they are not intended to represent fully the views of any individual. We adopt this device because it allows us to draw out differences in the research literature that we believe are fundamental, but that often go unrecognized.

4.1 The structural lag hypothesis

In its most general form, the first hypothesis supposes that reading demands more linguistic competence than many beginning readers command. Although learning to speak and learning to read are continuous processes, some researchers have supposed that reading requires more complex linguistic structures than early speech development. On this view, at the age at which children begin to learn to read, some are still lacking part of the necessary structural knowledge. It is assumed that the inherent complexity of certain structures makes them unavailable until the would-be reader has had sufficient experience with sentences that contain these structures. Thus, this hypothesis about the sources of reading difficulty rests on two assumptions about language acquisition: (1) that linguistic materials are ordered in complexity, and (2) that language acquisition proceeds in a stepwise fashion, beginning with the simplest linguistic structures and culminating when the most complex structures have been mastered.

An advocate of this view might point to evidence of late maturation of the spoken-language competence of poor readers, including late-maturing structures which are required for interpreting complex sentences (see e.g., Byrne, 1981; Fletcher, Satz, & Scholes, 1981; Stein et al., 1984; Vogel, 1975). One might also propose that reading engages linguistic structures or rules that require special experience for their unfolding. The earliest developments in language acquisition require only immersion in a speaking environment; instruction is unnecessary, even irrelevant. In contrast, the later development of language, as well as the early stages of reading, may require more finely-tuned experience.

Since this hypothesis turns out to be more appropriate for some levels of linguistic knowledge than for others, we consider two variants, one at the level of syntax and the other at the level of phonology.

4.1.1. The syntactic lag hypothesis

We ask first what consequences a syntactic delay would have for beginning readers. Let us suppose, for example, that children who are at the age at which reading instruction normally begins have not yet mastered the syntactic rules needed for generating restrictive relative clauses (e.g., "who threw the game" in *The referee who threw the game* ...). It is clear that these children would be unable to learn to read sentences containing relative clauses. A deficiency at this level, then, would establish a ceiling on the abilities of poor readers to comprehend text. Further, the impact of a lag in syntactic knowledge would presumably show up in processing spoken sentences; it could hardly be limited to reading. However, a syntactic deficiency could not explain why poor readers have problems at *lower* levels of language processing, such as deficits in phonologic analysis and orthographic decoding.

It is apparent then that this hypothesis, by itself, cannot explain why some children have special problems learning to read. If poor readers do in fact have structural deficits at the syntactic level, their reading problems are in no way special. One possibility is that they are a manifestation of a general deficit that depresses all language functions. Another possibility is that poor readers have specific deficits at more than one level of language. In that event, the sentence processing problems of poor readers would simply be unrelated to their deficiencies in orthographic decoding. But if, on the contrary, both the lower-level (orthographic-phonologic) and the higher-level (sentence understanding) problems have a common source in poor readers, then the latter problems could be *derivative*.

In succeeding sections we make a case for a derivational view by appealing to experimental studies that assess factors influencing the understanding of complex syntactic structures by preschool children and by schoolage children who are good or poor readers. First, however, we must consider another variant of the structural lag hypothesis: the view that reading problems are derived from delay in the appearance of needed phonological structures.

4.1.2. The phonological lag hypothesis

The phonological lag hypothesis draws support from empirical correlations between measures of reading skill derived from reading isolated, unconnected words and those derived from reading text with comprehension. There is abundant evidence, as we noted, that word recognition measures account for a large portion of the variance in comprehension-related measures of reading. Since, in addition, there is also evidence pointing to a close link between phonological segmentation abilities and ability to decode words orthographically, the hypothesis that the root problem for many poor readers is a structural deficiency at the phonological level has much to recommend it. It provides a theoretically coherent and empirically testable framework for research and it is consistent with many empirical findings on successful and unsuccessful readers.

There are strong grounds, then, for supposing that orthographic decoding abilities and the phonological knowledge on which they rest are necessary for reading mastery. But are they sufficient? Are orthographic decoding skills the only new thing a would-be reader must acquire in order to read with understanding up to the limit set by spoken-language comprehension? To suppose so would assume that the other abilities needed for understanding printed text are already in place and have long been in use in understanding spoken language. But such an assumption would appear to ignore the other two components of the symptom picture in poor readers: deficiencies in temporary verbal memory and failures in understanding complex spoken sentences. Therefore, at this juncture, we take another direction, and examine the alternative hypothesis that all the problems of poor readers are reflections of a deficiency in processing, rather than a deficiency in linguistic knowledge.

4.2. The processing limitation hypothesis

The processing limitation hypothesis maintains that all the necessary linguistic structures are mastered before the child begins to learn to read, and therefore that the source of reading difficulty lies outside of the phonological and syntactic components of children's internal grammars. This hypothesis acknowledges that decoding skills, and the metaphonological analytic abilities that support them, are necessary for reading mastery in an alphabetic orthography (the individual who lacks them has no means of identifying words newly encountered in print). On this view, however, these are not the only necessary abilities. The processing limitation hypothesis asserts that an additional skill is required by the internal language apparatus in order to interface an alphabetic orthography with preexisting phonological and morphological representations: the efficient management of working memory. This is needed for sentence understanding, both in reading and in spoken language, to bring about integration of the component segments for assembly of higher-level linguistic structures of syntax and semantics.

On this hypothesis, learning to process language in the orthographic mode places extra burdens on working memory with the result that, until the reader is quite proficient, comprehension of text is more limited than comprehension of spoken sentences. It is assumed that speech processing is usually automatic in the beginning reader. One consequence of automaticity is that processing spoken sentences, including even many complex syntactic structures, is conserving of working memory resources. Reading, on the other hand, is extremely costly of these resources until the reader has sufficient mastery of orthographic decoding skills. Moreover, the existence of working memory impairment adds another dimension to the picture of the poor reader. Given sentences that pose unusual memory demands, a poor reader with this impairment can be expected to manifest language deficits that extend beyond reading, involving comprehension of spoken language. In Section 6 we discuss the possibility that the structures that have been found to be stumbling blocks for poor readers in previous research are in fact structures that tax working memory resources.

In contrast to the structural lag hypothesis, the processing limitation hypothesis can, in principle, account for all the basic facts about reading acquisition. Therefore, in the following sections we adopt this standpoint, and we draw out its implications.

5. The language processing mechanism

Since the processing limitation hypothesis assigns an essential role to linguistic memory, it will be useful to sketch our conception of temporary verbal memory. Then we turn to consider the language processing system, and the place of verbal memory in it.

5.1 Short-term memory versus working memory

First, we emphasize that we do not equate "short-term memory" and "working memory," although the former is partly subsumed by the latter. Verbal short-term memory is commonly seen as a passive storage bin for information, whereas working memory is seen as an active processing system, although it has a storage component. Short-term memory is commonly understood as a static system for accumulating and holding segments of speech (or orthographic segments) as they arrive during continuous listening to speech or during reading. This form of memory is verbatim, but highly transient. Presented items are retained in the order of arrival, but are quickly lost unless the material is maintained by continuous rehearsal. Material in short-term memory can also be saved if it can be restructured into some more compact representation (replacing the verbatim record). Put another way, the system is limited in capacity, but the limits are rendered somewhat elastic if opportunities exist for grouping its contents. Finally, it has long been recognized that a phonetic code is important for maintaining material in short-term memory.

In place of the storage bin conception, some workers (Baddeley, 1979; Baddeley & Hitch, 1974; Daneman & Carpenter, 1980; Perfetti & Lesgold, 1977) have argued for a more dynamic notion, endowing this form of memory with *processing* and not merely *storage* functions. This conception of working memory makes it an active part of the language processing system. Working memory is seen to play an indispensable role in comprehension both of spoken discourse and printed text (Liberman, Mattingly, & Turvey, 1972). On the simplest analysis, working memory has only two working parts, although it has access to several linguistic structures. One component is a storage buffer where rehearsal of phonetically coded material can take place. The buffer has the properties commonly attributed to short-term memory. Its phonological store can hold unorganized linguistic information only briefly, perhaps for only one or two seconds. Given this limitation, working memory cannot efficiently store unorganized strings of segments.

The second component of working memory plays an "executive" role (Baddeley & Hitch, 1974). This component has received comparatively little attention, so its exact functions are still opaque. Pursuing an analogy with the compiling of programming languages, we view it as a control mechanism which is capable of fitting together "statements" from the phonological, syntactic, and semantic parsers. As we conceive of it, the control structure integrates written or spoken units of processing with preceding and succeeding material. It facilitates the organization of the products of lower-level processing by relaying information that has undergone analysis at one level to the next-higher level. The first duty of the control mechanism is to transfer phonologically analyzed material out of the buffer and push it upwards through the higher level parsers, thus freeing the buffer for succeeding material. In reading, it is this transfer of information that is constrained by the level of orthographic decoding skill, according to the processing limitation hypothesis.[3]

5.2 Working memory and the language processing mechanism

The thesis of modular organization of the language system leads us to expect a specific memory component for linguistic material. The question of domain-specific systems of memory has been the subject of considerable research. A good case can be made for the existence of a memory system that is specialized for verbal material. It has been found, in this regard, that verbal retention is selectively impaired by damage to critical regions of the left dominant cerebral hemisphere; damage to corresponding portions of the right nondominant hemisphere results in selective impairments of nonverbal material, such as abstract designs and faces (Corsi, 1972; Milner, 1974). The finding of dissociated memory deficits fits neatly with evidence discussed above, that

---

[3]For an insightful general discussion relating computer architecture and models of cognitive processing, see Pylyshyn (1984). See Hamburger and Crain (1984) for detailed discussion of the role of "cognitive compiling" in children's language processing.

the memory limitation in poor readers is restricted to linguistic materials.

Although the neuropsychologic evidence clearly points to the existence of a specific verbal memory system, we must ask, nevertheless, whether this system is a part of the language module. On Fodor's (1983) view, the language module as a whole is an "input system": its operations are fast; they are mandatory; they are largely sealed off from conscious inspection; they are also insulated from cognitive inferencing mechanisms external to language. Working memory, as we understand it, does not conform to all of these criteria. Some of its operations consume appreciable time, and some are open to conscious inspection, as in the rehearsal and reanalysis of linguistic material. Nevertheless, it seems to us that working memory belongs in the language module by reason of its intimate association with the parsers which assign phonological, syntactic, and semantic structure to linguistic input. In so far as the working memory system is understood to be a part of the language module, albeit as an "output system," we are forced to differ with Fodor's characterization of the language processing mechanism. For purposes of further discussion, though, we will assume that working memory is part of the language module.

In addition to its storage and rehearsal functions, working memory, as we have characterized it, controls the unidirectional flow of linguistic information through the series of parsers from lower levels to higher levels in the system. Each parser is taken to be a processor which accesses rules and principles corresponding to its level of representation. Each is, roughly, a function from input of the appropriate type to structural descriptions at the given level of representation. We maintain that each of the parsers meets Fodor's criteria for an "input system." Before leaving these architectural matters, we would append a disclaimer: we do not assume that higher-level processors beyond semantic parsing are accessed by the working memory system. Reasoning, planning actions, inference and metalinguistic operations are not taken to be parts of the language module, though they operate on its contents. We emphasize, therefore, that we are using the term "semantics" in a highly restricted sense, to describe the rule system which determines coreference between linguistic constituents, and "filler-gap" dependencies (see Section 6). Crucially, the term is not being used here to refer to real-world knowledge or beliefs.

5.3 Working memory in spoken-language understanding and reading

It is pertinent to consider how the components of the language module may interact. (We consider spoken language first, and address remarks specific to reading at the end of the section.) It seems reasonable to suppose that both the operations of the fixed-resource parsing mechanisms as well as the operations of the control mechanism of working memory are subject to the constraints of the limited buffer space. Limited space means that the parsers have a narrow window of input data available to them at any one time. On the one hand, understanding sentences clearly requires working memory, because syntactic and semantic structures are composed over sequences of several words. On the other hand, the assignment even of complex higher-level structures is ordinarily conserving of this limited resource; parsing does not ordinarily impose severe demands on memory in understanding speech. The combinatorial properties of the parsing systems are evidently so rapid that they minimize the role of memory in speech understanding.

Under some circumstances, however, working memory constraints apparently do produce problems in syntactic processing, especially in reading. Memory limitations may impair syntactic processing in two ways, corresponding to the two components of the working memory system. Here we build on the insight of Perfetti and Lesgold (1977), who proposed that if the limitations on the working memory are exceeded, for whatever reason, in the service of low-level processing, higher-level processing may be curtailed. This would apply, first, to poor readers who have inherent limitations in buffer capacity (Mann et al., 1980). They would have insufficient capacity to allow higher-level processing to occur uninhibited, although it may not be brought to a complete halt. We should caution, however, that variation among individuals in buffer capacity is not the most important factor in reading, because, in general, tests of rote recall account for only 10–25% of the total variance in the measures of reading (Daneman & Carpenter, 1980; Mann et al., 1984). It was this fact that led us to consider the other component of working memory.

A second way that working memory dysfunction can inhibit syntactic processing is by poor control of the flow of information through the system of parsers. The control structure must efficiently regulate the flow of linguistic material from lower- to higher-levels of representation in keeping with the inherent limitation in the buffer space. From the dual structure of working memory, it may be inferred, as Daneman and Carpenter (1980) and Perfetti and Lesgold (1977) have noted, that studies of retention and rote recall of unorganized materials may provide an incomplete and possibly misleading picture of the active processing capabilities of working memory. In relying exclusively on these measures as indices of working memory capacity, researchers may have overlooked a possibly more important source of variation among readers: in our terms this is the problem of regulating the flow of information between the phonological buffer and the higher-level parsers.

Whichever component of the system is most responsible for the functional limitation on working memory, it should be noted that only those sentence processing tasks that impose unusually severe memory demands are expected to offer significant problems for poor readers in spoken language comprehension. On syntactic tasks that are less taxing of this resource, we would expect them to perform as well as good readers. (This prediction is born out in two studies reviewed in the next section.)

It remains to compare the involvement of working memory in spoken language and in reading. Since reading and speech tap so many of the same linguistic abilities, it is easy to overlook the possibility that reading may pose more difficulties than speech for some of the language apparatus. In reading, the chores of working memory include the on-line regulation of syntactic and semantic analyses, after orthographic decoding and phonologic compiling have begun. Until the reader is proficient in decoding printed words, we contend that reading is more taxing of working memory resources than speech. We are aware, however, of a contrary claim: it is sometimes argued that the permanence of print, in contrast to the transience of speech, should have exactly the opposite effect, with the result that, other things equal, the demands on working memory in processing print should be *less*. The advantage of print would obtain because the reader can look back, whereas the listener who needs to reanalyze is forced to rely on the fast-decaying memory trace.

In evaluating this argument, we maintain that other things are *not* equal, and in the case of the beginning reader and the unskilled reader, the inequality favors speech over reading. In either case, what must be considered is the effect of rate of information flow through the short-term memory buffer. If the rate is too fast, as by rapid presentation in the laboratory, information will be lost; if it is too slow, integration will be impaired. An optimal rate of transmission of linguistic information is achieved so often in speech communications because the language mechanisms for producing and receiving speech are biologically matched (Liberman, Cooper, Shankweiler, & Studdert-Kennedy, 1967; Liberman & Mattingly, 1985). As a consequence, speech processing up to the level of meaning is extremely fast (Marslen-Wilson & Tyler, 1980). Perhaps it must be, given the constraints on the memory buffer.

Reading, on the other hand, is fast only in the skilled reader. It is reasonable to suppose, then, that only the skilled reader can take advantage of the opportunity afforded by print, to reanalyze or to verify the initial analysis of a word string. The unskilled reader cannot make efficient use of working memory because of difficulties in orthographic decoding. But until the reader is practiced enough to become proficient, there is no advantage in being able to look back. For these reasons, we would make the prediction that unskilled readers will be less able than good readers to recover from structural ambiguities that induce a wrong analysis (this so-called "garden path" effect is discussed further in the next section). This would hardly be surprising in reading tasks, but since the normal limitations on verbal working memory are magnified in many poor readers, we would expect them to be less able to recover from wrong syntactic analyses even in spoken language.

6. The role of working memory in failures of sentence comprehension

As sketched above, the structural lag hypothesis supposes that linguistic structures are acquired in order of complexity, so that late emergence of a structure reflects its greater inherent complexity. Poor readers, on this view, are language delayed, and would be expected to make significant errors on tasks which involve comprehension of sentences that have complex syntactic structure. However, as we have emphasized, failure on a comprehension task does not necessarily indicate a lack of the correct structure for the sentences that are misunderstood; inefficient or abnormally limited working memory can also interfere with understanding on some sentence comprehension tasks, as claimed by the processing limitation hypothesis.

In order to pursue the causes of poor readers' failures in comprehension, we first discuss experimental tasks which have been devised to test the contrasting predictions of these hypotheses as they have been applied in the investigation of the linguistic abilities of young children. Following this, two studies are presented in which the spoken language abilities of both good and poor readers were compared, and alternative interpretations of the findings are considered.

6.1 Assessing linguistic competence in young children

We sketch two experiments which were specifically devised to disentangle structural factors and working memory in the sentence comprehension of normal children. In each case we find that the children's comprehension improves dramatically when the processing demands on memory are reduced.

The first experiment makes use of the contrast between two structural phenomena, coordination and subordination. It is widely held that structures which involve subordination are more complex than ones involving coordination. Researchers in language acquisition have appealed to this difference to explain why children typically make more errors in understanding sentences bearing relative clauses (as in 1) than sentences containing conjoined clauses (as in 2), when comprehension is assessed by a figure manipulation ("do-what-I-say") task.

(1) The dog pushed the sheep that jumped over the fence.
(2) The dog pushed the sheep and jumped over the fence.

The usual finding, that (1) is more difficult for children than (2), has been interpreted as revealing the relatively late emergence of the rules for subordinate syntax in language development (e.g., Tavakolian, 1981).

However, it was shown by Hamburger and Crain (1982) that the source of children's performance errors on this task was *not* a lack of knowledge of the syntactic rules underlying relative clauses. By constructing appropriate pragmatic contexts, they were able to reliably elicit utterances containing relative clauses from children as young as three. In addition, when the pragmatic "felicity conditions" on the use of restrictive relative clauses were satisfied, they found very few residual errors even in the "do-what-I-say" comprehension task. These findings suggest that nonsyntactic demands of this task had been masking children's competence with this construction in previous studies.

One of the nonsyntactic impediments to successful performance involves working memory (for others, see Hamburger & Crain, 1982, 1984). To clarify this, we would note that even children's *correct* responses to sentences containing relative clauses can be seen to display the effects of working memory. In the Hamburger and Crain (1982) study, it was observed that many children who performed the *correct* actions associated with sentences like (1) often failed, nevertheless, to act out these events in the same way as adults. Most 3-year-olds and many 4-year-olds would act out this sentence by making the dog push the sheep first, and then making the sheep jump over the fence. Older children and adults act out these events in the opposite order, the relative clause *before* the main clause. Intuitively, acting out the second mentioned clause first seems conceptually more correct since "the sheep that jumped over the fence" is what the dog pushed. It is reasonable to suppose that this kind of conflict between the order of mention and conceptual order stresses working memory because both clauses must be available long enough to plan the response which represents the conceptual order. We propose that the differing responses of children and adults reflect the more severe limitations in children's working memory. Young children are presumably unable to compile the plan and so must interpret and act out the clauses in the order of mention (see Hamburger & Crain, 1984, for more detailed discussion of plans and planning).

Studies of temporal adverbial clauses have also yielded data which support the twofold claim that processing factors mask children's knowledge of complex structures and that working memory is specifically implicated. Temporal terms like *before*, *after* and *while* dictate the conceptual order of events, and they too may present conflicts between conceptual-order and order-of-mention, as (3) illustrates.

(3)   Luke flew the plane after Han flew the helicopter.

In this example, the order in which events are mentioned is opposite the order in which they took place. Several researchers have found that 5-year-olds frequently act out sentences like (3) in an order-of-mention fashion (Clark, 1970; Johnson, 1975). As with relative clause sentences, it is likely that this response reflects an inability to hold both clauses in memory long enough to formulate a plan for acting them out in the correct conceptual order.

There is direct evidence that processing demands created by the requirements of plan formation, and not lack of syntactic or semantic competence, were responsible for children's errors in comprehending sentences bearing temporal terms. The evidence is this: once the demands on working memory were reduced, by satisfying the presuppositions associated with this construction, most 4- and 5-year-old children usually give the correct response to sentences like (4).

(4)   Push the plane to me after you push the helicopter.

To satisfy the presupposition, Crain (1982) had children formulate part of the plan associated with sentences such as (4) *in advance*, by having them select one of the toys to play with before each trial. For the child who had indicated the intent to push the helicopter on the next trial, (4) could be used. Given this contextual support, children displayed unprecedented success in comprehending the temporal terms *before* and *after*.

This brief review shows how the apparent late emergence of a linguistic structure can result from the failure of verbal working memory to function efficiently. The methodological innovations which resulted in these demonstrations of early mastery of complex syntax have been extended to other constructions, including Wh-movement, pronouns and prenominal adjectives (Crain & Fodor, 1984; Crain & McKee, 1985; Hamburger & Crain, 1984). Although the possibility must be left open that some linguistic structures are problematic for children reaching the age at which reading instruction normally begins, this line of research emphasizes how much syntax has already been mastered by these children. The findings make it clear that the evidence cited above (Section 3) that poor readers have difficulty comprehending complex syntactic constructions is compatible with the processing limitation hypothesis. The proper interpretation of such findings is complicated by the existence of confounding factors. Unfortunately, the techniques discussed above have rarely been applied in reading research. But fortunately, other methods of teasing apart structural and processing factors have been applied, as we now show.

6.2 Assessing spoken language comprehension of good and poor readers

In Section 3, we noted evidence that poor readers have problems in comprehending some kinds of sentences, not only when these are presented to them in printed form, as would be expected, but also when the sentences are processed by ear. We have seen, however, that these findings would receive a different interpretation on each of the two hypotheses advanced in Section 4. The question can be put to the test by comparing the success of good and poor readers on structurally complex sentences. We can infer a processing limitation, and rule out a structural deficit, whenever the following four conditions are met: (i) there is a decrement in correct responses by poor readers but, (ii) they reveal a similar pattern of errors as good readers, (iii) they manifest a high rate of correct responses on some subset of sentences exhibiting the structure in question, and (iv) they show appreciable improvement in performance on problem cases in contexts that lessen the processing demands imposed on working memory.

It is germaine to consider two recent studies which have addressed the question of whether poor readers have a structural or a processing limitation, one by Mann et al. (1984), and the other by Fowler (1985). The study by Mann and her associates asked first whether good and poor readers in the third grade could be distinguished on a speech comprehension task involving sentences with relative clauses. Having found an affirmative answer, these researchers went on to ask whether malformation or absence of syntactic structures accounted for the differences in performance between the good and poor readers.

In the experiment on temporal terms discussed in the previous section, syntax was held constant and aspects of the task were manipulated in order to vary processing load. The experiment of Mann et al. adopted another approach, holding sentence length constant while varying the syntactic structure. Four types of sentences with relative clauses were presented, using a figure manipulation task. As (5) illustrates, each set of sentences contained exactly the same ten words, to control for vocabulary and sentence length.

(5) (a) The sheep pushed the cat that jumped over the cow.
     (b) The sheep that pushed the cat jumped over the cow.
     (c) The sheep pushed the cat that the cow jumped over.
     (d) The sheep that the cat pushed jumped over the cow.

It was found that the type of relative clause structure had a large effect on comprehensibility. Sentences of type (a) and (d) evoked the most errors. These are structures that earlier research on younger children also identified as the most difficult (Tavakolian, 1981).

Good and poor readers did not fare equally well, however. The study confirmed the earlier claims that poor readers can have considerable difficulties in understanding complex sentences even when these are presented in spoken form. But, given our criteria for distinguishing structural deficits from processing limitations, the findings of this study invite the inference that poor readers' problems with these sentences reflect a deficit in processing. First of all, the poor readers were worse than the good readers in comprehension of each of the four types of relative clause structure that were tested. But the poor readers did not appear to lack any type of relative clause structure entirely. In fact, their pattern of errors closely mirrored that of the good readers; they simply did less well on each sentence type. Thus, there was no statistical interaction of group by sentence type. Another reason to think that the source of the poor readers' difficulties is attributable to working memory is that they were also inferior to the good readers in immediate recall of these sentences and on other tests of short-term recall.

A further attempt to disentangle structural knowledge and processing capabilities in beginning readers was carried out by Fowler (1985). Two new experimental tasks were administered to second graders: a grammaticality judgement task, and a sentence correction task (in addition to other tests previously used at Haskins Laboratories to assess short-term recall and metaphonological abilities). The grammaticality judgement task was used to establish a baseline on the structural knowledge of the subjects, for comparison with the correction task. This expectation is motivated, in part, by recent research on aphasia showing that agrammatic aphasic patients with severe memory limitations were able to judge the grammaticality of sentences of considerable length and syntactic complexity (Crain, Shankweiler, & Tuller, 1984; Linebarger, Schwartz, & Saffran, 1984; Saffran, 1985). The findings on aphasics suggest that this task taps directly the syntactic analysis that is assigned. The correction task, on the other hand, is expected to stress working memory to a greater extent, because the sentence has to be retained long enough for reanalysis and revision.

As predicted, reading ability was significantly correlated with success on the correction task, but not with success on the judgement task. This is further support for the view that processing complexity, and not structural complexity, is a better diagnostic of reading disability. Two additional findings bear on the competing hypotheses about the causes of reading failure. First, the level of achievement on grammaticality judgements was well above chance for both good and poor readers, even on complex syntactic structures (e.g., Wh-movement and Tag questions). Second, results on the test of short-term recall (with IQ partialed out) were more strongly correlated with success on the sentence correction task than with success on the judgement task.

The poor readers in both of the foregoing studies appear to have the syntactic competence to compute complex structures (see also Shankweiler, Smith, & Mann, 1984; Smith, Mann, & Shankweiler, in press). We infer, however, from the studies of preschool children reviewed earlier, that some children may display comprehension of certain structures only when contextual supports are available, or where memory demands are minimized. Thus, when reading is put in the perspective of recent data on language acquisition, it is apparent that an explanation that appeals to processing limitations can account for the data. There is no need to impute to the poor reader, in addition, gaps in structural knowledge.

6.3 Other points of view

The contention that a deficit in working memory is responsible for errors in sentence understanding by poor readers has not gone unchallenged. Here we take up two challenges. First, it has been argued by Byrne (1981) that some differences in comprehension between good and poor readers cannot be attributed to verbal working memory. Comprehension data is presented from an object manipulation study in which good and poor readers responded to sentences containing adjectives like *easy* and *eager*. An appeal is then made to earlier findings by C. Chomsky (1969) that children master the syntactic properties of adjectives like *easy* later than those like *eager*.

Byrne's poor readers performed less accurately than age-matched good readers on sentences like (6) than sentences like (7). He argues that failures on sentences containing *easy* reflect the inherent syntactic complexity of this adjective, not its contributions to processing difficulty.

(6) John is easy to please.
(7) John is eager to please.

An explanation invoking the verbal memory system could not explain the difference between *easy* and *eager*, according to Byrne, because the two forms "load phonetic memory equally (having identical surface forms)" and, being short, impose relatively modest demands on memory (p. 203).

Results such as these can be accommodated within the processing limitation perspective, by attributing them to limitations in working memory function. As pointed out by Mann et al. (1980), short-term memory demands are not just a matter of sentence length or surface form. Despite their simple surface form and brevity, the inherent structural complexity of sentences with adjectives like *easy* may require additional computation and so may intensify the demands on working memory, as compared to sentences with adjectives like *eager*. The schematic diagrams below can be used to motivate an explanation invoking working memory to account for the greater difficulty poor readers have in acting out sentences with *easy*.

(8)   The bear is easy (__ to reach __).
(9)   The bear is eager (__ to jump).

As the diagram in (8) illustrates, the transitive verb *reach* has a superficially empty direct object position. In the terms of transformational grammar, the direct object has been "moved". In contrast, the subject position of the infinitival complement that bears the intransitive verb *jump* is empty in diagram (9), in this case by deletion. Comparing the two diagrams, it is apparent that the distance between the "gap" in the infinitival complement and the lexical NP that is interpreted as its "filler" is greater in (8) than in (9). Another relevant difference is that although both infinitival complements have missing subjects, the referent for the gap in subject position in (8) cannot be found anywhere in the sentence; it must be mentally filled by the listener.

It is widely assumed that holding onto a "filler" (or retrieving one for semantic interpretation) is a process that stresses working memory (see e.g., Wanner & Maratsos, 1978). This would explain why constructions with object gaps are more difficult to process than subject-gap constructions for normal children and adults. It would also explain why other populations with deficits in short-term memory are especially sensitive to this difference (Grodzinsky, 1984, for example, found the asymmetry with Broca-type aphasics). Given these considerations, poor readers also would be expected to perform with less success than good readers in response to structures like (8) even if they have attained an equivalent level of linguistic competence. In order to establish the level of competence of selected poor readers, we are currently investigating several constructions using tasks that minimize demands on working memory. The pursuit of optimal conditions for assessing linguistic competence was discussed in Section 7.1. The same methodological prescription has been followed in other areas of cognitive development, with considerable success (for a review, see Gelman, 1978).

The importance of working memory for sentence understanding has been challenged from another standpoint by Crowder (1982). This criticism is based on evidence that the syntactic parsing mechanism is fast. It is argued that claims for the centrality of working memory in language processing are weakened by evidence that the parsing mechanism extracts higher level structure "on line" (Frazier & Fodor, 1978; Frazier & Rayner, 1982). If there is little or no delay in attachment of successive lexical items into the structural analysis being computed, then there is no need, this argument goes, for the memory buffer to store more than a few items at a time.

Findings that indicate that higher-level processing is accomplished within very short stretches of text or discourse do not, in our view, undercut the position that sentence processing imposes burdens of major proportions on short-term memory. On the contrary, high-speed parsing mechanisms are exactly what one would expect to find in a system that has severely limited memory processing capacity. High-speed parsing routines may have evolved precisely to circumvent the intrinsic limitations.

Sentence parsing strategies, on one prominent view (Frazier & Fodor, 1978) are not *learned* maneuvers. Instead, they reflect the architecture of the language processor, which has several functions to perform and limited time and space for their compilation and execution. One parsing strategy that may have evolved to meet these exigencies encourages listeners or readers to connect incoming material with preceding material as locally as possible (the strategy called "right association" by Kimball, 1973, and "late closure" by Frazier, 1978). For example, the adverb *yesterday* is interpreted as related to the last mentioned event in (8); though at first reading this strategy may cause a momentary misanalysis, as in (9).

(8) Sam said he got his pay, yesterday.
(9) Sam said he will get paid, yesterday.

Although parsing strategies may enable the parser to function more efficiently in many cases, the existence of "garden path" sentences like (9) shows that these strategies are not powerful enough to overcome the liability of a tightly constrained working memory. Garden path phenomena make it clear that the need for working memory is not totally obviated by on-line sentence processing. Again, we should emphasize that some sentences will tax working memory heavily in certain experimental tasks, and those will be problem sentences for poor readers. It is worth noting, also, that there is evidence that children are even more dependent on these strategies than adults, presumably because children's working memories are more severely limited (see Crain & Fodor, 1984). As we have seen already, a clear prediction of the processing limitation hypothesis is that poor readers will be less able to recover from garden path sentences than good readers, even in spoken language tasks.

7. The hypotheses reconsidered

In the last section, we attempted to identify the reasons poor readers fail to comprehend complex sentences as well as good readers. In this final section, we return to the hypotheses raised at the outset, and to the question of a unitary underlying deficit that generates the symptom picture of the poor reader (as sketched in Section 3).

The fact that poor readers sometimes have difficulties in understanding spoken sentences raised the possibility that they have a structural deficit at the syntactic level (as the syntactic lag hypothesis claims). The existence of a deficit at this level would jeopardize a unified theory, because if poor readers' problems in sentence understanding are at least in part attributable to missing syntactic structures, then at least two basic deficits must be invoked to account for the total symptom picture. But, as we noted, comprehension difficulties could have another explanation: the problems could be caused by a limitation of a processor, namely, working memory, which is necessary for gaining access to syntactic structures and for their successful manipulation. In reviewing the evidence, we argued that the empirical data, such as they are, can better be accounted for by supposing that the syntactic structures are in place. Poor readers' failures in comprehension are only *apparently* syntactic: they occur on just those sentences that stress working memory.

An argument against a lag in the development of phonological structures is more difficult to make. We have pointed to the evidence that poor readers lack the necessary metaphonologic skills needed for partitioning words into their phonologic segments and mentally manipulating these segments. These deficits and others in the phonologic domain to which we have referred (e.g., Brady et al., 1983; Katz, 1986) could reflect delay in the establishment of some aspects of phonologic structure.[4] However, in the absence of any decisive evidence, we would seek to explain them as instead reflecting limitations on *use* of phonologic structures. Thus, whereas we believe the empirical evidence is sufficient to locate the problem underlying the syndrome of the poor reader at the phonological level, there is no need to suppose that any structures are missing. We recognize that the arguments against a structural deficit in poor readers cannot be conclusive without considerably more data. In the absence of such data we must leave the question open. However, the processing limitation hypothesis has an advantage: by invoking the concept of working memory it can tie together the diverse strands in the symptom complex of the poor reader.

Two properties of the working memory system play an essential role in explaining the language-related problems of poor readers: (i) limitations in either component of the working memory system supporting the analysis of

---

[4]Although it is easy in principle to draw a distinction between a deficiency in setting up phonological representations and an inefficiency in processing the representations, in practice the distinction is difficult to maintain. Recent work by investigators at Haskins Laboratories clearly points to poor readers' phonological deficiencies in identifying spoken words in degraded contexts (Brady et al., 1983) and in object naming and in judging metalinguistic properties of the retrieved names (Katz, 1986). However, neither study resolves the issue of defective representation versus defective processing.

input both in speech and reading, and (ii) the dependence of higher-level (syntactic and semantic) processing on preceding lower-level (orthographic and phonological) analysis of the contents of the buffer. From this combination of properties the possibility arises that unless the resources of working memory are managed efficiently in pursuing the phonological analysis of letter strings, higher-level analysis will be hobbled or inhibited altogether. The poor reader (and indeed any beginning reader) will fail to understand sentences in print that could easily be understood in spoken language. But, in addition, we know that poor readers often have special working memory limitations over and above the normal limitations. Therefore they have a double handicap: poor decoding abilities and unusually constrained immediate memory. The handicap would be expected to show up even in processing spoken language when sentences are costly of memory resources.

It is worth pointing out similarities between our hypothesis about the constraining factors in comprehension and the ideas of Perfetti and his associates. Perfetti and Lesgold (1977) advanced the idea nearly 10 years ago that slow decoding interferes with integration and inhibits reading comprehension in poor readers. The combined result of poor decoding skills and working memory limitations creates a "bottleneck." Like us, these researchers see inefficient low-level processing as a limiting factor in poor readers' reading comprehension, and they maintain, as we do, that poor readers' problems in comprehension are not confined to reading (see Perfetti, 1985 for a comprehensive summary). Perfetti and Lesgold even suggest that there may be a single deficit underlying the bottleneck, but they stop short of identifying the deficit. We have pursued the possibility that a unified explanation can be given of the problems that give rise to the bottleneck. Researchers at Haskins Laboratories have sought an explicit connection between working memory problems and orthographic decoding problems. The bridge currently being investigated is that both orthographic decoding and working memory access phonological structures (Liberman & Shankweiler, 1985; but see also, Alegria, Pignot, & Morais, 1982).

There is, in fact, much evidence that what we are calling verbal working memory (one component of which is verbal short-term memory, as traditionally conceived) uses a phonologic output code. Earlier, we noted the empirical basis for this belief: (1) in recalling linguistic material, verbatim retention of the phonologic units of the input is possible within narrow constraints of quantity and time, (2) interference with rehearsal causes errors in recall, (3) the error rate is increased when the items are phonetically similar (as when they rhyme with one another). The buffer component of working memory is surely phonologic in the sense that it incorporates these characteristics. The finding that poor readers show reduced confusability effects in comparison to good readers is evidence that a phonological deficiency may underlie their extra limitations in buffer storage capacity.

Poor readers' working memory problems have not heretofore been related explicitly to the other component of working memory, the control component. The primary job of the control mechanism as it relates to reading is to transfer the contents of the buffer from the phonological level to higher levels. Because we assume that reading is a bottom-up process, a disruption in flow of phonologic information to the other parsers would inevitably result in impaired reading performance. Of course it is possible that other control properties of this mechanism are also deficient. Such deficiencies would set a ceiling on reading, but would not give rise specifically to reading difficulties.

The problem of learning to read is largely to adapt the control component to accept orthographic input and to assign a phonologic analysis. As we have seen, the phonologic analysis of the speech signal is executed entirely within the speech module, whereas phonologic analysis of orthographic input demands the construction of algorithms for relating orthographic structure to phonologic structure. To construct this interface is an intellectual task, which requires overt attention and metalinguistic knowledge that doesn't come free with language acquisition. Until an entire set of analytic metaphonologic strategies are practiced enough to become largely automatic, higher-level processing will be curtailed because working memory is overloaded.

The idea of a computational bottleneck enables us to understand how constriction of the working memory system in handling phonologic information can inhibit higher-level processing of text. Clarification of the peculiar demands of orthographic decoding, together with the properties of working memory, enables us to explain why the poor reader is far less able to understand complex sentences in print than in speech, and it explains difficulties with spoken language that would otherwise appear mysterious. It is our conclusion, then, that deficits which implicate lower-level (phonological) components in the structural hierarchy have repercussions on higher levels. The hypothesis that language-related problems at different levels arise from a common source is the foremost reason, in our view, for adhering to the processing limitation hypothesis. It represents the strongest empirical hypothesis. The explanatory strength and further empirical consequences of this hypothesis are discussed in Crain and Shankweiler (in press).

References

Alegria, J., Pignot, E., & Morais, J. (1982). Phonetic analysis of speech and memory codes in beginning readers. *Memory and Cognition, 10*, 451–456.

Baddeley, A.D. (1966). Short-term memory for word sequences as a function of acoustic and formal similarity. *Quarterly Journal of Experimental Psychology, 18*, 362–365.

Baddeley, A.D. (1979). Working memory and reading. In P.A. Kolers, M.E. Wrolstad, & H. Bouma (Eds.), *The proceedings of the conference on the processing of visible language* (Vol. 1). New York: Plenum.

Baddeley, A.D., & Hitch, G.B. (1974). Working memory. In G.H. Bower (Ed.), *The psychology of learning and activation* (Vol. 4). New York: Academic Press.

Bradley, L., & Bryant, P.E. (1983). Categorizing sounds and learning to read—a causal connection. *Nature, 301*, 419–421.

Brady, S., Shankweiler, D., & Mann, V.A. (1983). Speech perception and memory coding in relation to reading ability. *Journal of Experimental Child Psychology, 35*, 345–367.

Byrne, B. (1981). Deficient syntactic control in poor readers: Is a weak phonetic memory code responsible? *Applied Psycholinguistics 2*: 201–212.

Chomsky, C. (1969). *The acquisition of syntax in children from 5 to 10*. Cambridge, MA: MIT Press.

Chomsky, N. (1975). *Reflections on language*. New York: Pantheon Books.

Clark, E.V. (1970). How young children describe events in time. In G.B. Flores d'Areais & W.J.M. Levelt (Eds.), *Advances in psycholinguistics*. Amsterdam: North-Holland.

Conrad, R. (1964). Acoustic confusions in immediate memory. *British Journal of Psychology, 3*, 75–84.

Conrad, R. (1972). Speech and reading. In J. Kavanagh and I. Mattingly (Eds.), *Language by ear and by eye: The relationships between speech and reading*. Cambridge, MA: MIT Press.

Corsi, P.M. (1972). *Human memory and the medial temporal region of the brain*. Unpublished Ph.D. thesis, McGill University, Montreal.

Crain, S. (1982). Temporal terms: Mastery by age five. In *Papers and Reports on Child Language Development Vol. 21*. Stanford University.

Crain, S., & Fodor, J. (1984). On the innateness of subjacency. In the proceedings of the *Eastern States Conference on Linguistics, 1*. Columbus, Ohio: Ohio State University.

Crain, S., & McKee, C. (1985). Acquisition of structural constraints on anaphora. In the proceedings of the *North Eastern Linguistics Society, 16*, University of Massachusetts, Amherst, MA.

Crain, S., & Shankweiler, D. (in press). Reading acquisition and language acquisition. In A. Davison, G. Green, & G. Herman (Eds.), *Critical approaches to readability: Theoretical bases of linguistic complexity*. Hillsdale, NJ: Erlbaum.

Crain, S., Shankweiler, D., & Tuller B. (1984). Preservation of sensitivity to closed-class items in agrammatism. Los Angeles, CA: Academy of Aphasia.

Crowder, R.G. (1982). *The psychology of reading*. New York: Oxford University Press.

Daneman, M., & Carpenter, P.A. (1980). Individual differences in working memory and reading. *Journal of Verbal Learning and Verbal Behavior, 19*, 450–466.

Denckla, M.B., & Rudel, R.G. (1976). Naming of object-drawings by dyslexic and other learning disabled children. *Brain and Language, 3*, 1–15.

Fletcher, J.M., Satz, P., & Scholes, R. (1981). Developmental changes in the linguistic performance correlates of reading achievement. *Brain and Language, 13*: 78–90.

Fodor, J.A. (1983). *The modularity of mind*. Cambridge, MA: MIT Press.

Fowler, A. (1985). Do poor readers have a basic syntactic deficit: Evidence from a grammaticality judgment task in second graders. Paper presented at New England Psychological Association, New Haven, CT.

Frazier, L. (1978). *On comprehending sentences: syntactic parsing strategies*. Unpublished Ph.D. dissertation, University of Connecticut.

Frazier, L., & Fodor, J.D. (1978). The sausage machine: A two-stage parsing model. *Cognition, 6*, 291–325.

Frazier, L., & Rayner, K. (1982). Making and correcting errors during sentence comprehension: Eye movements in the analysis of structurally ambiguous sentences. *Cognitive Psychology, 14*, 178–210.

Gelman, R. (1978). Cognitive development. *Annual Review of Psychology, 29*, 297–332.

Gough, P.B., & Hillinger, M.L. (1980). Learning to read: An unnatural act. *Bulletin of the Orton Society, 30*, 179–196.

Grodzinsky, Y. (1984). *Language deficits and linguistic theory.* Unpublished Ph.D. dissertation, Brandeis University.

Hamburger, H., & Crain, S. (1982). Relative acquisition. In S. Kuczaj, II (Ed.), *Language Development, Volume 1: Syntax and Semantics.* Hillsdale, NJ: Erlbaum.

Hamburger, H., & Crain, S. (1984). Acquisition of cognitive compiling. *Cognition, 17*, 85–136.

Johnson, M.L. (1975). The meaning of *before* and *after* for preschool children. *Journal of Experimental Child Psychology, 19*, 88–99.

Katz, R.B. (1986). Phonological deficiencies in children with reading disability: Evidence from an object-naming task. *Cognition, 22*, 225–257.

Katz, R.B., Shankweiler, D., & Liberman, I.Y. (1981). Memory for item order and phonetic recoding in the beginning reader. *Journal of Experimental Child Psychology, 32*, 474–484.

Kean, M.-L. (1977). The linguistic interpretation of aphasic syndromes. *Cognition, 5*, 9–46.

Kean, M.-L. (1980). Grammatical representations and the description of language processing. In D. Caplan (Ed.), *Biological studies of mental processes.* Cambridge, MA, MIT Press.

Keil, F. (1980). Development of the ability to perceive ambiguities: Evidence for the task specificity of a linguistic skill. *Journal of Psycholinguistic Research, 9*, 219–230.

Kimball, J.P. (1973). Seven principles of surface structure parsing. *Cognition, 2*, 15–47.

Kohn, B., & Dennis, M. (1974). Selective impairments of visuospatial abilities in infantile hemiplegics after right cerebral hemidecortication. *Neuropsychologia, 12*, 505–512.

Liberman, A.M., Cooper, F.S., Shankweiler, D., & Studdert-Kennedy, M. (1967). Perception of the speech code. *Psychological Review, 74*, 431–461.

Liberman, A.M., & Mattingly, I.G. (1985). The motor theory of speech perception revisited. *Cognition, 21*, 1–37.

Liberman, A.M., Mattingly, I.G., & Turvey, M. (1972). Language codes and memory codes. In A.W. Melton, & E. Martin (Eds.), *Coding processes and human memory.* Washington, DC: Winston and Sons.

Liberman, I.Y. (1983). A language-oriented view of reading and its disabilities. In H. Myklebust (Ed.), *Progress in learning disabilities* (Vol. 5). New York: Grune & Stratton.

Liberman, I.Y., Liberman, A.M., Mattingly, I.G., & Shankweiler, D. (1980). Orthography and the beginning reader. In J.F. Kavanagh, & R.L. Venezky (Eds.), *Orthography, reading, and dyslexia.* Baltimore, MD: University Park Press.

Liberman, I.Y., Mann, V.A., Shankweiler, D., & Werfelman, M. (1982). Children's memory for recurring linguistic and non-linguistic material in relation to reading ability. *Cortex, 18*, 367–375.

Liberman, I.Y., & Shankweiler, D. (1985). Phonology and the problems of learning to read and write. *Remedial and Special Education, 6*, 8–17.

Liberman, I.Y., Shankweiler, D., Fischer, F.W., & Carter, B. (1974). Explicit syllable and phoneme segmentation in the young child. *Journal of Experimental Child Psychology, 18*, 201–212.

Liberman, I.Y., Shankweiler, D., Liberman, A.M., Fowler, C., & Fischer, F.W. (1977). Phonetic segmentation and recoding in the beginning reader. In A.S. Reber, & D.L. Scarborough (Eds.), *Toward a psychology of reading: The proceedings of the CUNY Conferences.* Hillsdale, NJ: Erlbaum.

Linebarger, M.C., Schwartz, M.F., & Saffran, E.M. (1983). Sensitivity to grammatical structure in so-called agrammatic aphasics. *Cognition, 13*, 361–392.

Mann, V.A., & Liberman, I.Y. (1984). Phonological awareness and verbal short-term memory: Can they presage early reading problems? *Journal of Learning Disabilities, 17*, 592–599.

Mann, V.A., Liberman, I.Y., & Shankweiler, D. (1980). Children's memory for sentences and word strings in relation to reading ability. *Memory and Cognition, 8*, 329–335.

Mann, V.A., Shankweiler, D., & Smith S.T. (1984). The association between comprehension of spoken sentences and early reading ability: the role of phonetic representation. *Journal of Child Language, 11*, 627–643.

Marslen-Wilson, W., & Tyler L. (1980). The temporal structure of spoken language understanding. *Cognition, 8*, 1–71.

Mattingly, I.G. (1972). Reading, the linguistic process, and linguistic awareness. In J.F. Kavanagh & I.G. Mattingly (Eds.), *Language by ear and by eye*. Cambridge, MA: MIT Press.

Mattingly, I.G. (1984). Reading, linguistic awareness, and language acquisition. In J. Downing & R. Valtin (Eds.), *Language awareness and learning to read*, New York: Springer-Verlag.

Milner, B. (1974). Hemispheric specialization: Scope and limits. In F.O. Schmitt & F.G. Worden (Eds.), *The Neurosciences: Third study program*. Cambridge, MA: MIT Press.

Morais, J., Cary, L., Alegria, J., & Bertelson, P. (1979). Does awareness of speech as a sequence of phonemes arise spontaneously? *Cognition, 1*, 323–331.

Netley, C., & Rovet, J. (1983). Relationships among brain organization, maturation rate, and the development of verbal and nonverbal ability. In S. Segalowitz (Ed.), *Language functions and brain organization*. New York: Academic Press.

Olson, R.K., Davidson, B.J., Kliegl, R., & Davies, S.E. (1984). Development of phonetic memory in disabled and normal readers. *Journal of Experimental Child Psychology, 37*, 187–206.

Perfetti, C.A. (1985). *Reading ability*. New York: Oxford University Press.

Perfetti, C.A., & Goldman, S.R. (1976). Discourse memory and reading comprehension skill. *Journal of Verbal Learning and Verbal Behavior, 14*, 33–42.

Perfetti, C.A., & Hogaboam, T. (1975). The relationship between single word decoding and reading comprehension skill. *Journal of Educational Psychology, 67*, 461–469.

Perfetti, C.A., & Lesgold, A.M. (1977). Discourse comprehension and sources of individual differences. In M.A. Just & P.A. Carpenter (Eds.), *Cognitive processes in comprehension*. Hillsdale, NJ: Erlbaum.

Pylyshyn, Z.W. (1984). *Computation and cognition: toward a foundation for cognitive science*. Cambridge, MA: Bradford.

Saffran, E.M. (1985). Short-term memory and sentence processing: Evidence from a case study. Paper presented at Academy of Aphasia, Pittsburgh, PA.

Shankweiler, D., Liberman, I.Y., Mark, L.S., Fowler, C.A., & Fischer, F.W. (1979). The speech code and learning to read. *Journal of Experimental Psychology: Human Learning and Memory, 5*, 531–545.

Shankweiler, D., & Liberman, I.Y. (1972). Misreading: A search for causes. In J.F. Kavanagh & I.G. Mattingly (Eds.), *Language by ear and by eye: The relationships between speech and reading*. Cambridge, MA: MIT Press.

Shankweiler, D., Smith, S.T., & Mann, V.A. (1984). Repetition and comprehension of spoken sentences by reading-disabled children. *Brain and Language, 23*, 241–257.

Smith, S.T., Mann, V.A., & Shankweiler, D. (in press). Good and poor readers comprehension of spoken sentences: A study with the Token Test. *Cortex*.

Stanovich, K.E. (1982). Individual differences in the cognitive processes of reading: 1. Word decoding. *Journal of Learning Disabilities, 15*, 449–512.

Stein, C.L., Cairns, H.S., & Zurif, E.B. (1984). Sentence comprehension limitations related to syntactic deficits in reading-disabled children. *Applied Psycholinguistics, 5*, 305–322.

Tavakolian, S.L. (1981). The conjoined-clause analysis of relative clauses. In S. Tavakolian (Ed.), *Language acquisition and linguistic theory*. Cambridge: MIT Press.

Treiman, R. and Baron, J. (1981). Segmental analysis ability: Development and relation to reading ability.

In G.E. MacKinnon & T.G. Waller (Eds.), *Reading research: Advances in theory and practice* (Vol. 3). New York: Academic Press.

Vellutino, F.R. (1979). *Dyslexia: Theory and research.* Cambridge, MA: MIT Press.

Vogel, S.A. (1975). *Syntactic abilities in normal and dyslexic children.* Baltimore, MD: University Park Press.

Wanner, E., & Maratsos, M. (1978). An ATN approach to comprehension. In M. Halle, J. Bresnan, & G. Miller (Eds.), *Linguistic theory and psychological reality.* Cambridge, MA: MIT Press.

Wolf, M. (1981). The word-retrieval process and reading in children and aphasics. In K. Nelson (Ed.), *Children's language* (Vol. 3). New York: Gardner Press.

Résumé

Dans cet article, nous étudions un ensemble de problèmes qui ont été identifiés chez des enfants qui éprouvent des difficultés de lecture, et nous essayons de les expliquer en tenant compte des propriétés du système de traitement du langage. Le fait de considérer les troubles de lecture du point de vue de la structure linguistique et de l'acquisition du langage nous permet de faire des hypothèses spécifique sur leurs causes. Ces hypothèses sont ensuite examinées à la lumière d'une analyse des exigences de la tâche de lecture et de l'évaluation de l'état du lecteur qui ne parvient pas à satisfaire à ces exigences. Le reste de l'article étudie plus en détail une proposition quant à la source des troubles de lecture, dans laquelle le système de mémoire de travail joue un rôle central. Cette proposition est évaluée à la lumière d'investigations empiriques qui ont essayé de séparer le savoir structural et la capacité de mémoire chez des enfants normaux et chez des enfants éprouvant de sérieuses difficultés de lecture.

Index

Italicized page numbers following names indicate reference entries.